Contemporary Latin American Classics

Contemporary Latin American Classics

J. CARY DAVIS, *General Editor*

JOSÉ MARTÍ

MARTÍ

ON THE

U.S.A.

Selected and translated, with an

Introduction by LUIS A. BARALT

Foreword by J. CARY DAVIS

Southern Illinois University Press

CARBONDALE AND EDWARDSVILLE

Foreword
J. Cary Davis

"PRESIDENT DIES FROM ASSASSIN'S BULLET . . . CROWDS BOO
SPEAKERS FOR NEGRO RIGHTS . . . DEMOCRATIC LANDSLIDE BURIES
INCUMBENTS . . . POET'S WORKS BANNED AS OBSCENE . . .
WELL-KNOWN PASTOR ACCUSED OF IMMORAL RELATIONS WITH ONE
OF HIS OWN FLOCK . . . PRESIDENTIAL CANDIDATE DEFIES TAMMANY
HALL . . . MOB VIOLENCE IN NEW ORLEANS, RIOTS AND LYNCHINGS
. . . LOCAL LAW OFFICERS POWERLESS . . . CHEAP IMMIGRANT
LABOR RUINING SOUTHWEST . . . KANSAS TO GO REPUBLICAN? . . .
INDIAN LANDS DOOMED BY GOVERNMENT PROJECTS . . .
EARTHQUAKE DESTROYS COASTAL CITIES . . . DEPRESSION
THREATENED BY HIGH TARIFFS AND AUTOMATION . . . WOMEN TO
HOLD BALANCE OF POWER"

HEADLINES of the 1960's, without a doubt?!
Not so: all these and more were current topics which engrossed
the general public three-quarters of a century ago when Martí
wrote his news articles which were published and avidly read in
newspapers and journals throughout Latin America. In them we
see the image of the United States of the 1880's reflected through
the eyes of a distinguished foreigner, sympathetic toward this land
that gave him a generous welcome, appreciative of her strength
and virtues, yet fully conscious of her many flaws and weak-
nesses.

It is eminently fitting that this Cuban patriot and man of
letters, in exile from dictatorial rule in that sadly oppressed island of the Caribbean, should be interpreted to an American
audience of the present day by another man of letters, likewise
a refugee from a more modern, but no less ruthless, dictatorship
in Cuba. Luis A. Baralt was born in New York City, April 12,
1892, of Cuban-American parentage. He learned English as a
young lad in that metropolis. In 1900 his parents moved to Cuba,
where he later graduated with a Ph.D. (*Summa cum laude*)
from the University of Havana (1914). He holds an A.M. from
Harvard and an LL.D. from the University of Havana (1917).

v

He has studied in Paris, at Columbia University, and elsewhere.

Dr. Baralt has taught courses in Spanish, Spanish-American literature, and Latin American culture in universities both here and abroad. Among them are the University of Miami, Middlebury College, and the University of Colorado. He was Professor of English at Havana Institute, 1918–34; Director of the Havana University Theatre, 1946–60; Professor of Philosophy and Aesthetics at the University of Havana, 1934–60; and Dean of its faculty of Philosophy and Letters, 1957–60. Since 1960, when he decided to leave Cuba because of the Castro regime, Dr. Baralt has been Visiting Professor at Southern Illinois University in the departments of Philosophy and Foreign Languages.

In Cuba, Luis A. Baralt was Undersecretary (1933) and Secretary (1934) of Education; a member of several important commissions and embassies for his country; president of the Philharmonic Orchestra Society of Havana, 1926–36; and president of the National Author's Guild, 1944–46. In addition, Dr. Baralt has been active in the work of the International Committee for Intellectual Cooperation (of the League of Nations) and of UNESCO. The roster of his memberships in academic and cultural organizations is a long one. He has lectured on many phases of cultural and philosophic thought, written and published a number of plays, traveled widely in Europe and in Central and South America. Because of his outstanding achievements in the academic world and the cause of international good will and understanding, Dr. Baralt is a Chevalier de la Légion d'Honneur (France) and a Caballero de la Orden del Sol (Peru). He was a decisive factor in the development of the Cuban theatrical movement, having founded "LA CUEVA" (the Art Theatre of Havana), produced several of his own plays, and directed various theatrical groups. Thoroughly conversant with a number of languages, he has translated a considerable number of plays from English, French, German, and Portuguese into his native tongue.

Dr. Baralt's acquaintance with Martí began at an early age. His mother, Doña Blanca Zacharie de Baralt, in her biography of the poet, *El Martí que yo conocí*, relates that she met Martí and her future husband, Luis A. Baralt y Peoli, on the same day in the home of the latter at a gathering in which the former was

a guest. The poet was a constant visitor in the Baralt home in
New York in those trying days of his exile and often held the
infant Luis in his arms. Hence Dr, Baralt's interest in Martí is
both a personal and an intellectual one, as well as that of a
compatriot in exile from his native land. As a student and critic
of literature, Dr. Baralt is well fitted for the task of revealing
his illustrious fellow countryman to an American audience; as
a Cuban thoroughly familiar with the American way of life, he
has found it a stimulating experience to reaffirm Martí's evalua-
tions of the United States and his reactions thereto; as the son
of intimate friends of the author, the work of translation has
been for him a true Labor of Love.

MEMORIA ENIM VERA INMORTALITAS

Southern Illinois University
February 23, 1965

Contents

3   LIFE IN THE U.S.A.

Introduction
Luis A. Baralt

TO THE average English reader the name José Martí means little or nothing. The publication of this volume is therefore an urgently needed contribution in response to a deeply felt demand. Complaints are often heard of the scarcity of information available to scholars and the general public concerning Latin America's great men, be their field politics, philosophy, or belles-lettres. In the case of José Martí such paucity of material in English is especially lamentable, since it contrasts with the profusion of original texts, biographies, critical studies, and commentaries which have appeared in the last decade in both Latin America and Spain.

For some time Martí's significance as a man of letters and a thinker was overshadowed, even in Latin America, by his fame as a political leader, the inspirer and *artifex* of Cuba's independence. His importance as a master of the Spanish language, as a powerful innovator of literary form both in prose and in verse, as an original and profound thinker was not at first apparent save to a few scholars. The main reason for this is the fact that most of his writings had been published in periodicals of different lands and other literary masterpieces had their origin as improvised, although well-meditated, speeches. Fortunately Martí reconstructed the most important of these or else they had been taken down in shorthand. But many have been lost forever. His letters, so revealing of the man and of the writer, only came to the attention of the recipient and a limited number of friends. It was years after Martí's death that his beloved pupil Gonzalo de Quesada, following the general scheme laid out by the master, combined in several volumes the most outstanding items of his literary production, together with numerous articles and opinions about the author.

With the passing of years, devoted scholars have gathered together an impressive mass of written material which has created a literary image of Martí greatly surpassing that of him as the political leader of Cuba's revolution against Spain, important as this fact was as a facet of the man's nature. Now Martí's writings are accessible in two practically exhaustive collections of complete works: the *Editorial Lex* edition in two volumes and the *Trópico* edition in seventy-four volumes.

Such an array of eloquence, of beauty, of wisdom, running the gamut from economics and politics to every aspect of art and philosophy, has produced a powerful impact in Spanish-speaking countries, but remains little known to the rest of the world. One need not be a Cuban, naturally indebted to him for the gift of political emancipation, to feel Martí's service to humanity, for his voice was ecumenical. A full acquaintance with his work now reveals that his message was only accidentally addressed to his countrymen. It was a message to America, to mankind. Those who have received that message acknowledge the greatness of Martí as a creator of beauty and as a moral and spiritual guide for all men. It is time that the world, beginning with Anglo-Saxon America, concur in this acknowledgment.

It has seemed appropriate, as a starter, to offer a selection of Martí's writings dealing with this country which he admired and where he found refuge during the most critical years of his life. The timeliness of this publication also springs from the fact that a recent trend has developed which makes Martí out to be a forerunner of the Communist takeover in Cuba. Nothing could be farther from the truth. Though he was always a passionate defender of the humble and the downtrodden, with whom he said he would always cast his lot (*"Con los pobres de la tierra quiero yo mi suerte echar"*), though he was a progressive, typical nineteenth-century liberal, there is nothing in his writings that smacks of anti-capitalist extremism, nor did he advocate the absorption of the individual by an over-inflated state. The words "full dignity of man" were always on his lips. His abundant political studies, more than the impressions on the United States gathered in this book, prove that he was a decided believer in the democratic philosophy of government. But even these articles contain ample evidence of his admiration of this country's democratic structure. When he criticizes, it is the deviations in practice he attacks, not democracy itself. Many passages will be found where he praises the better fruits of free enterprise (see the article on Peter Cooper).

Much is made of his anti-clericalism. In matters of religion, no doubt, he was definitely against bigotry and all forms of misguided dogmatism, but his spirituality — for some even his mysticism — is so apparent that it has often been pointed out as one of his essential characteristics. He conceived of a new religion free from dogmatic fetters, much in the manner of the Emersonian tradition. On the score of anti-imperialism, quotations from Martí are likewise trumped up to show him as an enemy of the United States. His metaphorical phrase *"Conozco al monstruo, he vivido en sus entrañas"* (I know the monster, I have lived inside him), where the word "monster" is used in the same sense Hobbes uses the word "Leviathan" and no more, has been worn to rags by those who would capitalize on Martí's always fair criticisms of what he saw in this country. They do not mention all the praises he lavished upon the men, institutions, and customs he found and loved here. His anti-imperialism, if it can be so called, was but a warning to the weaker nations to the south against the "manifest destiny" doctrine he foresaw and advice to Latin America to prepare itself to withstand the foreseeable economic expansion of its powerful northern neighbor.

All forms of coercions that might in any way curtail man's freedom, whether exercised by the masses or by an individual dictator, were abhorrent to Martí. Much of this transpires from the present articles. The reader will become convinced that there was nothing of the totalitarian or the materialist in Martí, whose position was in all matters diametrically opposed to the one International Communism would glady assign to him.

As Henri Bergson has shown philosophically, and common sense corroborates, there can be no such thing as a perfect translation when the text to be translated has any artistic (intuitive) value. Translating is always the lesser of two evils, the other being to remain in complete ignorance of what has interested and moved the readers of another language. But what sense of frustration always accompanies a translator's task! At every step he feels the truth of the Italian adage: *traduttore, traditore,* and how right was whoever said that the best translation is but the reverse side of a tapestry. The present translator has tried to be as little of a traitor as possible and to bring forth as much as he could of the tapestry's original colors, and hopes to have saved at least some of the aesthetic qualities of the original. His constant concern has been (1) to convey with the greatest possible accuracy the main train of thought of each segment of the text and (2) to preserve something of the essential rhythm of words and images and of the peculiar style of the author.

Martí once said that when he wrote in English he was really writing Spanish with English words. Perhaps the reader will at times feel that the present translator has been doing the same. I submit that when this is done consciously the procedure may have its virtues; it helps to convey the "Latin" qualities of the author's thought and speech. The crux of the translator's art is to hit upon the optimum balance between the respect for the morphological and grammatical structure of the original and the laws that govern the language into which he is translating. To make the rendition readable, some violence must perforce be done to the original. But it is no less true that the more liberties a translator takes in order to comply with the strictures of the language in which he is writing the farther he is removing his rendition from the original work. If at times the reader finds this version exotic or foreign the chances are that the effect has been consciously sought. Many liberties have nevertheless been taken with the purpose of relieving the effort required of the reader if he is to project himself into the author's extraneous thought and manners of expression. Overlong paragraphs to which the English reader is unaccustomed have been broken down and intricate clause structures simplified, but the translator has reduced such liberties to a minimum.

The reader would do well to bear in mind that much of Martí's exuberance and floridity is characteristic of his time, a tendency he shared with contemporaries writing in English or any other language. Whitman's prose, for instance, is strongly reminiscent of Martí's prose. A translation into present day English forms of expression would be absurd.

In comparing versions of the articles as they appear in the three collections of Martí's works divergences have been found indicative of successive revisions by the author, especially when the same article was published in two different periodicals. In such cases the translator has chosen either the most concise or that which lent itself best to an English rendition.

Most of the articles appearing in Part I and Part II are included *in toto*. Those in Part III have been more or less abridged. They all fall under the headings of *Norte Americanos* (North Americans) or *Escenas Norte Americanas* (North American Scenes), two of the various groups under which the author wished his works to be collected, according to the instructions he gave Gonzalo de Quesada y Aróstegui in a letter written shortly before his death and known as his "literary testament." Volumes of selections of Martí's works have appeared in French, Russian, and Portuguese translations. In English, apart from scattered items in scholarly reviews, only one selection of Martí's writings, as far as I know, has been published up to now in book form, Juan de Onís' excellent *The America of José Martí* (New York: Noonday Press, 1953). The contents of his book do not coincide with those of the present volume, except for a few essays, and the two versions of those are different.

I am deeply indebted to the Ford Foundation and the Southern Illinois University Press for having made possible the publication of this book, and to Albert William Bork, Boyd George Carter, and J. Cary Davis, all of Southern Illinois University, for their careful revision of my manuscript and their intelligent and useful suggestions. I appreciate the assistance of Mr. Genaro Marin of the Southern Illinois University Latin American Institute in the research for the Notes.

José Martí all

A biographical sketch will help place José Martí's sojourn in the United States in the proper context. Martí was born January 23, 1853, in a humble two-story house on Paula Street in Havana, now preserved as a shrine to his memory. His father, Mariano Martí, who had come from Spain as a sergeant in the Spanish army, married in Cuba a girl likewise from Spain, Leonor Pérez, and decided to make his home there. He obtained transference to the police force where he served as a night-watchman in Havana and other towns and cities. Several daughters had been born to the humble couple before José. In spite of their meagre resources, Don Mariano and Doña Leonor did not neglect their son's education. One of the schools he attended was run by a man of great distinction, Rafael María Mendive, a poet and a man of high ideals who had a decisive influence in molding the child's mind and character. Before reaching adolescence the precocious José had acquired a mass of knowledge unusual in a boy and began to show the mettle which marked in the child the man that was to be. When adversity soon struck he was quick in acknowledging his indebtedness in a letter to his revered teacher. "I have suffered much," he wrote, "but I am convinced that I have learned how to suffer. If I have had strength for it all and if I possess the qualities that make me a man, I owe it to you alone. From you I have acquired whatever virtue and kindness there is in me."

The occasion for this letter was the beginning of Martí's career as a patriot. From Mendive he had learned to love his country. When the Ten Years War of emancipation broke out in 1868 Martí was only fifteen years old, too young to join the *mambises* in the battlefields. He and his schoolmates contributed as best they could to the cause of Cuban independence: they published clandestine tracts and periodicals. In one of these, *La Patria Libre,* a shortlived weekly, appeared his first literary work, a two-act play, *Abdala,* in which the still immature but phenomenally talented poet poured forth all his patriotic ardor. It was not long before Mendive, who far from discouraging his pupils set them the example of resisting tyranny, was exiled, and Martí and his close friend and collaborator Fermín Valdés Domínguez were jailed for "disloyalty" to Spain. José was sentenced to six years at hard labor and Fermín to six month's imprisonment. A library and lecture room dedicated to Martí now stand on the spot, then in the outskirts of Havana, where the frail seventeen-year-old patriot worked for months under inhuman conditions. The heavy chains that he was forced to drag at all times maimed him for life; the quicklime of the quarry where the gang of prisoners was taken daily burned into his flesh and nearly blinded him. Through an influential friend, Martí's parents succeeded in having the harsh sentence changed to that of deportation to Spain. From 1871 until a Spanish bullet at Dos Ríos put a tragic end to his short life in 1895, Martí was to visit his beloved Cuba on only two brief occasions. From that time forth, liberation of his country was to be the dominant impulse and motivation of all his actions.

The years in Spain between 1871 and 1874 were definitive in Martí's development. His first concern was to make known the horrors he and so many others had endured for opposing the Spanish rule and aspiring to the independence of their native land. The resulting tract, entitled *El presidio político en Cuba* (Political Imprisonment in Cuba), written at the age of eighteen, revealed in Martí not only an ardent patriot but a writer of original, vibrating style. At the universities of Madrid and Zaragoza he completed his academic education. He read the classics, voraciously acquiring that wealth of vocabulary and that flexibility in the use of idiomatic and expressive forms which, despite the many novelties which later were to distinguish his style, placed Martí the writer squarely within the best tradition of the language of Cervantes and Calderón.

These years in Spain were perhaps the happiest in Martí's short life. He was in the flower of his youth; he frequented literary coteries; he went to the theatre (often with his bosom friend Fermín, who had joined him); he knew love and rejoiced in everything that was good and noble in the mother country, even as he abhorred Spanish colonialism. The capacity to distinguish between the Spain he loved, breeder of mystics and heroes, and the Spain he was to devote his life to combat, is one of the most admirable traits in Martí. Later he was to write of Aragón specifically:

> Para Aragón en España
> Tengo yo en mi corazón,
> Un lugar todo Aragón:
> Franco fiero, fiel, sin saña.
>
> .   .   .   .   .
>
> Amo la tierra florida,
> Musulmana o española,
> Donde rompió su corola
> La poca flor de mi vida.

> For Aragon in Spain I hold
> A warm place in my heart,
> A place which is like Aragon:
> Frank and gentle, loyal, bold.
>
> .   .   .   .   .   .

> I'll always love that flowery land,
> Be it Moorish, be it Spanish,
> Where the slim blossom of my life
> Opened to the air its chalice.

(From number VII of *Versos sencillos*)

But his still more beloved Cuba was always present in his heart. In defense of her cause he worked unflinchingly. The advent of the Republic in Spain in 1873 raised his hopes. To the new government he addressed the second of his great political tracts, entitled *La Republica española y la revolución cubana* (The Spanish Republic and the Cuban Revolution). It was his belief that both causes were identical. "If Cuba declares her independence," he wrote, "based on the same right Spain has to declare herself a republic, how can Spain deny Cuba the right to be free, which is the same right Spain invokes to achieve her own freedom?" The authorities turned a cold shoulder on Martí's appeal; their alleged liberalism stopped on the threshold of misguided national pride.

When the sentence of confinement to Spain was finally lifted, Martí, after short stopovers in Paris and London, joined his parents in Mexico. There his formation as a writer made rapid strides. He soon was able to earn his livelihood as a journalist, and achieved local prestige as a lecturer and orator of unusual merit. Mexico was a revelation for Martí. For the first time he established direct contact with a Latin American country other than his own. It was probably there that what had been his all-absorbing concern for the political emancipation of Cuba took on a broader scope. In Mexico he sampled the many shortcomings of the young nations that Spain had spawned over the vast territory he was fond of referring to as *Our America*. The problems of one were the problems of all. Mexico opened her arms wide to Martí. The intellectual groups took him in as one of their own, for the young exiled poet, passionate and imaginative, fitted admirably in the romantic atmosphere of the times. He became an habitué of the literary salon of "Rosario la de Acuña," a sort of Mexican Madame de Récamier, beautiful and brilliant. It was rumored that at her nightly gatherings of admiring poets Pepe stayed on later than the rest.

There was also Concha Padilla, the Spanish actress for whom he wrote a charming, *apropos* play in one act, *Amor con amor se paga* (Love for Love). But these were just flares of a fiery poet in his early twenties. An admirer of beauty, whether he found it in woman, in nature, in art, or in the heart of a friend, Martí was never prone to frivolous gallantry. It was therefore not surprising that when he met Carmen Zayas Bazán, a beautiful compatriot, he saw in her the future mother of his children. Yielding perhaps to some slight pressure on the part of his family, Martí became engaged to her.

Martí was not to lay aside his lifelong preoccupation with the destiny of Cuba. In private gatherings with other exiles, writing in newspapers, or speaking in public he pleaded eloquently for Cuba's cause. He likewise actively participated with the Mexicans in discussing their own socio-political problems: the anti-Catholic "reformation" which the Lerdo de Tejada administration had inherited from Juárez, education, the incorporation of the Indian in civic life — Martí's heart went out especially to the kindly, downcast Indian. Nevertheless, being a foreigner, he refused to participate in party politics.

When the unrest which foreshadowed Porfirio Díaz' long dictatorship became acute, Martí decided to move on. The fighting in Cuba still raged. General Martínez Campos had arrived at the head of a powerful army. In one hand he wielded a menacing weapon while with the other he tendered conciliatory offers of leniency, reform, and reconstruction. Feeling that perhaps his presence might revive the fighting spirit of his compatriots, exhausted after nine years of war, Martí decided to return to Cuba, using a fictitious name. He soon realized that his beloved cause was lost for the time being. He swore to begin again from scratch.

A month later he was in Guatemala, which a liberal-minded president, Justo Rufino Barrios, was trying to modernize and uplift. Thanks to a distinguished Cuban, José María Izaguirre, who had been appointed Director of the Normal School, Martí soon found employment there as professor of history and literature. But Martí was not one to remain concealed in a humble teaching position. He immediately gained notoriety. Asked to express his opinion on a new civil code that was being drafted

(Martí had graduated in law in Spain but had never yet practiced as a lawyer) he wrote on the subject with such competence and deep understanding of the needs and nature of the emerging peoples of Latin America, that soon the young Cuban was looked up to as a providential mentor on all cultural and political matters. He was promoted to a professorship in the university, where he taught a variety of subjects, all of which afforded him opportunity to instill in his students his own lofty conception of man and of the New World's position in an era of increasing enlightenment. His teaching, as might have been expected, was not without some opposition from the more conservative and privileged quarters, to whom his doctrines smacked of heterodoxy and extremism. But the young reformer was always cautious and refrained from becoming involved in domestic politics. His activity was tireless and unlimited. He founded cultural clubs and stimulated those that already existed, he helped edit the *Revista de la Universidad,* and he enthralled an ever-growing public with his forceful, dazzling oratory.

Martí's sojourn in Guatemala, brief as it was, left a deep impression upon its people. A monument in Guatemala City bears testimony to their gratitude. Among his writings, two outstanding works are associated with Guatemala: his unfinished *drama indio,* a play which if completed might have been Martí's best dramatic effort and is important for the understanding of his political ideas because it is a strong indictment of the country's bigoted, backward clergy; and *La niña de Guatemala,* a beautiful, ballad-like poem which children in Cuba learn by heart.

Then it was back to Cuba again. A grave injustice done to Izaguirre by the generally well-meaning but often rash and violent Barrios, prompted him to resign his teaching position. Besides, the recently signed Pact of Zanjón (1878) had brought the war to a close and offered him the opportunity to return to Cuba. He sailed once again for the city which had given him birth but which knew him not. Accompanying him was his expectant wife whom he had shortly before gone to Mexico to marry and had taken back to Guatemala.

The political climate in Cuba was characterized by mixed feelings of hopes for peace within the Spanish fold, well-grounded

misgivings as to the interpretation and implementation of the
concessions made by Spain in the Pact, and unflinching separa-
tism. The latter position was no more than an undercurrent.
Most of the spiritual and intellectual leaders wanted a respite:
peace above all, peace and reconstruction under the mother country's now benevolent guidance. The strong, victorious despot had
to be propitiated, won over. Cuba was too exhausted to even
dream of stirring up insurrection again. At least a cooling off
period had to be taken advantage of before launching a new
war. But Maceo and a few other chiefs had not been signatories
to the Pact of Zanjón. In New York a junta or committee-in-
exile had been set up and was calling for funds to purchase arms
for future actions. Martínez Campos, the Governor General and
head of the powerful army which had finally defeated the Cuban
patriots, appealed to the Madrid government to grant Cuba the
same status enjoyed by the Spanish provinces. His request fell
on deaf ears. When Martínez Campos became suspected of excessive partiality toward the Islanders he was recalled and the
stern, harsh General Blanco sent to replace him.

Martí knew well where his duty lay. His house and his none-
too-active law office soon became meeting places for conspirators.
The old Guanabacoa Liceo, a cultural society a few kilometers
from Havana, offered him a rostrum from which to preach his
doctrines. Though his friends warned him to be cautious, his
libertarian ideas were only too evident behind the brilliant fab-
ric of his orations, regardless of the subject. As always, his
oratory drew increasingly large crowds. In Juan Gualberto Gómez, an intelligent, cultured Negro lawyer, he found enthusiastic
support. Juan Gualberto was appointed Delegate of the New
York junta, Martí subdelegate.

Carmen Zayas Bazán could not see eye-to-eye with her husband, predestined to greatness. A child, Pepito, had been born
to them. Her motherly concern was naturally for him, for her
home. But Martí, though a tender, homeloving man, could not
refrain from fulfilling his destiny. Nothing should stand in his
way, regardless of what might happen to him, to his dear ones.
Domestic arguments ensued: she was a conformist; he was a
dreamer. His devotion to a lofty cause only prompted in her
harsh words which he heard patiently but unmoved. Carmen

was right in her fears. One day a knock was heard at the door. The police had come to arrest her husband. The sentence this time was less severe. Thanks to the good offices of many friends, Martí was only banished once again and put on a ship bound for Spain. He had in fact been offered his freedom if only he would publicly proclaim his allegiance to Spain. Appeasement was the present policy of the government. He replied: "Tell the General that Martí is not of the race of those who are for sale."

There was little he could do during his banishment other than revive the memories of the Spain he loved. To the Spaniards the Cuban question was still important, though only one among a number of political issues. The ascent of Martínez Campos to the premiership raised hopes of a more favorable deal for suffering Cuba. But such hopes were shortlived, and when his government fell Martí decided to find his way to New York, which he did as soon as he was able to elude the vigilance of the authorities.

After a stop in Paris, he arrived in this country where he was to spend almost all of the rest of his short life (1880–1895). Fifteen years of ceaseless activity directed to the accomplishment of his one goal: the liberation of Cuba. He immediately contacted the junta, then presided over by José Francisco Lamadriz, but mostly guided in its planning for war by a general of great prestige, Calixto García, whose name Elbert Hubbard was to popularize in his little essay *A Message to García*. There were spontaneous uprisings in Oriente province and in central Cuba, but Maceo awaited in Jamaica orders to take command. As for Máximo Gómez, the previous general-in-chief, he was taking no part in the venture. The support of the people themselves, on the island and among the exiles, was only half-hearted. Martí did not like the situation nor how things were being run, but who was *he* to impose his ideas? Yet he immediately placed himself at the junta's service. Calixto García was not too favorably impressed by the newcomer who had no war experience nor had even lived much in Cuba. As always, Martí soon won the old veteran's esteem and brought him around to some of his fundamental views. A change in a nation's status, Martí believed, was not to be achieved by a few military leaders alone, no matter how respected; it had to surge from the base up, it had to be willed by the people. To begin with, the Cubans in exile had to be mobilized. Towards this end no serious attempt had been made. Martí knew this was the one contribution he could make. Then began what has been called his apostolate, an unceasing campaign in which he preached a new patriotic gospel through word of mouth, speeches, letters, and articles. His first important speech, given in New York at Steck Hall, was not only the revelation of a powerful mind, of an inflamed patriot who could be trusted, but the placing of the first stones of his political philosophy. He made clear to all what the past war had meant and to what the definitive war should lead.

Martí quickly gained prestige, but in the Cuban revolutionary setup during these first months in New York he was only one more pawn. His development as a commanding figure was still to follow a long, slow process. In the meantime he continued to mature intellectually and spiritually. Startled and stimulated by his contact with the great city, he delved into every aspect of the young democracy which he saw budding into full bloom all around him, but not without pitfalls and growing pains. He began to absorb and to evaluate this "great land conquered by a peace loving people who rose from their knees in prayer to put their hands to the plow." The throbbing "city of iron" filled him with mixed feelings of awe and puzzlement.

During his long years in New York Martí lived humbly, but always decorously. He earned a measly pittance as a bookkeeper in a business firm, giving Spanish lessons, and with his pen. His English was soon good enough for him to contribute articles on art to *The Hour,* articles written, as he confessed, "in Spanish with English words." When his small income at last permitted him to do so he sent for his wife and child. This was a great joy for the tenderhearted father who had not seen his son since birth. He gave the child strange names of endearment: "my little king," or "the dwarf prince," or "my little shepherd." It was then he composed those precious short poems dedicated to his son which he was to publish later under the title of *Ismaelillo.*

The so called *Guerra Chiquita* (Little War) was not going well, as Martí had feared. He would have wanted it otherwise and had done all he could to avert the debacle, but the disaster was only too evident. Calixto García had been taken prisoner and deported. Some chieftains surrendered. One, Emilio Núñez, refused to do so without first obtaining authorization from the New York junta. Martí, then in charge *ad interim,* sent the authorization, adding these words: "We are not, nor do we deserve to be called, professional revolutionaries . . . capable of sacrificing noble lives to keep alive a cause . . . whose triumph is not probable . . ." Martí was expressing his political philosophy. Only "just and necessary" wars were excusable. A great probability of success is their only justification. He knew the times were not yet ripe: Cuba would have to wait.

It was during this period of frustration for the patriot that his ever-dissatisfied wife abandoned him and returned to her father in Camagüey, taking with her Martí's beloved son. The brokenhearted father felt lonelier than ever. New York was an alien, overwhelming boiling pot to which he had still not become adapted. He craved to renew contact with the countries to the south which had become a foremost concern of his. So he sailed for Venezuela, the cradle of Latin American independence, the birth place of Simón Bolívar.

In Caracas he made the acquaintance of a great man, Cecilio Acosta, whom the "Illustrious Dictator" Guzmán Blanco forced to live in seclusion and to whom Martí was to pay tribute in one of his most beautiful essays. As in Guatemala, he exerted a profound influence upon the younger generation and stimulated the country's cultural life. He founded the *Revista Venezolana.* But in spite of Martí's caution, the intelligent Guzmán Blanco saw in the young Cuban apostle of liberty a menace to his regime. He invited Martí to write an article in his praise or otherwise leave the country. Martí took the only course compatible with his integrity.

Again we find our hero in New York in the summer of 1881. For the ensuing few years Martí was to intensify his literary pursuits. Shortly after his return he contributed regularly to the Caracas *La Opinión,* under a pseudonym of course, until his ideas and his unmistakable style revealed his identity to the local censorship. But his reputation as a writer soon reached the editors of the Buenos Aires *La Nación,* the leading newspaper in Latin America, who invited him to contribute articles on the United States. This was not only a much needed prop to his always precarious finances but an opportunity to reach a vast public. No Latin American was better qualified for such an undertaking. There was no aspect of the life of this country which had not awakened his interest. Step by step he was forming in his mind a vivid image of the United States, both of its over-all scheme and of the minutest workings of the body politic. All these impressions he poured out periodically in brilliantly written articles that conveyed to Latin Americans a detailed and on the whole accurate picture of the United States. A large proportion of the articles appearing in this book have been selected from his contributions to *La Nación*. He also wrote for other Latin American newspapers and for *La América* and *El Latino Americano* published in this country.

Until the very eve of the definitive war against Spain his activity as a journalist was prolific. To the New York *Sun* he contributed frequently, sometimes writing his articles in French when there was no Spanish translator on the paper's staff. He founded and directed *Patria*, the official organ of the Revolutionary Party, and a delightful magazine for children, *La Edad de Oro*. For Appleton and Company he translated several books into Spanish: Hugh Conway's *Called Back* (Misterio), Helen Hunt Jackson's *Ramona*, Jevon's *Logic*. He also published in *El Latino Americano* his only novel, *Amistad funesta* (Untoward Friendship). For a while politics occupied less of his attention, to the great satisfaction of his wife who had come back from Cuba to join him. For a time he served as Vice-Consul and later Consul of Uruguay. Argentina also appointed him Consul in New York.

The story of Martí's groundwork activity in preparation for the Cuban Revolution, which was not to break out until 1895, is too long and complicated to be told here. Let it suffice to say that the process was characterized by ups and downs, free lance actions in Cuba, conferences between the chieftains, and agreements upon various plans only to be abandoned when found impractical. Though Martí's collaboration in the successive plans was always wholehearted, there were times when he despaired at not being able to impress the leaders with the necessity of first laying solid foundations before engaging in actions that might prove rash and harmful. His counsel was not always heeded.

From heroes whom he worshiped, like the grand old warrior
Máximo Gómez, he received harsh rebuffs that wounded his sensitive soul. Loose tongues had disparaging things to say of this
man who seemed now to stand in the way of action by preaching
caution. Martí, in fact, gradually developed one of the most surprising aspects of his personality. From behind the visionary, the
dreamer, the poet, emerged a level-headed, at times even tough,
realist capable of analyzing the possible consequences of every
step taken, no matter how unimportant it might seem, a great
organizer who was slowly transforming a motley crowd of Cuban exiles scattered over the face of the earth into a veritable
community, a nation without a territory but still a nation. He
knew that only when this collective consciousness were achieved
would it be possible to make concrete military plans and engage
in active warfare.

Martí's predominance in the movement was not won in a
day. Not even on the eve of war when everything was in readi-
ness to strike might it be said that he controlled the movement.
He always acted as what he really was: the mouthpiece of the
people, the interpreter of the collective will. His whole moral
philosophy was based on the idea of duty, sacrifice, and service.
As a leader he felt it was his mission to preach, to indoctrinate,
to convince. But once his compatriots acquired the necessary
spiritual coherence and unanimity of purpose, he became their
servant. Nothing was more abhorrent to this great democrat
than a dictator. Thus his growing authority was won step by
step without his ever assuming full control. The task ahead was
a collective one, and he had the gift of making each man and
woman feel equally important, no matter how humble his or
her contribution might be. All knew that if he asked others to
give of their labors and their money, he gave his all. No one gave
more than he. He gave, gave, gave: his time, his health, ultimately his life. He wrote letters everywhere, to Gómez in Jamaica, to Maceo in Honduras, to the Cuban refugees in Philadelphia or Paris. He traveled to Key West and Tampa to talk
to the Cuban tobacco factory workers there. He organized patriotic clubs wherever there was a Cuban colony. When the time
came to organize the definitive Cuban Revolutionary Party it
was he who drafted its bylaws, its proclamation, its manifestoes.

He visited Santo Domingo, Haiti, Jamaica, Honduras, Costa Rica, and Panama to discuss plans with leaders there.

Before war broke out again on February 24, 1895, Martí saw his ideal gradually take shape, despite the many stumbling blocks he valiantly had to hurdle: misunderstandings, false accusations, and military setbacks, as, for example, the loss of three ships carrying an expeditionary force, arms, and ammunition which were seized by U.S. authorities in the port of Fernandina, Florida, at the very outset of hostilities. But the greatest task had been accomplished: Cuba already existed even before its separation from Spain; Cuba was now and forever a national entity, conscious of its essences, its destiny, and its political philosophy. This spiritual creation had been Martí's own work.

He still had more to do. A man who loved all men, even his adversaries, who made a friend of whoever approached him, who made the humble, the poor, the ignorant, the Negro feel they were his equals, this angelic man, nevertheless, had spent all his life calling to arms, convinced that, no matter how hateful, war sometimes is necessary. Necessity and justice, he believed, are the only excuse for war, but when war is necessary and just it becomes unavoidable, nay, imperative. Yet Martí had never had a weapon in his small, delicate hands. There were some who held his love for belles-lettres and art against him, who whispered that his was a comfortable position, writing letters while others shed their blood on the battlefield. Martí knew very well that his work would not be complete until he wrote with his own blood the last stanza of the beautiful poem which was his life. So, against the better judgment of those who felt he was indispensable to the work of coordination from New York, he decided to meet Máximo Gómez in Santo Domingo and land with him on his beloved island.

The saga of Martí's last days is as beautiful as the rest of his life. We have of those days in Montecristo, Santo Domingo, and the days that followed his landing in a frail rowboat at Playitas, Cuba, his own testimony in a touching diary, in letters to María Mantilla, in whose home Martí had for years found the warmth his wife had never been able to give him, to Manuel Mercado, his Mexican friend, to his mother, and in the Manifesto which lays out the directives the coming Republic should follow. He rejoiced like a child when he saw again the Cuban countryside, the royal palms which to him symbolized the Fatherland, when he talked to the simple, intelligent, hospitable *guajiros* (peasants). When Máximo Gómez, the glorious general-in-chief, conferred upon him on landing the rank, more honorary than effective, of General of the Army of Liberation, he was ashamed. But he knew his mission was a simple one. He had not come to command armies; there were others much better fitted than he to take on that responsibility. He had come to die, only to die. When a few days after landing he charged against a small detachment of Spanish troops at Dos Ríos followed by a single aide, it looked like a suicide. Indeed he had written on the eve of his death: *"Para mí ya es hora"* (My hour has struck).

Charles Dana, the editor of *The Sun,* published in his journal this obituary: "We learn with poignant sorrow of the death in battle of José Martí, the well-known leader of the Cuban revolutionists. We knew him long and well, and esteemed him profoundly. For a protracted period beginning twenty years ago (Dana miscalculates the years of his association with Martí, whose total residence in New York did not exceed fifteen years.), he was employed as a contributor to *The Sun,* writing on subjects and questions of the fine arts. In these things his knowledge was solid and extensive, and his ideas and conclusions were original and brilliant. He was a man of genius, of imagination, of hope, and of courage, one of those descendants of the Spanish race whose American birth and instincts seem to have added to the revolutionary tincture which all modern Spaniards inherit. His heart was warm and affectionate, his opinions ardent and inspiring, and he died as such a man might wish to die, battling for liberty and democracy. Of such heroes there are not too many in the world, and his warlike grave testifies that, even in a positive and materialistic age, there are spirits that can give all for their principles without thinking of any selfish returns for themselves.

"Honor to the memory of José Martí and peace to his soul!"

Martí the Writer

The importance of Martí as a literary figure has been growing constantly in the last few decades. The articles in the present collection will reveal to the reader some of his stylistic peculiarities. Here we encounter primarily the journalist. With the exception of a few, as, for instance, the remarkable studies on Emerson and Walt Whitman, the articles are impressionistic "stories," written hurriedly to catch the first mail. They are nevertheless personal in the sense that Martí was not merely an objective expositor, as modern reporters are trained to be. The most valuable part of his accounts of men and happenings are not so much the facts themselves and how he relates them, as his "Ah's!" and "Oh's," his enthusiastic approvals or harsh condemnations, his analyses and explanations, his critical appraisal of whatever attracted his attention. The reader will learn that Martí was a man of strong likes and dislikes. In his eulogies, generous; in his censures, vehement.

But important as Martí's journalistic writings may be, they constitute a minor part of his literary production, if not in quantity, in significance. His poetic works stand out conspicuously and rank among the best written in Spanish in his time. They are not numerous. We have mentioned *Ismaelillo,* dedicated to his son and published in 1882. In 1891 Martí published his *Versos sencillos* (Plain Poems). Other poems were published only after his death. *Versos libres* (Blank Verses) gathers poems written mostly at the age of twenty-five. *Flores del destierro* (Flowers from Exile) is a collection of poems of different periods joined together because of their thematic harmony. It is impossible to characterize in a few lines Martí's poetic production. Even the metric form varies substantially from one book to another. The verses of *Ismaelillo* are spritely, scintillating, never longer than seven syllables; those of *Versos sencillos* are all written in classic quatrains with assonant rhyme; the *Versos libres* are ponderous, majestic, sometimes blazing hendecasyllables. The first are like porcelain bric-a-brac; the second are like a picture gallery of dreams and remembrances, smacking strongly of autobiography; the third have a heroic ring and strike the graver, fuller, more vibrating chords of the poet's passionate spirit.

Despite this variety there is a quality common to all Martí's poems: the peculiarities of his language. If ever the definition *Le style c'est l'homme* were true, it is certainly true in the case of Martí. Sending a copy of *Ismaelillo* to a friend, he says in the letter: "Do not read it once or you will find the poems strange, read it twice so that I may gain your indulgence." This "strangeness" is Martí's greatest charm: new, exciting choice of adjectives; fresh, unhackneyed metaphors. He claimed absolute spontaneity for his every line, for they came directly from the heart. "You will not find here," he says in the same letter, "a single cerebral line. I am scarcely responsible for the images that come to me unsolicited." Perhaps this confession—like the introspections of all poets—must be taken with a grain of salt. Martí was never a facile scribbler of trivialities, and his manuscripts reveal considerable revision and correction. He always aimed at formal perfection. Nevertheless, the reader always finds in his poems that miraculous, magic quality which is the essence of true lyricism. As we read, we are swept away into a world of dreams where the things of reality are stripped of the veils that cover them in actual existence and show themselves as clear, meaningful, autonomous entities.

Though the "modernist" movement was already under way when Martí's poetic works began to be known around 1882, many historians and critics have insisted that he must have greatly influenced the later development of that school of poetry. It is a fact that Rubén Darío, the indisputable highpriest of "modernismo," met Martí and was deeply impressed by the man and the poet, on whom he wrote four articles in *La Nación*. But to what extent the younger poet's stylistic innovations might have been determined by the Cuban is still a debatable problem into which we cannot enter here. What is evident is that Martí's manner was as much a new departure as that of the famous Nicaraguan.

Martí's contribution to dramatic literature is the weakest part of his production. It includes *Abdala*, the two-act play written at the age of sixteen, *Adúltera*, a *Sehlen Drama* in prose, conceived while in Spain, which makes good reading but is not too satisfactory when performed; the short *Amor con amor se paga* of his Mexican days, delightful but of little consequence, and the unfinished Guatemalan play on the problem of clericalism which he called his *drama indio* but left untitled. If completed, it might have been his best dramatic work.

As for Martí's prose works (speeches, essays, articles, letters, etc.), the originality of style, the unequivocally personal stamp he imprinted on every line is, if anything, more striking than in his poems. He believed that metaphor was not the exclusive property of poetry and thus imparted to his prose a rhapsodic swing that is often disconcerting to the reader but which gives his utterance an incredible warmth and allows the author's thought to delve into unexpected substrata of his subject. Few writers have possessed as Martí did the faculty of using prose to entrance and to reveal. And no wonder, because Martí's whole person exuded poetry. Even his ordinary speech, his friends recalled, was rich in imagery—not bookish or conventional, but original, evoking, stimulating. Indeed, he endowed his very actions with a poetic turn. His life, it has been said, was his most beautiful poem.

José Martí was a smallish man, slender and frail, with a pear-shaped face under a broad, luminous forehead, and serene, inquisitive eyes. He bore himself with dignity but never ponderously. He gave the impression of weightlessness. He might be likened to a quivering leaf or, as my mother remembers him in her book *El Martí que yo conocí* (Martí as I Knew Him), to a living flame. This creature of fire, creator of beauty, apostle of spiritual values preached his gospel in stirring, immortal pages, yet most of the world has not yet hearkened unto his message. When it does, it will be a better world, a world of men who love beauty as he did, who respect one another, who are governed by an inner sense of duty, and who enrich their lives through giving rather than receiving, through sharing rather than grasping.

February, 1965

I

MEN

WALT WHITMAN

"LAST night he looked like a god, sitting in his red plush chair, with his gray hair, his beard on his breast, his smokey eyebrows, his hand on a cane." This is what one of today's papers says about Walt Whitman,[1] the seventy-year-old man to whom the sharpest critics, who are always a minority, assign an exceptional place in the literature of his country and his times. Only the sacred books of antiquity offer a doctrine comparable in language and vigorous poetry to that expounded in grandiose, priestly apothegms, like outbursts of light, by this old poet whose astounding book has now been banned.

Why, of course! Isn't it a natural work? Universities and Latin have made men ignore one another; instead of falling in each others' arms attracted by the essential and eternal, they separate, nagging each other like fishwives at the slightest disagreement; man is molded by a book or a teacher in contact with whom he has been placed by chance or fashion as a pudding is molded by its container; philosophic, religious, or literary schools disguise men as a livery does a lackey; men let themselves be branded like horses and bulls and go around in the world showing their brands. So, when they find themselves in front of a naked, virginal, loving, sincere, and potent man — in front of a man who walks, loves, fights, rows — who, not letting himself be blinded by misfortune, reads a promise of ultimate felicity in world equilibrium and grace; when they find themselves in front of the fatherly, sinewy, and angelic man, Walt Whitman, they flee as from their own conscience and refuse to recognize in this fragrant and superior humanity the prototype of their drab, becassocked, dollish species.

The daily paper tells us that yesterday, when that other adorable old man, Gladstone,[2] had just set his opponents in Parlia-

---

Dated New York, April 19, 1887, published also in *El Partido Liberal*, Mexico, 1887, and in *La Nación*, Buenos Aires, June 26, 1887.

3

ment right as to the justice of granting Ireland self-government, he seemed like a powerful mastiff standing unrivaled amid the mob of curs at his feet. Thus Whitman appears with his "natural person," [3] his "unharnessed nature with original energy," his "myriad beautiful and gigantic youths," [4] with his belief that "the smallest sprout shows there is really no death," [5] with his formidable account of peoples and races in "Salut au Monde," [6] his determination to "be silent while they discuss, and to go and bathe and admire himself, knowing the perfect fitness and harmony of things." [7] Thus appears Whitman, "who doesn't say these things for a dollar"; [8] who is "satisfied and sees, dances, sings and laughs"; [9] who "has no chair, no church, no philosophy"; [10] that is what Whitman is like compared to those rickety poets and philosophers, one-detail, one-aspect philosophers; honey and water, rhetorical poets; philosophical and literary mannequins.

He must be studied, because if he is not the poet of best taste, he is the most intrepid, comprehensive and uninhibited poet of his time. In his little frame house, which verges on poverty, there hangs by the window a picture of Victor Hugo, [11] bordered in black mourning; Emerson, [12] whose books purify and exalt, used to put an arm around his shoulder and call him his friend; Tennyson, [13] one of those who sees to the roots of things, sends from his oaken chair in England tender greetings to the "grand old man"; Robert Buchanan, [14] that outspoken Englishman, thunders to the North Americans: "what can you possibly know about letters when you are letting your colossal Walt Whitman's old age pass without honoring him as he deserves?"

The truth is that on reading him, though at first astounded, our soul, tormented by universal pettiness, feels a delightful sensation of recovery. He creates his own grammar, his own logic. He reads in the ox's eye and the sap of the leaf! "That man who cleans the filth out of your house is my brother!" His apparent formlessness, which is at first disconcerting, turns out later, except for brief instants of portentous extravagance, to be like the sublime order and composition of mountain peaks on the horizon.

He does not live in New York, his "beloved Manhattan," [15] his "superb-faced, million-footed Manhattan," which he visits when he wishes to intone "the song of what he beholds in Libertad";[16] he lives, since his books and lectures yield him barely enough to buy bread, with "loving friends" [17] who care for him in a little out-of-the-way country house, from which he goes in his carriage, pulled by the horses he loves, to see the "athletic young men" in their virile pastimes, the "camerados" [18] who are not afraid of rubbing elbows with this iconoclast who wishes to establish the institution of comradeship, to see the yielding fields, the friends who pass arm in arm singing, the loving couples gay and sprightly like quails. So he tells us in his "Calamus," [19] the enormously strange book in which he sings of love between friends: "City of orgies . . . Not the pageants of you, not your shifting tableaux, your spectacles, repay me . . . Nor the processions in the streets, nor the bright windows with goods in them, nor to converse with learned persons . . . Not those, but as I pass O Manhattan, your frequent and swift flash of eyes offering me love . . . Lovers, continual lovers, only repay me." [20] He is like the old man he announces at the end of his forbidden book, his "Leaves of Grass": "I announce myriads of youths, beautiful, gigantic, sweet-blooded, I announce a race of splendid and savage old men." [21]

He lives in the country, where the man of nature can toil in the free earth, under the tanning sun, but not far from the city, amiable and warm, with its noises of life, its diversity of occupation, its variegated epic, the dust wagons raise, the smoke from panting factories, the all-seeing sun, "the loud laugh of work people at their meals," [22] "the flap of the curtained litter, a sick man borne inside to the hospital," [23] the "exclamations of women taken suddenly who hurry home and give birth to babes." [24] But yesterday Whitman came from the country to recite for a gathering of loyal friends his oration on that other man of nature, that great and sweet soul, "that great star early droop'd in the western sky," [25] Abraham Lincoln. All New York's intelligentsia attended in religious silence that brilliant lecture which, because of its sudden breaks, its vibrant tones, its hymn-like fugue, its olympic familiarity, seemed at times like the chatter of stars. Those sucklings fed on Latin, French, or academic milk will perhaps not understand this heroic graciousness. Man's free and secure life in a new continent has created a

wholesome, robust philosophy which is emerging upon the world
in Herculean epodes. Only a poetry of togetherness and faith
becomes this largest conflux of freemen and workers the world
has ever seen, a soothing and solemn poetry which rises like the
sun from the sea, burning clouds, festooning the wave crests with
fire, awakening in the prolific inland forests the drowsy flowers
and nests. Pollen flies, mountain peaks exchange kisses, branches
intermix, leaves seek the sun, everything exhales music. Such
is the language of piercing light in which Whitman spoke of
Lincoln.

Perhaps one of the most beautiful creations of contemporary
poetry is Whitman's mystic dirge on Lincoln's death. All nature
escorts the lamented deceased to his grave. The stars had proph-
esied, since a month before clouds had been turning black. There
was a gray bird in the swamp singing a desperate song. Between
thought and the certainty of death the poet wanders in the
mournful fields as between two comrades. Like a musician he
arranges, hides, restates these sad themes in a total twilight
harmony. When the poem comes to a close it is as though the
whole world were in mourning and possessed by the deceased
from one ocean to another. We see the clouds, the heavy moon
that forebodes the catastrophe, the gray bird's long wings. It is
much more beautiful, strange, and profound than Poe's "The
Raven." The poet has brought to the coffin a twig of lilac.

Such is his poetry.

Willows no longer wail over graves; death is "the harvest,
the opener and usher into the heavenly mansion, the great re-
vealer"; what is, was, and shall be again; the apparent opposi-
tions and sorrows merge with each other in a calm, celestial
spring; a bone is a flower. One hears, close by, the noise of suns
moving majestically as they seek their definite places in space;
life is a hymn; death is a hidden form of life; sweat is holy and
the entozoan is holy; men should kiss each other on the cheek
when they meet; those who live should embrace with ineffable
love and love the grass, the animals, the air, the sea, pain, death;
souls possessed by love suffer less; life holds no suffering for
him who grasps its meaning in time; honey, light, and kisses are
spawned together. In the resplendent peace, under the massive,
starry vault, to the tune of a soft music there rises over the

slumbering worlds stretched like hounds at its feet, a peaceful, gigantic lilac tree!

Every social condition contributes to literature its own expression, so much so that the history of nations can be told more truthfully through their literary movements than through their annals and chronicles. Nature cannot contradict itself; even the human aspiration to find in love, during this life or after death, a perfect type of grace and beauty, shows that the elements which in our present span of life seem disjointed and hostile will, in the totality of life, become happily adjusted. A literature which announces and promotes the ultimate and felicitous accord of apparent contradictions; a literature which promotes through nature's spontaneous advice and teaching, the identity, in a superior peace, of rival dogmas and passions which divide and bloody nations still in a primitive state; a literature which imparts to men's restive spirit so deep-rooted a conviction in definitive justice and beauty that life's distress and ugliness cease to dishearten and embitter them, will not only reveal a social condition nearer to perfection than any known so far, but will provide humanity, thirsty for wonders and poetry, by a fortunate combination of reason and grace, with the religion it has vaguely awaited since it discovered the emptiness and insufficiency of its ancient creeds.

Who is the dunce who maintains that poetry is not indispensable to nations? Some people are so short-sighted that they think a fruit is nothing but rind. Poetry, which unites souls or disbands them, fortifies or fills them with anguish, uplifts or defeats them, which gives to or takes from men hope and courage is more necessary to a people even than industry. Whereas industry provides the means for living, poetry affords the desire and the strength to live. What is to become of a nation of men who have lost the habit of thinking, with faith, of the significance and scope of their actions? The best, those whom nature has anointed with the sacred thirst for the future, will lose in a painful, muted undoing, all incentive to bear the ugly sides of life; and as for the masses, the vulgar, the children of lust, the common, they will breed empty offspring without sanctity, raise mere instruments to the category of essential faculties and will confuse the soul with the bustle of an ever incomplete prosperity, the soul whose incurable affliction only finds satisfaction in the beautiful and the great.

Liberty should be blessed, among other reasons, because its enjoyment affords modern man — previously deprived of the calm, the stimulus, and the poetry of existence — that supreme peace and religious well-being which an orderly world brings to those who live in it with the pride and serenity that free will brings. Look beyond the mountains, you poets who water deserted altars with childish tears!

You thought religion was lost because it was changing form over your heads. Arise, for you are the priests. The definitive religion is liberty. And the poetry of liberty is the new cult. It is poetry that soothes and embellishes the present, infers and illumines the future and explains the ineffable purpose and seductive goodness of the universe.

Let us hear what this hardworking, contented people sings; let us hear Walt Whitman. Self-assertion raises this people to majesty, tolerance to justice, order to happiness. He who lives according to an autocratic creed is like an oyster in its shell, which only sees the prison which holds it and in the darkness believes it to be the whole world. Liberty gives wings to oysters. And what, heard from inside the shell, seemed an uproarious battle, turns out in the open to be the natural flow of sap in the world's vigorous pulse.

To Walt Whitman the world was always as it is today. That a thing is, is sufficient reason for its having to be, and when it no longer should be, it will no longer be. What is no longer, what can no longer be seen, can be proved by what is and can be seen; because everything is in everything and one thing explains another; and when what now is is no longer, it will in turn be proven by what then will be. The infinitesimal collaborates with the infinite and everything is in its place, turtle, ox, birds, those "wing'd purposes." [26] It is as fortunate to die as to be born, because the dead are alive: "no array of terms can say how much he is at peace about God and about death!" [27] He laughs at what we call disillusionment and he knows the vastness of time, which he accepts absolutely. All is contained within him; all of him is contained in all; if another is debased, he is debased; he knows he is in the ebb and flow of every tide, no wonder he is proud, feeling himself to be a living and intelligent part of nature! What does he care if he returns to the womb that bore him, and the loving moist earth converts him into the useful vegetable or the lovely flower? He will nourish men after having loved them. His duty is to create; the atom that creates is of divine essence; the act of creation is exquisite and sacred. Convinced of the identity of the universe he sings the "Song of Myself." This song of himself is woven out of everything: of creeds that quarrel and pass, of man who breeds and toils, of animals who help him, oh! those animals among which "not one kneels to another, not one is respectable or unhappy, nor sweats nor whines about his condition." [28] He considers himself heir to the world.

Nothing is alien to him and he takes everything into account: the snail that drags itself along, the ox that gazes on him with its mysterious eyes, the priest who defends part of the truth as though it were the whole truth. Man should open his arms and then press everything against his heart, virtue as well as crime, filth as well as cleanliness, ignorance as well as wisdom; in his heart everything should fuse as in an oven; above all he should let his gray beard grow. But, to be sure, "we have had ducking and deprecating about enough." [29] He scolds the unbelievers, the sophists, the chatterers: procreate instead of quarreling, add to the world! Create with the reverence with which a devout believer kisses the altar steps!

He belongs to all castes, creeds, and professions, and finds justice and poetry in all of them. He measures religions without wrath, but believes the perfect religion to be in nature. Religion and life are in nature. If there is a sick person in the house, he will tell both the doctor and the priest to go home: "I seize the descending man and raise him with resistless will . . . I will open windows, love him, speak to him in his ear; you will see him cured; you are words and grass, but I am stronger than you because I am love." [30] The Creator is "the Lover divine and the comrade perfect"; [31] men are *camerados* and the more they love and create the more they are worth, even though whatever occupies their place and time is as good as anything else; but let everyone see the world for himself, for Walt Whitman, who feels within himself the world since its beginning, knows, from what the sun and open air have taught him, that a sunrise reveals more than the best book. He thinks about the orbs above, desires women, feels himself possessed of a universal, frantic love. He hears rising from the scenes of creation and the toils of man a concert that fills him with joy, and when he looks toward the river at the hour factories are closing and the setting sun tints the water, he feels he has an appointment with the Creator, recognizes man is definitively good and from his head, reflected upon the surface, he sees rays of light emerging.

How can I convey an idea of this man's sweeping, flaming love? He loves the world with Sappho's [32] fire. To him the world is like a gigantic bed and this bed an altar. "The words and ideas men have prostituted with secrecy and false modesty I shall make illustrious; I praise and consecrate what Egypt did." [33] One of the sources of his originality is the Herculean strength with which he subdues ideas as though to rape them, when he means only to kiss them as would a saint. Another source is the material, brutal, corporal, manner in which he expresses his most delicate ideals. Those who are incapable of understanding his greatness have found this language lewd; there even have been imbeciles, with a prudishness worthy of evil-minded school boys, who believed they found in "Calamus," when he praises the love between friends in the most ardent images possible, a return to Virgil's [34] vile desire for Cebetes or Horace's [35] for Gyges and Lyciscus. And when in "The Children of Adam" [36] he sings of the divine sin in images beside which the most passionate images of "The Song of Songs" seem pale, he trembles, shrinks, surrenders, expands, goes mad with pride and satisfied virility, he recalls the god of the Amazon,[37] who crossed over forests and rivers sowing the seeds of life: "my duty is creation!" [38] "I sing the body electric!" [39] he says in "The Children of Adam"; and to find anything comparable to the satanic strength with which he enumerates, like a hungry hero smacking his bloody lips, the parts of a woman's body, one must have read in Hebrew the genealogies of Genesis or followed through the forests primeval the naked, flesh-eating bands of primitive men.

You say this man is brutal? Listen to this poem, "Beautiful Women," a two verse poem as are many of his poems: "Women sit and move to and fro, some old, some young, / the young are beautiful, but the old are more beautiful than the young." [40] And this other, "Mother and Babe": "I see the sleeping babe nestling the breast of his mother, / the sleeping mother and babe hush'd, I study them long and long." [41] He foresees that, even as in men of genius extreme virility and tenderness are joined, so in the delightful peace where life will come to rest, the two forces which have necessarily separated to continue the task of creation will reunite solemnly, jubilantly as becomes the Universe.

When he walks on the grass he says the grass caresses him, that he "feels his joints moving"; [42] and the most restless youth would not find such fiery words to describe the joy of the body, which to Whitman is part of the soul, when he feels the sea's embrace. All living things love him: the earth, the night, the sea. "You sea . . . dash me with amorous wet." [43] He relishes the air. He offers himself to the breeze like a trembling lover. He favors doors without locks, bodies in their natural beauty; he believes he sanctifies whatever he touches or touches him and finds virtue in all corporal things. He is "Walt Whitman, a kosmos, of Manhattan the son. / Turbulent, fleshy, sensual, eating, drinking and breeding / . . . no stander above men and women or apart from them." [44] He describes truth as a frenzied lover who assaults his body and strips himself of his clothes in the anxiety of possession. But when the soul, free of drudgery and books, emerges whole, silent, as it looks back on the well-employed day, it meditates on the most pleasing subjects: night, sleep, death, the song of the universal for the benefit of the common man, the sweetness of dying, "advancing on," [45] and falling at the foot of the primeval tree, ax in hand, bitten by the last serpent in the forest.

Imagine what new and strange effect is obtained by this language, filled with superb animality, when it praises the passion which should unite mankind. In one of the "Calamus" poems he enumerates the liveliest pleasures he owes to nature and fatherland; but he finds that only the ocean waves are worthy of accompanying his joy when by moonlight he sees the friend he loves sleeping by his side. He loves the humble, the fallen, the wounded, even the wicked. He has no disdain for the

great, since for him only the useful are great. He throws an arm
about the shoulder of teamsters, sailors, country laborers. He
goes hunting and fishing with them and at harvest time climbs
with them atop the hay wagons. The muscular Negro who, standing on the pole behind his horses, drives his wagon calmly
through the turmoil of Broadway, seemed to him more beautiful
than a victorious emperor. He understands all virtues, receives
all prizes, works at all trades, shares all sorrows, feels a heroic
pleasure when from the smithy threshold he sees the young
blacksmiths, stripped to the waist, brandishing their sledges
over their heads and striking alternately. He is the slave, the
prisoner, the fighter, the fallen one, the beggar. When the slave
knocks at his door, pursued and sweating, he fills the bath tub
for him, sits him at his table; he has his loaded gun in the
corner ready to defend him, should anyone try to attack his
guest, he will kill the pursuer and sit again at the table as
though he had only killed a viper!

Walt Whitman, therefore, is contented; why should pride
prick him, since he knows one ends up being a blade of grass or
a flower? Is a carnation, a sprig of sage, a branch of honey-
suckle proud? How else can he look upon human tribulations
but serenely, knowing that they will be followed by eternity for
him who awaits his blissful merger with nature? Why should he
hurry, since he believes everything is where it should be and
that one man's will cannot change the course of the world? He
suffers indeed; but the part of himself that suffers he considers
a minor, perishable being, and he feels, over and above his trials
and mysteries, that there is in him another being who cannot
suffer because he knows universal greatness. It suffices him to
be as he is and he witnesses, with impassivity or joy, the course
of his life, be it unnoticed or praised. With a single stroke he
puts aside romantic lamentation as a useless excrescence: "Not
asking the sky to come down to my good will!" [46] What majesty
there is to that phrase in which he says he loves animals because
"they do not sweat and whine about their condition!" [47] The
truth is there are too many scaremongers; it is urgent for us
to see the world as it is, so as not to make mountains out of
molehills; to make men strong instead of taking from them
through lamentations whatever strength sorrow has left them;

for lepers do not go around exhibiting their sores. Neither doubts nor science disturb him. "Gentlemen, to you the first honors always! / Your facts are useful, and yet they are not my dwelling, / I but enter by them to an area of my dwelling." [48] "How beggarly appear arguments before a defiant deed!" [49] "Lo! Keen-eyed towering science / . . . Yet again, lo! The soul, above all science; . . ." [50] But where his philosophy has entirely conquered hatred, as wise men order, is in this phrase which partakes of the melancholy of defeat but uproots all reason for envy: Why should I be jealous, he says, of my brother for doing what I cannot do? "He that by me spreads a wider breast than my own, proves the width of my own. Let the Sun interpenetrate the Earth until it all be sweet and pure light, like my blood! Let the rejoicing be universal. I sing the eternity of existence, the happiness of our life and the beauty beyond change of the Universe. My signs are the calfskin shoe, the open collar and a staff cut from the woods." [51]

All this he says in apocalyptic phrase. Rhymes or accents? Oh, no! His rhythm lies in the stanzas which he joins, amidst an apparent chaos of superimposed and convulsive phrases, according to a wise pattern that distributes ideas in great musical groups, a poetic form natural to a people who do not build stone by stone but in enormous blocks.

Walt Whitman's language, a complete departure from that used heretofore by poets, corresponds in its strangeness and power to his cyclic poetry and to a new humanity gathered on a fertile continent full of such portents that they cannot be expressed in affected, set, rhetorical forms. It is no longer a question of hidden loves, of ladies that break their troth, the sterile complaint of those who lack the necessary energy to conquer life nor the cunning that becomes cowards. It is no longer a question of jingles, of alcove complaints, but of the birth of a new era, the dawn of the definitive religion and man's renovation, of a faith which is to replace a dead one and arises radiantly clear from redeemed man's arrogant peace; of writing the sacred books of a people who, emerging out of the old world, absorbs at savage nature's udders all the virgin forces and cyclopean pomp of liberty; it is a question of painting with words the bustle of settling masses, working cities, conquered seas, and

enslaved rivers. Will Walt Whitman seek rhymes with which to
mold into soft couplets these mountains of merchandise, bristling
forests, crowds of ships, battles where millions of men lay down
their lives to uphold a right, the sun prevailing over everything
and spilling its limpid fire across the vast panorama?

Oh, no! Walt Whitman speaks in biblical verses, with no
apparent music, though soon we realize they sound like the crust
of the earth being trodden upon by barefooted, glorious, victorious armies. At times Whitman's language is like a butcher's
window where carcasses hang; again it is like the chant of
patriarchs singing in a circle full of the world's sadness in the
hour when smoke rises to the clouds; other times it sounds like
a stolen kiss, like a rape, like the snapping of a dried-out parchment in the sun. But his phrase never loses the rhythmic movement of the wave. He himself tells us how he speaks in "prophetical screams," [52] which are, he says, a few "indicative words for
the future." [53] That precisely is his poetry — an index. A sense
of the universal pervades his book and gives it, despite the
superficial confusion, a grandiose regularity; but his disjointed,
lashing, incomplete, loose phrases emit, rather than express; "I
send my imaginings over the hoary mountains." "Earth! . . .
Say, old top-knot, what do you want?" [54] "I sound my barbaric
yawp over the roofs of the world." [55]

He is not one to turn out a beggarly thought in regal garments
to go stumbling, crawling along under the weight of its showy
opulence. Nor does he blow up warblers to make them look like
eagles; whenever he opens his fist he sows eagles as a farmer
would grain. One verse will have five syllables, the next forty,
the next ten. He does not press a comparison, in fact he does not
compare, but tells what he saw or remembers, adding a graphic
or incisive commentary and, with a masterful control of the
general impression he is trying to create, without showing his
hand, he uses his art in reproducing things in his picture with
the same disorder in which he observed them in nature. Even
when he raves there is no dissonance, because that is how the
mind wanders unhampered from one subject to other analogous
ones. But then, as though he had only slackened the reins, he
suddenly pulls on them and regains full control over the run-
away quadriga of his verses, as they gallop on devouring the

land; at times they neigh eagerly like lustful stallions; at times, covered with lather, they trample clouds with their hoofs; at times they sink into the earth — daring and black — and are heard rumbling on for a long while. He sketches; but one would say he does so with fire. He can bring together in five lines, like a bundle of freshly gnawed bones, all the horrors of war. An adverb is all he needs to stretch out or shrink a phrase, an adjective to reinforce it. His must be a great method, since its effect is great. But it might seem that he proceeds with no method at all, especially in the use of words, which he combines with unheard of audacity, putting august and almost divine words next to others which seem the least appropriate and decent. Certain pictures he does not paint with epithets, which in him are always lively and profound, but by means of sounds, which he arranges and juggles with consummate skill. By thus alternating his procedures he sustains the reader's interest, which one monotonous mode might cause to lag. As savages do, he brings forth melancholy through repetition. His unexpected, impetuous caesura changes constantly and respects no rule, though one can perceive a wise order in its meanderings, stops, breaks. He prefers to describe by accumulation, and his reasoning never resorts to the vulgar form of argument nor the high-sounding form of oratory, but to the mystery of insinuation, the fervor of certitude and the fiery turn of prophecy. We find in his book at every step these words of ours: *viva, camarada, libertad, americanos.* And what could reveal his character better than the French words with which, with evident delight, he studs his verses, as though to expand their meaning; *ami, exalté, accoucheur, nonchalant, ensemble? Ensemble,* especially, seduces him because he sees the sky that embraces the life of peoples, the life of worlds. From the Italian he has taken one word: *bravura!*

Thus, praising muscles and boldness, inviting passers-by to put their hand on his shoulder without fear when he crosses, listening with open palms to the song of things, joyously catching and proclaiming gigantic fecundities, gathering in epic verses seeds, battles, and orbs, pointing out to these times filled with astonishment the radiant human hives that cover the American vales and mountains and graze with their bee's wings the garment of vigilant liberty, shepherding the friendly ages toward the tranquil waters of eternity, while his friends feast him rustically with champagne and the first fish caught this spring, Walt Whitman awaits the happy hour when his body will leave him, after having revealed to the world a real, resounding, loving man, and when, returned to the purifying airs, he will germinate and perfume them "disembodied, triumphant, dead." [56]

PRESIDENT GARFIELD

WHEN one witnesses humanity's great outbursts of love one is proud of being a man, but when one witnesses its downfalls or its rages, one is ashamed. Death is useful, virtue is useful; misfortune is necessary and awakens in the hearts of all those who see it a noble desire to remedy it. In proof of this, behold the whole world tremulous and moved, palaces and thrones of monarchs in mourning, and the most populous nation on earth kneeling in front of a humble casket on which the palms of martyrdom rest, and in which lies, beneath the cupula of the Washington Capitol, a man who once bought his Greek books with the price of the wood he planed, who enjoyed one of the cleanest reputations on earth

Garfield [1] is dead.

He died September 19 when somber night was not half spent, and since then the signs of admiration, of affection, veneration and sorrow have been unending. The city, all the cities of the nation, are hung in black; hearts too. A martyr is like a father or a brother to the men he dies for. That is how everybody feels: as though he had lost a father or a brother. This man has been killed by a hidden element which, from within humanity's forces of destruction, operates against the forces of construction: a spiteful, yet intelligent, implacable element: the hatred of virtue.

I once wrote as follows in one of those sad books which are never published, because only spirited, active books should be published, books that fortify and open ways: "Virtuous man, thou shalt be hated!" He who becomes discouraged looks with irate eyes upon one who doesn't, as does the lazy man upon the hard worker; he who yields to adversity and precipitates his undoing by being a coward, hates the man who smiles at adversity, who charms, seduces, and tames it as a magician does a

From an article dated New York, October 1, 1881, published in *La Opinión National*, Caracas, October 19, 1881.

serpent. Impatient people hate those who are patient; the over-proud people who hope to reap a great and premature harvest where they have neither toiled, nor tilled, nor watered, detest and persecute the meek who have carried their reward with their virtue, their good name with their efforts, their glory with their pains. Reward is a prize, not a right; it is only after a soldier has fought his battle honorably that a medal shines on his breast. Mount Tabor is Calvary's reward. Men watch the struggle filled with fear and veneration. They praise in the fighter the heroic energy they lack. They feel virtuous when they see a virtuous man. All celebrate his victory as though it were theirs. He becomes the symbol, the precursor, the evangelist. So now it seems as though all men were covered by one funeral pall.

It was a warm night; the air was humid, the world quiet, the sea calm. There were two girls strolling on the beach. A woman prayed in her room. An old lady, in a far-off state, sat up awaiting news of her son. Those who had been out riding were returning, the foaming coach horses shook their harnesses. The house lights were going off while the lights in heaven began sparkling as if to light the grand stage for the great son's homecoming. In New Jersey the Long Beach villas were quiet and wrapped in sleep: a distant watchman's steps were heard, a boy messenger fluttered around like a butterfly, running in and out of the wounded President's house. And in those restful hours which always precede catastrophes, as though nature stored up forces to meet the great blow that was to put them to the test, scattered groups roamed the avenues, or commented in hotel lobbies on the news of the day, or took refuge in a parlor to remark sadly that the sick man's hands had been so cold and rigid today, that they seemed incapable of holding onto the reins of life any longer.

Night, shadowy night, is death's favorite hour: at nightfall she was sitting at the head of the President's bed. There stood energy on one side, goodness on the other, but the springs of the body were broken: his lungs were purulent, his heart gone mad, an aneurysm about to give way.

"There's plenty of pus today," said the doctor as he dressed his wound.

"Well, put it in the income column!" said the martyr smiling, already sure of his end.

Then the doctor wrote on a pad the instructions for the night treatment and tore off the sheet; it was the last. Lights had been dimmed; Mrs. Garfield was praying; General Swain, a faithful friend, had begun his watch; trusty Daniel, a Negro, entered the room. A muffled scream was heard.

"Oh, my God! Swain! I am in terrible pain right here" — and the patient put his hand to his heart — "what a terrible pain!"

Those lips said not another word. The household was notified, the bed surrounded. The hour had come. The time had come for the soul to leave his body majestically, serenely. His wife, her eyes dry because they had no more tears to shed, entered the spacious chamber.

"Is there no hope, doctor?"

"He is dying, Madame!"

Doctors, friends, children, servants stood around. The daughter approached her mother to ask: "Is he dying?" Her mother embraced her closely: "Oh, my daughter!"

The sea could be heard as it pounded and dissolved on the beach even as this dying man dissolved in the bosom of the unknown. Sometimes he struggled like a giant about to be defeated, or again his heaving breath softened like a panting locomotive pulling into a far-off station. Gradually the vague moans became hoarser and more muffled, slower; the heart, love's mansion, broke; and the doctor in a weeping voice announced: "It is all over." [2]

The wife still wept, sinking her head among the sheets; the daughter sighed in her friend's arms; the brave sleepless mother awaited news of her beloved James, when first Long Beach and then the nation awakened horrified. The sad news flew to the cities, towns, villages. Bells, from the Hudson to the Rio Grande, from Baltimore to San Francisco, began to toll. Their sounds rent the air like funeral birds ousted from the belfries by the cold wind. On all lips laughter ceased, and all eyes wept together. Theaters were closed. Compact, alarmed crowds filled the hotels. In Brooklyn a group of men, filled with indignation,

silenced some passengers who were singing in a streetcar on their
way home from a party, unaware of the tragic event. Newspaper
extras were called in loud voices on the streets and sold at exor-
bitant prices. The powerful presses of the important dailies
filled many columns with the smallest details of the event, the
news of which had been rushed to them by special trains!

It was one o'clock in the morning when the Vice-President,
in his shirt-sleeves, swore loyalty before Judge Brady to the duties inherent in his new office. Then, sobbing, he dropped in an
armchair and sat many hours with his face in his hands.

How sad the dawn was at daybreak! People walked about
silently, slowly! Morning did not gladden men's faces as it is
wont to do. The city looked like an immense temple. Streetcars,
trains, river ferries, where the sprightly, garrulous crowds gather
in the early hours, were like hearses. Not a voice was heard
among a thousand people, only the rustling of newspapers of
which incredible quantities had been sold. What magnificent
sadness and venerable mourning! And thus it was throughout
the Union. Thus grieved the energetic Northerner, the brilliant
Southerner, the rough Californian, the cultured Bostonian; the
Spaniard, the German, the Irishman, the poor fruit vendor, the
husky teamster, the elegant lady, the wealthy gentleman.

New York that morning was like a sun without rays or an
ocean run dry. If one went out on the street it was hard to hold
back one's tears. Here, a man risked his life to hang a black
cloth as a sign of mourning on the highest cornice of his house;
there, a child with his toy hammer nailed a black crepe bow to
his door, while far down the street, a church showed its massive
columns wound with funeral drapes; elsewhere a woman of
humble birth hung a small American flag with somber trimmings
from her window. Everywhere, in the streets, whether sumptuous or miserable, on pompous Broadway or popular Bowery, on
humble Third Avenue or in the slums by the rivers, wreaths,
garlands, banners, allegorical figures, and frames were being
made from merino wool, rich gauze, glossy satin, or pieces of
dresses. Floral offerings were displayed in shop windows. Without warning shops, which had opened languidly, began to close.
The loss of this man seemed to leave all minds devoid of light,
all hearts deprived of gayety. A collection started by the founder

of the submarine cable [3] for the President's family brought in a fortune. Bells tolled; black trimmings sheathed the tall church towers and the domes of important buildings. Country folk hung on their doors the emblem of woe: a black and white rosette. Over locomotives a tuft of black gauze waved next to their tuft of smoke. From over the oceans heartfelt messages arrived from Emperors and Liberators, from corporations and cabinets, from countries and kings.

Southerners, over whose heads Garfield had wielded his shining sword, wept as did the Northerners. Mercantile Philadelphia closed her books and wrapped them in crepe. Proud Boston, classic Washington, immense Chicago, fashionable Saratoga, the bastions of the South together with the bastions of the North, first bowed their heads, and then in praise and honor of this man they raised their eyes from earth that day and turned them heavenward. The plow remained stationary just where the farmer had heard the news; the fire remained unstoked in the bowels of the steamer ready to take off to sea.

At the same time, as a tribute to the law and out of respect for the nation which demands to know everything that concerns the life or death of its chief, physicians investigated the great man's corpse. His illness had been a superb struggle between a man's will and death's voracity. The autopsy revealed that the immediate cause of death had been a secondary hemorrhage of the mesenteric arteries which the murderous bullet had severed. The bullet, flouting human science and the various instruments used to locate it, had lodged under the peritoneum about two and a half inches to the left of the spine. It had gone through the skin, fractured the eleventh right rib, traversed the spinal column in front of the spinal channel, fractured the first lumbar vertebra, dragging numerous splinters into the soft adjacent parts, and stopped its devastating course under the pancreas. It carried with it the victim's death sentence.

It was possible to prolong his life, allowing his fortitude to be admired, his virtues to be recognized as the highest, and public indignation to abate by dint of the generosity such great grief awakened in all; but to save him was impossible.

In the meanwhile, even as the trembling hands of the doctors searched in the feverish wound for the deadly bullet, the in-

famous, ambitious murderer slept in his cell gloating because he
had gained weight in jail. Indeed the villain had. Perhaps he is
placing his trust in human goodness! Perhaps he trusts his own
wits which he values highly! Perhaps he trusts the gratitude of
those who have profited from his deed and on whom he relies!
He craved glory, but lacking the courage to work out his own
he intercepted another man's glory. This fellow destroyed a
modern temple: an honest, sensible, inquiring, hard-working,
free man! What a meager price is this murderer's corrupt blood
— people comment — for the magnificent life he has snatched
from us! Holland,[4] the author of *Kathrina* and a celebrated poet,
has written: "How can such a miserable life possibly extinguish
such a great one?" In the streets one sees the murderer hanged
in effigy between balconies. In public squares dummy likenesses
are hanged and then burned without police opposition, with a
sign on the dummy's back which reads: "This is the people's
verdict!" In the woods well-groomed, masked conspirators swear
they will see to it that he dies an ignominious death, worthy of
his crime, not the regular death to which the court will sentence
him.

But this thirst for vengeance, the brutal and violent expression of a generous wrath, is found only among the humbler
people, in lowly neighborhoods.[5] The vast masses of the nation
are sadly convinced of the uselessness of ire, and that the dagger
with which they might stab the culprit would never serve to
cut the mourning drapes from their hearts. A great man departed surely demands better homage than a useless death.
Surely the assassin does not even deserve to pay the price of his
crime. Let his heart of stone and iron have no other companions
than stone and iron for the rest of his infamous life! Men who
are busy making themselves and becoming worthy of their
heroes, have no time to kill a villain! Such is the measure of
goodness and kindness which minds have been given by the
admirable spectacle of this gentle, heroic man on whose dying
lips there was never a question full of hate or a word of ire!

This immense sorrow has come in due time to this business-
like people to level their sickly spiritual life and their commercial life, which is wholesome in its proper domain, but otherwise
hard and corrupt. Lives engaged only in love of self are lost,

and only those that mingle with others in sorrow and love, in toil and tears are saved.

Once the autopsy was over and the body prepared, the colossal apotheosis began. The funeral crossed a whole nation: on flowery paths; amidst sighs and tears; amidst prostrate crowds; amidst armies in mourning; amidst flags, wreaths, festoons, garlands; amidst offerings from monarchs and popular love, which is the highest offering; through palmed arches; over carpets of roses; under gilded vaults; between marble walls!

From the waterfront he is taken to Washington, the historic dramatic capital; from Washington, the city of his glories, to Cleveland, the city of his toils, his beginnings, his struggles as pastor and teacher, of his candid friendships, of his saddest and sweetest memories.

The apotheosis began in Long Beach. The well-dressed neighbors of that stylish place, the many who had come from Washington and New York, the numerous wealthy residents who in summer favor the beaches of this famous bathing resort, putting aside all convention, oblivious of the frigid aloofness apparently imposed by the silly mutual exhibition of luxury in which these moderns live — as though the warmth of the sun of virtue had melted away all the ice which rivalry and ambition accumulate on man — here all press upon the house of death silent, humble, sad as a black tide that surges and falls under melancholy night's dark canopy. This house, the scene of so much hope, of so much anxiety, was now first opened to the eager crowds. The grief-stricken visitors filed by for an hour. There, in a plain, black casket, adorned only with heavy silver rings, lay the man who leaves behind him a warmth like the sun's and a splendor like the moon's. He now was wearing the clothes in which, six months before, he had sworn loyalty to his duties as President. A man does not know on donning a garment whether he is dressing to enter the house of Glory or the house of Death. At his feet lay two palm leaves forming a V for "Victory!" A silver plaque on the casket read as follows:

JAMES ABRAM GARFIELD
BORN NOVEMBER 19*th*, 1831
DIED, PRESIDENT OF THE UNITED STATES
SEPTEMBER 19*th*, 1881

Alas! death's claws had left ridges on his handsome face,
where the black angel's merciless wings had swept away all
flesh. His eyes seemed like empty nests; his beard fell on his
breast like the wave of a dead sea; his forehead was like a
plowed field. As in life, his hand rested on his heart.

When the doors of the house were closed to the masses the
doors of the Church were opened to them. The Pastor of the
Presbyterian Church, standing by this apostle's head, read from
the Apostles; he read from the Epistle to the Corinthians, so full
of divine faith and human wisdom, and then, he raised his tremulous voice to God in prayer.

An anxious train awaited near the home, eager to carry him
away; its panting clamor smothered the panting rumble of this
Christian man of God; the hero was to return to Washington in
its powerful arms, arms worthy of bearing its burden. He was
placed in a car all draped in mourning, where twelve soldiers
stood guard. Flags hung in festoons from the vaulted ceiling as
if watching over the martyr. The train, so as not to interrupt
that glorious sleep, moved slowly, then crossed the countryside
bordering the wide ocean and disappeared in the vast distance,
while the Long Beach residents, like families deprived of their
father-head, returned to their deserted houses.

All the way to Washington the train moved between walls of
people. In Princeton where the tracks had been strewn with
fresh-cut roses by school children, college students showered the
funeral coach with garlands and wreaths. As the train entered
Philadelphia tens of thousands now uncovered their heads. The
imposing silence provoked weeping. In Wilmington the crowds
were so thick the train could scarcely move through them. Washington was paved and decked with people: avenues and squares,
balconies and windows, sidewalks and rooftops; everything over-
flowed with people, from the station, all covered with black dra-
peries, to the Capitol, in sober funeral attire. For three hours not
a covered head could be seen. Lines of select Union troops made
way for the casket, carried on artillery men's shoulders to the
hearse, which was pulled by six horses arrayed in black. There
was not a harsh noise, not an uncalled-for word, not a murmer
to mar that solemn silence, only muffled sighs. Those sighs that
were held back through respect or timidity found their way out

and tears appeared in every eye when the vast procession reached
the foot of the triumphal staircase before the rotunda. When the
casket passed before honest Washington's statue the band began
to play the melancholy strains of a beautiful, sad hymn so dear
to every American heart: "Nearer My God to Thee!" The most
illustrious men of the Judiciary and Congress awaited the coffin
on either side of the imposing stairway. When one looked from
the upper steps upon that reverent, silent, loving mass of griev-
ing, bareheaded, weeping people which extended farther than
the eye could see in the directions of the several avenues leading
to the magnificent Capitol building; when one met face to face
this generous award, this loving tribute paid to a martyr, one
felt possessed of all the sublimity of human grandeur and the
intoxicating seductions of martyrdom. The bitter enemies of the
eve: Arthur,[6] the new President, and Blaine,[7] Garfield's Cabinet
head, followed the coffin, united by a visible common sorrow.
There also followed Windom, the much-praised Secretary of the
Treasury, the head of the Judiciary, General Grant who has been
deeply affected by this death, and General Beale, Garfield's close
companion. There also walked along with them two Cabinet
members, Swain and Rockwell, both Garfield's dear friends, his
Maecenas, the former, the latter his Pilades; the dead President's faithful secretaries; outstanding functionaries, and brilliant officers of the Union's well-trained Army and Navy. They
scaled the last marble steps, passed through the bronze door and
placed the casket on the same bier on which Lincoln's body had
rested many years ago. The crypt which Congress had destined
for Washington was opened. Inside, the simple catafalque was
adorned with silver stripes on black velvet: thus should death
be to him who has lived well: on black velvet a stripe of silver!

The next day this broken wheel is replaced by a new one.
The incoming head of the nation who, in his art-filled New York
home, had sworn loyalty to his position amid dramatic incidents
at a time of real manly bereavement, has now repeated his oath
in the Vice-President's office in the Capitol, according to tradition. It was a dignified occasion, as have been so far all the new
chief's personal acts. Only a small group of high-ranking officials
and close friends were present, by special invitation, not the
usual prying multitude.

The political rivalries which in these last few days have
arisen with the semblance and vigor of novelty were not apparent
during the week of funeral ceremonies. Then they seemed to have
shrunken, ashamed of themselves, and the forlorn national family
was not aware of them. Democrats and Republicans alike grieved
for the loss of their honest chief, and in that immense living mass
that gathered in Washington to see the remains of the deceased
Executive, it was wondrous to observe how, for the first time
since the war, men's hatred softened before the tomb of a man
who knew no hatred. He fought against the South, for the glory
of the nation, the redemption of slaves, and the insurance of
liberty; but he loved the South. No hydra nested in his apostolic heart. He reserved justice to strike at the wicked, but his
judgment was by nature prudent, and goodness was his heart's
condition. And so Negro invalids from the rebel states, waiting
to enter the Capitol since dawn, stood in line next to stylish
Washington ladies, big-bodied Californians, and lively New
Yorkers. The imposing rotunda saw 150,000 human beings that
day. Mothers carried children in their arms. A blind man was
led by a friend. Poor people from nearby cities and villages arrived covered with dust after traveling all night and carrying a
basket of food. Six thousand people an hour saw the body.
Scarcely a murmur could be heard outside among the respectful
crowd: once inside, overcome by grief, they wept.

Children stopped in awe in front of the bier as though they
were approaching the sun or gazing toward a mountain. In the
rotunda the pungent smell of flowers filled the air. At the foot
of the catafalque was placed a majestic, rich wreath of Neil
roses, white carnations, odorous jasmines and geranium leaves
with the following inscription, which does honor to both the
deceased and the sender: "Queen Victoria, to the memory of the
late President Garfield. An expression of her sorrow and sympathy with Mrs. Garfield and the American Nation." How the
Queen has allowed her heart to shine through cold etiquette!
During Garfield's sickness her concern had been a maternal
anxiety. Her telegrams arrived at the President's house with the
dawn. She showed a deep, constant interest. She wanted direct,
not official reports. She had stood in spirit at the patient's bed-
side. She had descended from her regal throne to sit in the home

of the Mentor farmer. She had greeted the President's admirable wife as a friend. She had repeatedly inquired about her health and that of the children and his aged mother.

Washington never saw a more imposing procession than the one which accompanied Garfield's body to the station from whence the train left to take it to where, in the shade of the native willows, the walls of the coffin would struggle in vain to resist the earth's voracious work of transformation. Washington was full of outsiders and city residents. Her streets are broad as squares, her squares are like arenas, yet both could scarcely hold such multitudes. Offerings to God had been made in the beautiful rotunda; before two thousand fortunate spectators, foreign ministers, high Army and Navy officers, and the most important Government personnel, the Bible had been read. The Rev. Isaac Erret had offered an eloquent prayer and the Pastor of the church Garfield had attended in Washington had devoted eloquent phrases to praising the man he called Garfield the Good.

The soft music of "In the Sweet By and By" like a rising vapor or a flame that is dying, accompanied the corpse to the pompous funeral hearse. When the procession reached the train, the band played a mystic tune, "Safe in the Arms of Jesus," and the coffin was placed in the funeral coach, from the vaulted ceiling of which hung a great butterfly of white and yellow flowers with outstretched wings.

Along the way, gardens had been despoiled and trees plundered of all fresh branches so as to honor the deceased. Wherever the train stopped roses had been strewn. Leaving their villages deserted, people lined the track. His faithful wife was on the funeral train. She had come from Long Beach with her husband's body, but hid from strangers' eyes. She had closed the doors of the rotunda behind her so that she might speak undisturbed with her dead husband. Now, with him, she was bound for Cleveland, where the burial would take place. Oh, what a long, sad journey! Oh, the black night, the endless fields, the pungent air, the speeding train and, there, her dead man!

In the meantime, Cleveland turned night into day preparing to receive the glorious guest. Quiet, religious, modest Cleveland was hurriedly erecting in its principal square an imposing monument. But where were the hundred thousand spectators to be lodged? How to feed them? Private homes were turned into hotels; the railroad companies rented out coach seats; he was lucky who found a stretch of lawn or a chair to sleep on; rolling of drums was heard throughout the city; military delegations from all over the country showed their dress uniforms; helmet tufts waved in the air; ladies wove beautiful wreaths; streets and buildings were strewn with immortelles and laurel leaves. The whole town was a camp.

The coffin arrived and was placed on its monument; the crowds paid homage. These words could be read on a tall arch behind:

LIFE'S RACE WELL RUN,
LIFE'S WORK WELL DONE,
LIFE'S CROWN WELL WON,
NOW COMES REST.

The hospitable city boiled as would a body suddenly receiving an extraordinary inflow of blood. All day the parade marched past the corpse. That night was an unforgettable, romantic, historic one. A golden dome rested on four tall arches sustained by black pillars striped in gold. The arches were adorned with immortelles and ivy. By the strong pillars were placed cannons draped in mourning. Black banners hung from the high cornices, alternating with the national colors. The mysterious electric light reflected on the backs of shields, on the coffin's silver bands, on the bold golden dome. The wind murmured in the trees; the branches, stirred by the breeze, bowed over the catafalque; sentries marched silently up and down; a pale light shone over crosses of moss and flower offerings simulating Egyptian urns, an empty chair, a lyre, a star, a lighthouse, a compass, a Bible. On the Bible, by the soft amber light, could be read, written in red immortelles: "Thy will be done!"

Monday, the day of the burial, was to be an official day of mourning, of humbling, of prayer for the whole nation. These fifty million people set aside their instruments of toil. Bibles were opened and organs resounded. The city rose at dawn to accomplish its sad task. All hearts were filled with anguish. On a spacious platform behind the monument, the most famous men in the land gradually took their places, where the loyal multitude had milled around since morning.

Now the funeral service begins. A group of heavily veiled women ascends to the platform. The eighty-three-year-old mother looks sadly at her son's face. She is his life-long companion, faithful beyond the grave! At her side, his trembling sister. The notables come in groups and sit silently. Finally the platform is filled with governors, soldiers, famous politicians, clergymen, orators, the most loyal hearts and the most brilliant minds in the nation. Hundreds of voices intone a hymn. A sad voice reads from the Scriptures the passage beginning: "Man, that is born of woman, is of few days and full of trouble." [8] Then a clergyman rises and says: "Oh, God! We thank Thee for that noble, grand character of our departed President, which stood out so prominent before the Nation and before the world; and we pray that the righteousness which he so loved and which he exemplified may prevail in all the land." [9]

The Vocal Society [10] sang "He loved in Thee, oh, Lord, he died in Thee." [11] Upon the last strain, the Reverend Erret, the passionate, eloquent preacher, stood up. To him had come the honor of speaking of the deceased. It was not one of those winged speeches, one of those transports of eloquence which on grave occasions spring like a golden-maned lion or a cloud-piercing condor from the lips of brilliant Hispanic-American orators. It was an appropriate, wise, calm oration: an enumeration of merits, a summary of appraisals, some rational warnings, and honest advice. The quiet discourse of the grave Reverend was followed by a sad, prolonged, painful silence. A clergyman then sang, supported by the Vocal Society, the hymn the deceased loved, a hymn to work, a call to war, a verse to labor:

> Oh, reapers of life's harvest
> rise to the mountain
> of wisdom
> and bring down errors, defeated:
> Let there be no strange word
> or science hidden from men, oh reapers!
> Serve as I do the God I love,
> and a golden temple shall be thy reward.[12]

And indeed his destiny had, with a soft, posthumous caress, placed him to rest under a golden temple.

Then the colossal cortege started moving toward the far-off cemetery. Artillery men carried the President on their shoulders; relatives and friends followed in closed carriages. The immense throng was preceded by distant, rhythmic cannon shots, bugle calls, and a melancholy funeral march. Companies from all the divisions, commissions from all forces, delegates from all lodges, wearing dress uniforms, feathered hats, showy trappings, followed the coffin. The lodge he belonged to, the regiment he commanded during the war, corporations, colleges, election campaign centers, universities, Hebrews, Hungarians, Swiss, Bohemians, Germans, workers of all kinds, formed a long, endless accompaniment.

Those who stand for the struggle for life, those who are stimulated by holy labor accompanied the body of that hard worker, that hard struggler, to its cold resting place. Catholic, rationalist, Israelite societies, temperance societies, benevolent societies, were with him. White citizens and Negro citizens, solemnly grouped together, were with him. In the rear came a gigantic display of troops. Following a group of prominent people, ten National Guard regiments. Folded, battle-torn flags; languid, piercing tunes as though they came from gusts of wind playing on dying harps; then the brave people with their picturesque disorder, their neat array, their worn hats, their tanned faces, their calloused hands, their sorrowful demeanor, their loving word, their little crosses fastened to their sleeves or hats.

He entered the cemetery through an arch covered with inscriptions: "Lay him to sleep whom we have learned to love," read one; "Lay him to sleep whom we have learned to trust," read another. Another, atop the arch, read: "Come to rest." He was placed in the ground. The chaplain of his gallant regiment spoke by the open grave. The German Choral Societies sang in Latin Horace's "Integer Vitae." Then the great crowds outside joined the choir in singing again:

> Oh, reapers of life's harvest
> rise to the mountain
> of wisdom

and bring down errors, defeated:
Let there be no strange word
or science hidden from men, oh, reapers!

The hymn stopped; the casket was lowered into the grave. The leader, who had fostered mercy, charity, truth, goodness, and piety among men; who had lived in that prudent moderation which Don Diego Hurtado de Mendoza [13] recommended to Boscán; [14] who, filled with Divine love, had conquered all spite and human frailties and from the steel of his farmer's tools had forged his Senator's and President's pen; who had placed his word by the side of justice, his sword by the side of liberty, and his fortune behind his duty; who, like the God of the primitive Hebrews, had assumed all shapes, spoken all voices, and suffered all his people's tribulations; who had battled in the hour of battle, preached in the hour of peace, argued in the hour of debate, suffered in silence and loved unceasingly; who, through his outstanding virtue, rose from the lowest echelons of human status to resplendent heights; now returns to dust as white as the fleece of unborn kids that Spanish nobles gave their brides. He, a man of all mankind, of his nation, of his times, self-made, industrious, loving, a martyr fallen in the everlasting battle between the Satanic forces that devour and the Divine forces that construct. He who died among hymns, was mourned with equal tenderness from one confine of the world to another, with a queen's wreath on his coffin and the canticles of a colossal people reaching the heights of his luminous spirit.

Slowly the carriages returned. It rained sadly. The faithful mourners returned to their hearths; the unhappy old lady sat in her chair gazing absently; in her terrible loneliness she gathered her children around her.

In the meantime New York offered an admirable picture. All the city's temples were open: the Catholic cathedral, the synagogue, the pagoda, the Methodist church, the free thinkers' hall . . . Beecher, Talmage, Adler, Collyer, Chauncey Depew spoke. The echo from the churches died on the street. New York, richly clad in mourning, rested and sobbed. There were buildings — Babylonian buildings, like the jeweller Tiffany's — covered from top to basement with black merino. On the streets they

sold tuberoses tied with black ribbons. Black streamers streaked
the walls as tears ran down faces. Mourning emblems could be
seen on boat masts, iron steeple crosses, and weather vanes. All
house entrances were adorned appropriately, as were the roofs
of porticos.

The nation is still under the black canopy. The days of
mourning have passed and still the insignia have not been taken
down from columns and walls. The noble tenacity of a grateful
nation! The President has announced in vain that the Senate
should meet in an extraordinary session to elect, in case of a catastrophe, a successor, who now does not exist, to the presidency
of the nation. The new President's studied reserve and show of
sorrow is commented on favorably. Still the nation, with hands
full of myrtle and immortelles, stunned by the blow, stands over
the open grave gazing on its departed. It shows its love in offerings and prayers. The collection for the widow has reached three
hundred and sixty thousand dollars. Large offerings are beginning to reach the trembling old mother who has no further desire to live. It has been reported that European churches remained open during the hours of the funeral, as an homage to
the deceased President.

Sorrow nourishes, sorrow purifies, sorrow uplifts. The wealth
of countries is in their heroes. Men are like little jugs that knock
against each other and break, letting forth the fragrance of love
for the encouragement of the living. Broad, marvelous earth,
with its brave who fall, its knaves who wound, its high-placed
ones; earth, that astonishes us with its repugnant stubbornness,
its progressive forces, its unyielding forces, its flying passions,
and retarding appetites; the earth, a picturesque, immense circus
where a splendid battle is ever being fought between the servants
of the flesh, with their golden bucklers, and the servants of light,
bare-breasted; the earth, that tempestuous arena where men like
diamond points or bright sparks jump, flutter, shine, and perish;
the earth is a mortal hand-to-hand battle, wrath against wrath,
tooth against tooth, law of love against law of hatred! This time
the law of love was the victor.

JESSE JAMES

THESE days, festive in New York, have been exciting ones in Missouri where there lived a bandit with a high forehead, a handsome face, and a hand for killing. He robbed, not purses, but banks; not houses, but towns; assaulted not coaches, but trains. He was the hero of the wilderness. His town-folk had more praise for his bravery than censure for his crimes. He was not the son of a ruffian, but of a clergyman; he did not look like a villain, but like a gentleman; he did not marry a harlot, but a school teacher. And they say that he was a political boss during one of his periods of inactivity, that he went under an assumed name and attended the recent Democratic convention as a political boss to elect a president. Missouri and Kansas are covered with wilderness and thick forests. Jesse James [1] and his followers knew the trails through the woods, the hideouts on the roads, the fords in the swamps, the hollow trees. His house was an armory, as was his person, for he girded himself with two great belts of revolvers. He began life in times of war, and before a beard appeared on his cheek he had killed many a bearded man. In Alba's [2] day he would have been a captain in Flanders. In times of Pizarro, [3] he would have been a good lieutenant. In these times he was a soldier first, [4] then a bandit. He was not one of those magnificent soldiers of Sheridan who fought to make this country one and to abolish slavery, or who hoisted the flag of the North on obstinate Confederate forts. Nor was he one of those patient soldiers of silent Grant who rounded up dumb-stricken rebels as a cool hunter would a hungry wild boar. He was a southern guerrilla fighter, for whom a banner was nothing more than a shield for looting, his hand an instrument of murder. He would leave his victim on the ground and carry away the booty to distribute generously among his henchmen, minor tigers who licked the greater tiger's hand.

Published in *La Opinión Nacional*, Caracas, 1882.

When the war was over a formidable duel began. On one side were the young bandits, who rode through towns knocking at bank doors, walked out of them in broad daylight with all the gold and, drunk with danger which intoxicates like wine, fled shouting among the horror-stricken townsfolk who only realized a crime had been committed after it was all over. After a weak pursuit the townsfolk returned to the bank door and contemplated the golden fleeing figures, the brave riders embellished by the beauty of daring. On the other side were the incompetent judges in that region of small towns and vast forests; the district's soldiery, who always returned wounded or didn't return at all; the restless people, who, blinded by the glamour that always goes with bravery, saw in the bold thief a gentleman robber and their hearts throbbed as hearts always do (when the soul's good doctrine does not purify them) in the presence of an extraordinary deed, no matter how vile. Thus do Spanish ladies, watching bulls die at the hands of men in the bloody arena, throw their enormous fans in the air, take off a diminutive satin slipper to throw to the *matador,* or take from their *mantilla* the red rose pinned thereon, and clap their dainty hands!

Once there was a fair going on in Missouri. No less than thirty thousand people had gathered in a large town to gamble, dine, frolic, and watch the horse races. Suddenly there was a panic. Jesse James had heard of the fair and when all eyes were fixed on the jockeys' whips, he and his followers fell upon the ticket office, ran down the guards, and went off with all the admittance money. Such was the daring and magnitude of the crime that some Missourians concluded that it deserved pardon. Other times the knaves sank their arms elbow-deep in blood. They would rip a rail out near a railway curve, then hide in the thicket on their fast mounts. When the train came, they fell to, sparing no one, seizing all the money, loading their horses with gold ingots. Those who might man the train again were nailed to the ground. If there was a nearby bar or a local bully, they would repair there to start a row, lest the world believe there were other braver, quicker-drawing, harder-riding men than James's men. If there was a dance in Texas with the town belles, Jesse James would knock at the hall door with the butt of his gun and claim what he considered his due: the fairest for the bravest! Once they sent a famous spy after him; the spy was found with a bullet-riddled sign on his chest threatening future pursuers with a similar fate.

Life in those far-off regions is most singular. In the wilderness life develops in men all the appetites, all the arrogance, all the impulses, all the elegance of the wild beast! It is understandable that the buffalo hunter, used to challenging that powerful animal and then sitting, as on a throne, on the defeated monster's rump, should let his hair grow down to his shoulders, teach his broad feet to trample logs and his hands to bend them, train his heart to conquer tempests, and take on that solemn, sad look that comes from gazing much on nature and on the unknown. But, how can newspapers and chroniclers possibly find quixotic heroism in the deeds of this highway killer? It is fitting he should have been shot in the back by a friend, who was paid by the governor for his efforts.[5] It is fitting that a man who relies on the murderer's dagger rather than on the emblem of justice in order to govern should be expelled from the governor's mansion. Yet it is a fearful and shameless thing that a state executive and a young cutthroat should, on a dark night at the back entrance of the palace of the law, set a price on a bandit's life. How can one respect a judge who commits the same crime as the criminal? Shady was the thicket where James's gang waylaid trains; just as shady was the office where the guardian of the law set a price on the gangster's head. And the very same magistrates who persecuted him laid him in a sumptuous coffin, for which they paid from their own pocket or the state's treasury: in a special train — not the regular one — they took him to be buried at his mother's estate. Local magistrates held the cordons of the bier; thousands of people gathered to watch with tearful eyes as the man who had so often put bullets through men's skulls with no more compunction than a squirrel cracking a nut was lowered into his grave. Meanwhile police officers squabbled over who would keep the bandit's fleetfooted mare.

LONGFELLOW

NOW the celebrated poet sleeps in his grave as in a cold urn. No longer will he peer from his window at the children playing; the leaves hovering about and falling; the snowflakes, like butterflies, dancing jovially in the air; the trees stooped by the wind as men are stooped by sorrow; the bright sun so warming to a limpid soul; those slight visions of subtle wings that poets see in the air; that solemn calm that floats on the blue hills; the wheat fields; the stately trees like incense over a vast altar. Longfellow [1] is dead! Oh, what company good poets are! What gentle friends they are even when we know them not! What benefactors they are when they sing of heavenly things and console us! How soothing they are when they make us cry! How they push and uplift us when they make us think! How they fill our souls with soft music when they sorrow and pluck the air and make it sing as if it were a lyre and they held the secret of playing on it!

Life left his body like a departing bird. They clothed him in black. They kissed his generous hand. They gazed on his broad forehead as on an empty temple. They laid him in his satin coffin and on his body placed a humble bouquet of wild flowers. They dug a hollow under a majestic elm. There he sleeps!

How beautiful he was in life! He had that mystic beauty of good men; the wholesome color of those who are chaste; the magnificent arrogance of those who are virtuous; the goodness of the great; the sadness of all who live, and the craving for death that makes life beautiful.

His chest was broad, his gait was sure, his courtesy was genuine, his countenance was indescribable. His gaze was warm and caressing. He had lived among literary cliques which is no small merit in a man of his stature. His studies served him as a crucible, which is as it should be, and not as fetters as studies serve

Published in *La Opinión Nacional*, Caracas, April 11, 1882.

many others. He had in him so much light that the reflection of other lights never blinded him. He was of those who give of themselves, not of those who take from others. Some crows croaked at him, as crows always do at eagles. Some envious men nibbled at him with their green teeth. But teeth cannot bite into light. While glancing anxiously into the sky, he fixed his eyes on the high clouds and the tall mountains, and shed peace by describing beautiful things which are calming. He saw the beautiful land where men work, and that other land which is more beautiful still, where perhaps men also work.

He had no desire to rest, as he did not tire; but having lived long he had the desire a son would have who has not seen his mother for a long time. At times he felt the soft sadness of one who sees moonbeams far off in the black shadows, and at other times he felt a hurry to end it all, or doubt as to life hereafter. The fear of knowing himself filled his eyes with lightning. Then he would smile at having conquered himself, as a man who has tamed an eagle.

His poems are like resounding urns or Greek statues. To the frivolous eye they seem small, as everything great seems at first sight. But then, as from Greek statues, the soft charm of harmony and proportion emerges from them. In the bottom of those urns no rebel angels combat among burning clouds; nor do we hear winged laments arising that fly like wounded condors with dismal glance and scarlet breast; nor do we see tender lovers, stretched in a flowery vale and lulled by their gentle kisses and the swaying oat stalks; his poetry is rather a vase of myrrh from which human essences ascend fragrantly as an homage to what is high. The long-lived poet sang of Finns and Norwegians, of students from Salamanca, of Moravian nuns, Swedish ghosts, picturesque colonial things, and of wild America. But these diversions of the mind, though beautiful, do not represent well the poet's soul, nor are they his real creation, as are those wanderings of his eyes and spiritual exaltations and long, tender dialogues with nature, who was as this lover's betrothed, for whom she donned her finest garments and to whom, sure of his love, she showed the treasures of her splendid beauty. Then from his lips, born to song, emerged the harmony of song. Thus did he look out through his windowpanes on evening, not as one who feared night, but as one awaiting a tardy bride. To him little boys were flowers, little girls roses, and he was to them an old wall on which they could climb.

The thought of being lost like a wavelet in a boundless sea filled him with apprehension, and he rebelled, asking himself what might be the use of so much sorrow and the reason for so much martyrdom, but he felt pity for himself and others and kept this sorrow from his fellow men. He would have them live like Hector, not like Paris, with gratitude, not wrath, and know the beauty there is in sorrow, in death, and in work. He did not incite men to unfruitful wrath, but to the brave cultivation of themselves. It was his belief that since we have a soul we should live by the soul and not by vanity, and neither by buying nor selling pleasure, for real pleasure cannot be bought or sold. Life to him was a mountain: to be alive involved the obligation of carrying a white banner to its summit. He lived in peace, far from the noisy market place, midst murmuring bowers and where under a spreading chestnut tree a sturdy blacksmith toiled, sparks flying from the forge like kernels of golden corn while thoughtful groups of school children stopped to watch.

Now he has died serenely as a wave that disappears at sea. The children bear his name. The tall, ornate and cozy armchair made from the blacksmith's chestnut tree, given him by the children, is now empty. The grandfather clock which survives the watchmaker who made it, the warrior who counted by it the hours of battles, and the poet who praised it, still moves on lazily. And when, more like the voice of vengeance than the words of consolation, the religious chant which reminds us that we come from dust and to dust return resounded over the open grave. Nature, in whose bosom her beloved now rested, seemed to show her displeasure by lowering on the newly opened tomb a strong wind which bowed the elm's high bough, and whose voice repeated, as a consolation and a promise, Longfellow's noble lines: "Dust thou art, to dust returnest, / Was not spoken of the soul." [2]

Earth was thrown into the grave; it snowed; sadly, silently all found their way back to the city — the poet Holmes; [3] the orator Curtis; [4] the novelist Howells; [5] Louis Agassiz,[6] the son of the sage; gentle Whittier;[7] and tremulous Emerson[8] in whose lean visage could be read the solemn, majestic concentration of one who feels his head already bowing toward the pillow of the unknown!

EMERSON

A WRITER'S pen trembles at times, as if he were a priest, capable of sin, who believes himself unworthy of performing his ministry. When stirred the spirit soars high. It would rather have wings to lift it than a pen to chisel and shape it. There is pain and debasement in writing: it is like hitching a condor to a cart. For when a great man disappears from this earth, he leaves behind pure light, a craving for peace, and hatred of noise. The Universe becomes a temple; the business of the city, the tumult of life, and man's bustle, seem like a profanation. We feel as though we had lost our feet and had grown wings; as though we lived by starlight and sat in a white-flowered meadow. A fresh, pale light fills the silent, immense atmosphere. Everything moves to an apex and we rise to the top. The earth is at our feet like a far-off, forgotten world shrouded in shadows. Those rolling carts, those hawking merchants, those tall chimneys blasting into the air and all that crossing, caracoling, fighting, living that men indulge in, seem to us, from our chaste, comfortable refuge, the fracas of a barbarian army scaling our heights, trampling up the slopes, angrily rending the mighty shadow and revealing, behind it, like a colossal battlefield, the tumultuous city, vast, resplendent with warriors of stone in gold armors and helmets, wielding red spears.

Emerson [1] is dead; and our eyes are filled with sweet tears. We feel not grief, but envy. Our breast fills not with anguish, but with tenderness. Death is a victory, and when one has lived well, the bier is a triumphal chariot. We weep for pleasure, not for mourning, because the wounds life has left on the hands and feet of the deceased are already covered with rose petals. A just man's death is like a festival where all the world sits to watch the heavens open. Men's faces shine with hope, their arms bear sheaves of palms to scatter on the ground, they raise their com-

Published in *La Opinión Nacional,* Caracas, May 19, 1882.

bat swords to form an arch under which will pass, covered with boughs of oak, the victorious warrior's body. He who gave fully of himself and did well unto others rests at last. He who has bungled his work in life, must work anew to right it. And the young warriors, having seen with jealous eyes the great victor's body pass, aglow in grandiose tranquility, return to their worldly tasks to earn some day the right to be honored likewise with palms and arches of swords!

Who was this man who has died? All the world knows who he was. He was a man who discovered he was alive, who shook from his shoulders the cloaks and from his eyes the blindfolds inherited from by-gone times, and looked at Nature face to face as though all the earth were his home, the sun, his sun, and he the patriarch of it all. He was one of those to whom Nature shows herself, opens herself, to whom she stretches forth her multiple arms, as though wishing to cover all her son's body. One of those to whom the highest wisdom, the highest calm, the highest enjoyment was given. In his presence all Nature quivered like a bride. He lived happily, because he placed his love beyond earth. All his life was the dawn of a wedding night. What raptures did his soul not know! What visions did his eyes not see! What Tablets of the Law were his books! His poems what flights of angels!

When he was a boy he was timid, slender, and those who saw him likened him unto a young eagle, a young pine tree. Then he grew serene, amiable, and radiant: children and men would stop to see him pass. He had the firm gait of one who knows where he is going. His body was tall and frail like such trees as reach up their branches to the purest air. His face was lean as became a man accustomed to withdrawing within himself, but who wished to give of himself. His forehead was like a mountain slope; his nose like the beaks of high-soaring birds; his eyes winning as of one who was full of love, and quiet as of one who sees what others do not. It was impossible to see him without wanting to kiss his forehead. To Carlyle, the great English philosopher, who rose up against the earth with satanic strength and splendor, Emerson's visit was "a celestial vision." To Whitman, who has found in Nature a new poetry, to look upon him was to "live a blessed hour." [2] To Stedman, a good critic, "there was in

the sage's town a white light." [3] To Alcott, a noble, youthful old
man, who thinks and sings, "not having known him seemed a
misfortune." [4] People who saw him felt they had seen a living
monument or a supreme being. Such men towering like mountains do exist, before and behind whom all the land seems flat.
He was not familiar, but he was kind, because in his imperial
family all members had the qualities of emperors. He loved his
friends as he would a sweetheart: friendship to him had something of the solemnity of twilight in the woods. Love surpasses
friendship in that it creates offspring. Friendship surpasses love
in that it does not create desires, nor the fatigue of having gratified them, nor the pain of leaving the temple of gratified desires
for the temple of new desires. He radiated charm. One heard his
voice like that of a messenger from the future, speaking from a
luminous cloud. Those who gathered to listen seemed to be
bound by an impalpable tie fashioned of moonbeams. Wise men
visited him and came away at once rejoicing and reprimanded.
Young men walked leagues to see him. He would receive the
trembling pilgrims smiling, ask them to sit around the massive
mahogany table littered with ponderous tomes, and with his own
hands, pour them old sherry. Some, who read him without understanding him, accused him of lack of tenderness, because, used
to dealing with greatness, he deemed small what was his alone,
the accidental, essentially undeserving to be told! Such wailing
poetasters are Phrynes [5] of their grief! One should tell man what
is worthy of man and likely to exalt him! To sing one's petty
pains in mournful numbers is a task for ants! Sorrow should
be modest.

His mind was priestly; his gentleness, angelic; his wrath,
holy. When he saw men enslaved and pondered over them, he
spoke and it was as if once again the Tablets of the Law were
being shattered on the slopes of a new biblical mountain. His
wrath was Mosaic. He shook off the trifles of vulgarity as a lion
would gadflies. To him arguing was time stolen from the discov-
ery of truth. As he spoke of what he saw, he became impatient
with those who doubted what he said. Thus wrath did not spring
from vanity but from sincerity. How could it be his fault if
others lacked the revealing light that was in his eyes? Will not
the caterpillar deny the eagle's flight? He despised sophistry and

since for him the extraordinary was the common, he was amazed at the necessity of having to demonstrate the extraordinary. When he was misunderstood he shrugged his shoulders: Nature had spoken to him: he was Nature's high priest. He feigned no revelations, nor built mental worlds; nor added will power or mental effort to his writings in verse or prose. His prose is verse; his verse and prose are like echoes. Behind him he heard the Creative Spirit speaking through him to Nature. He saw himself as an all-seeing, all-reflecting, transparent eye; and nothing else. His writings seem like bits of shattered light which had shone upon him, bathed his soul, made it intoxicated with its dazzling brightness, and emerged again. What was he to think of those vain little minds, perched on their conventions as on stilts? Or of those unworthy men who have eyes and will not see? Or of those lazy gregarious men who use not their eyes, but see through those of others? Or of those clay figures who strut about fashioned by tailors, shoemakers, and hatters, and embellished by jewelers, who have senses and the gift of speech, but no more? Or of those pompous ranters who do not even dream that every thought is a mental ache, a flame that burns the oil of one's life, a mountain peak?

Never was there a man freer from the pressure of other men or of his time. The future did not make him tremble or blind him as he passed it. The light he carried within led him safely on this trip through the ruins we call life. He knew no limits nor fetters. Nor was he a man of his country, for he belonged to mankind. He saw the earth, found it unlike himself; he felt the pain of answering questions men do not ask, and withdrew within himself. He was tender towards men, loyal to himself. He was brought up to teach a creed, but he returned to the credulous his pastor's cassock because he felt upon his shoulders Nature's august mantle. He obeyed no system — doing so seemed to him a blind and servile act — nor did he create a system, for this he deemed the act of a weak, lowly, envious mind. He plunged into Nature and came forth radiant. He felt himself a man and, as such, God. He spoke of what he saw; where he could not see, he said naught. He revealed what he perceived, and revered what he failed to perceive. He looked into the Universe with his own eyes and spoke a language of his own. He

was a creator, through not wanting to be one. He felt divine
bliss and indulged in delightful, celestial communion. He knew
the ineffable sweetness of ecstasy. Never did he hire out his
mind, his tongue, or his conscience. Like a star he gave forth
light. In him the human being attained full dignity.

Thus did he live: seeing the invisible and revealing it. He
lived in a sacred city, for it was there, in the sage's Concord,
where men, tired of being slaves, decided to be free and against
the British redcoats fired the first bullet from the metal of which
this people was wrought. Concord is a place like ancient Tuscu-
lum, where thinkers, hermits, and poets live. In the sage's room
books looked more like guests than books: all dressed familiarly,
with faded pages, worn backs. He read everything, leaping like
an eagle from one book to another. The roof of the house was
lofty in the center, as was becoming to the home of one used to
soaring high. At times he closed his books and his eyes to enjoy
the bliss of seeing with his soul, or he restlessly paced about as
though moved by a will not his own, all afire, when an idea,
craving for a precise expression, as though trapped among bram-
bles, whipped his lips to force its way out into the air. At other
times he would sit fatigued and smile softly, like one who sees
something solemn and gratefully caresses his own spirit for having found it. Oh! What a joy it is to think well! What pleasure
to understand the object of life — a monarch's pleasure! When
a truth appears, one smiles as in the presence of a beauteous
maiden. One trembles as in the mystery of betrothal.

Here was a subtle seer who saw the delicate air change into
melodious, wise words in men's throats and who wrote as a seer,
not as a meditator. Whatever he wrote was a maxim. His pen
was no brush that dilutes; it was a chisel that sculptured and
cleaved. He turned out pure phrases as a sculptor does pure
lines. An unnecessary word seemed to him a wrinkle in the con-
tour. He chiseled off the wrinkle, which snapped in pieces, leaving the sentence clean. He abhorred the unnecessary. When he
spoke he exhausted his subject. At times he seemed to jump
from one thing to another, and at first sight we fail to see the
relation between two adjacent ideas. It is simply that what to
any other is a leap was to him a natural step. He walked, like
a giant, from peak to peak, not along trails and footpaths, like

pack-burdened pedestrians, to whom, when they glanced up from their depth, the giant seemed small. He did not write in periods but in schemata. His books are summae, not demonstrations. His thoughts seem isolated only because he saw much at one glance and would like to say everything at one time. He related things as he saw them, as one who reads by the glare of lightning or sees by a light so beautiful that it cannot possibly last. He leaves to others the task of developing ideas: he could not lose time; he announced! His style is not luxuriant but limpid. He cleansed it, assayed it, examined it, tested it. He kept only the marrow. His style is not like a verdant hillock covered with fragrant flowers; it is a basaltic mountain. He was the master of his tongue, not its slave. Language is the work of man; he should never be its slave. There are those who do not understand him well, but one cannot measure a mountain inch by inch. They say he is obscure. When were great minds not accused of being obscure? It is less humiliating to blame a writer for being unintelligible than to confess our incapacity to understand him. Emerson does not argue, he states. He preferred what Nature taught him to what man teaches. He believed a tree knows more than a book; a star teaches more than a university. A farm is like a gospel; a child on that farm is closer to universal truth than an antiquarian. For him there were no better candles than stars, nor better altars than mountains, nor better preachers than deep, throbbing nights. Angelic emotions filled him when he saw the morn, fair and happy, shed her veils. When he watched a sunset or the laughing dawn he felt more powerful than an Assyrian monarch or the King of Persia. To be good it sufficed him to see the beautiful. By these flames he wrote. His ideas fell upon his mind like white pebbles on a luminous sea: what sparks! what flashes! what tongues of fire! One feels dizzy as though one rode on a flying lion's back. He too felt dizzy, but emerged fortified. Then one presses the book to one's breast as one would a good and generous friend, or perhaps one caresses it tenderly as though it were a faithful woman's pure forehead.

He thought about everything that was deep. He wished to penetrate the mystery of life, to discover the laws of the existence of the Universe. As a creature he found himself strong and went out in search of his Creator. He returned elated, saying he had found Him. After this colloquy, he spent the rest of his life in a state of beatitude. During these spiritual elations, these surrenderings to the universal spirit, he would tremble like a leaf and then, fragrant and fresh as a leaf, return to himself.

When he was born, men piled before him all those obstacles which presumptuous men for centuries have heaped up around the cradle of new men. Books are full of subtle poisons that inflame the imagination and sicken judgment. He drank from all those cups, but the poison scarcely touched him and he went his way. It is man's torment that to see well he must be wise and forget he is. The possession of truth comes only from the struggle to select wisely between opposite revelations. Some, mere voices of other spirits, succumb. Others triumph and add to Nature a new voice. Emerson triumphed: behold his philosophy.

Nature [6] is the title of his best book: in it he abandons himself to his exquisite delights, tells of his marvelous promenades, rebels high-spiritedly against those who ask for eyes to see, forgetting they have eyes; in it he sees man, the Master; the Universe, mild and yielding, and all live things springing from its bosom or sinking into it, and, in all that lives, the Spirit which will continue living, and, in its arms, Man. He gives an account of himself and of what he sees, but no account of what he has not felt. He prefers to be called inconsistent rather than a Jack o' Dreams. Whenever his eyes no longer see he tells us so. He does not deny that others see, but holds to what *he* has seen. If there are contradictions in what he sees, he leaves to others the task of commenting on them and finding distinctions: he merely narrates. He sees only analogies: he finds no contradiction in Nature: he sees that in Nature everything is a symbol of man, and that whatever there is in man is in Nature. He sees that Nature influences man and that man makes Nature cheerful or sad, eloquent or dumb, absent or present, as he chooses. He sees man's idea as the master of universal matter; physical beauty invigorating man's spirit and preparing it for moral beauty. He sees that to a desolate spirit the Universe is desolate. He sees that the spectacle of Nature inspires faith, love, reverence. He feels that the Universe, while it abstains from answer-

ing man through formulas, does answer him by inspiring sentiments that calm his anxieties and allow him to live strong,
proud, and happy. He holds that everything resembles everything, that everything has the same object, that everything re-
volves about man, who embellishes everything with his mind,
that all the currents of Nature pass through each creature, that
the Creator is in every man and that every creature has within
something of the Creator, and that everything in the end will
return to the creative Spirit's bosom; that there is a central
unity in all facts — in thoughts and in actions; that the human
soul, in its wanderings through Nature, finds itself in all of her;
that the beauty of the Universe was created to breed desire, to
alleviate the pains of virtue and stimulate man to seek himself
and find himself; that "within man is the soul of the whole;
the wise silence; the universal beauty, to which every part and
particle is equally related; the Eternal ONE." [7] Life does not
worry him: he is happy because he does good: the important
thing is to be virtuous: "Virtue is the golden key / Which opes
the palace of eternity." [8] Life is more than relationships, or
danger, it is communion with the forces of Nature and self-
control, the latter following from the former: universal order
inspires individual order. Happiness is real, it is the highest
impression; therefore, no matter what the truth may be about
all mysterious things, it is sensible that one should do that which
produces real pleasure, pleasure which is higher than any other,
pleasure which is virtuous: life is but "a stopping-place in Nature." [9]

And as to death? Did it not make Emerson grieve? Death
holds no grief or fear for him who has lived nobly; only he who
has reason to fear fears it. Whoever deserves to be immortal
shall be: to die is to return the finite to the infinite: there is no
good in rebelling: life is a fact for which there is a reason,
namely that it is a fact: only for imbeciles is it a toy, for real
men it is a temple: rather than rebel, it is preferable to live
improving ourselves through the honest exercise of feeling and
thinking.

And as to science? Science confirms what the spirit has
grasped: the analogy of all forces of Nature; the similarity of
all living beings; the identical composition of all elements in the

Universe; the sovereignty of man, whose inferiors we know, but
not his superiors. Spirit foresees; beliefs confirm. Spirit, sub-
merged in the abstract, sees the whole; science, crawling over
the concrete like an insect, sees only details. The fact that the
Universe was formed by long, methodical, analogous processes,
neither announces Nature's end nor contradicts the existence of
spiritual facts. When science completes its cycle and men know
everything, they will only know what the mind already knows,
and nothing more.

And what about life's object? Life's object is to satisfy our
craving for perfect beauty, because just as virtue beautifies
whatever it touches so do beautiful things affect virtue. There is
a moral character in all the elements of Nature; since these
elements liven the moral character in man, it follows they have
it also. Thus are identified: truth, which is beauty in judgment;
goodness, which is beauty in affection; pure beauty, which is
loveliness in art. Art is nothing but Nature created by man.
There is no evading this intermixture. Nature bows to man and
presents her differences on which for him to sharpen his wits,
her marvels to move his will into imitating them, her exigencies
to educate his spirit through work, through disappointments,
and through virtue which overcomes them. Everything in this
multiple Universe happens as a symbol of man, as it happens in
man. Smoke vanishes in the air like thought in infinity. Sea
waves seethe and roll as affections do in the soul. The mimosa
is weak like a sensitive woman. Every quality of man is represented in one of Nature's animals. Trees speak to us in a language we understand. Night must surely leave something in our
ears, since she so fills with peace the hearts of those who take to
her their tribulations. The apparition of truth suddenly illuminates the soul, as the sun illuminates Nature. Morning makes
birds sing and men talk. Dusk folds the wings of birds and
silences the words of men. Virtue, which everything in Nature
stimulates, brings peace to man and rounds out his task, in the
manner of a curve that, folding back upon itself, completes its
course and closes the circle. The Universe is slave; man, king.

He stretched out his arms and held in them the secret of life.
Among painful labors and mortal anxiety, he rose from his body
— that fragile basket which held his winged spirit — to those

lofty peaks from which the wayfarer beholds — as a prize for his efforts — infinite beings garbed in light-spangled tunics. He experienced the mysterious overflow of the soul in the body, a rare fortune which fills the lips with kisses, the hands with caresses, the eyes with tears, and recalls the sudden swelling and bursting of Nature in the springtime. Then he felt the calm that comes after conversing with the divine and that magnificent regal arrogance with which man is endowed by the consciousness of his power. What man who is ruler over himself does not laugh at the impotence of a king?

There were times when, dazzled by those resplendent Hindu books in which the human creature, purified by virtue, flies like a fiery butterfly from its worldly dross to Brahma's bosom, he sat and did what he had censured, that is, he saw Nature through the eyes of others. This was because he had found an agreement between the vision of those eyes and his own. Then his own visions were blurred and tarnished. For that Indian philosophy makes one drowsy as does an orchard of orange blossoms. It is like seeing a flock of birds that makes us crave to fly. When we delve into it we feel as though we have sweetly swooned, wafted upwards on flames of blue. And one wonders whether Nature is not a phantasmagoria; man, a fancier; all the Universe, an idea; whether God is not the pure idea, and man, the aspiring idea which will end eventually in God's bosom like a pearl in its shell or an arrow in the trunk of a tree. And he begins to erect scaffolding and to build the Universe. But soon he tears down the scaffoldings, ashamed of the meanness of his edifice and the inadequacy of the mind, which, when it attempts to construct worlds, achieves no more than an ant trying to drag along a chain of mountains.

When once more he felt mystic, vague effluvia running through his veins he repaired to the woods to appease the tempest of his soul in the friendly reassurance of their tranquility. He observed that whenever the mind runs aground, like a ship on a craggy shore, intuition, escaping from the broken cage of mind, soars aloft like a sky-bound bird. He translated in ruffled, brutal, and rebellious language intuition's lucid raptures and the chaste swoons, the balmy delights, and the ravishing pleasures of a tremulous spirit which captive Nature, as though astonished

by her lover's boldness, admits to her communion. Emerson proclaimed to man that, since the Universe reveals itself to him
fully and directly, this revelation implies the right which every
man has to see it for himself and to quench with his own lips
the burning thirst it creates. Having learned through this communion that pure thought and pure affection produce such vivid
pleasure that the soul feels in them a sweet death, followed by
a radiant resurrection, he proclaimed to man that there is no
felicity save in being pure

When he had discovered this, and that man wears a crown of
stars, and that when man's skull grew cold his serene spirit
would cleave the air wrapped in light, he placed a loving hand
on tormented mankind and focused his lively, penetrating eyes
on the world's rude strife. His glance cleared away much rubbish. He sat familiarly at the table of heroes. He told with Ho-
meric tongue about conflicts among peoples. He was candid as
extraordinary men are. He followed his intuition, which opened
to him equally the bosom of a tomb or of a cloud. Having sat
and waxed strong in the senate of the stars, he now sits, as
though among brothers, in the senate of peoples. He tells of
ancient history and of modern history. He analyzes nations as
a geologist would fossils. His sentences stand out like vertebrae
of mastodons, like gilded statues, or Greek porticos. Of other
men we can say: "He is a brother"; of this one we must say:
"He is a father." He wrote a marvelous book which is a human
Summa, in which he consecrates great men, studying them by
types. He visited old England, land of his Puritan fathers, and
set his impressions down in another powerful book which he
titled *English Traits.*[10] He grouped in sheaves the facts of life,
and studied them in magical "Essays," [11] setting down their
laws. All his laws of life turn about the axis of this truth: "all
Nature shudders before a child's conscience." [12] He decomposed
and analyzed religion, destiny, power, wealth, illusions, and
greatness as with a chemist's hand. He leaves the beautiful
standing; razes the false; submits to no conventions. What is
vile, though it may be consecrated, he calls vile. It was time man
began to be angelic. Tenderness is a law; resignation is a law;
prudence is a law. These essays are like statutes. Their excessive
substance crushes us. They have the grandiose monotony of a

range of mountains. They are enhanced by an indefatigable fancy and a singular good sense. There is for him no difference between the big and the small, nor between the ideal and the practical; the laws that will provide the definitive triumph and the right to be crowned with stars, also provide felicity on earth. Contradictions are not in Nature; they stem from men's not knowing how to discover her analogies. He did not disdain science for being false but for being slow. His books are full of scientific truths. Tyndall [13] says he owes him all his science. All evolutionism is contained in a sheaf of Emersonian sentences. But he did not believe intellect suffices to penetrate the mystery of life, to give man peace, to provide him with the means for his growth. He held that intuition finishes what intellect begins; that eternal spirit guesses what human science traces. Science scents like a dog; spirit flies like a mighty condor over the abyss where the naturalist is absorbed in his delving. Emerson always observed, took notes of what he saw, grouped together in his notebooks similar facts, and when he found something to reveal he spoke out. He had something of Calderon, of Plato, of Pindar. Also of Franklin. He was not like the leafy bamboo whose copious foliage, ill-sustained by hollow trunks, bends to the ground, but like the baobab, or the savin, or the mighty genisaro whose robust top sits proudly on a massive trunk.

Idealism then roamed disdainfully about this earth and was not much loved by sensible men. Emerson humanized idealism: he did not wait for science — birds need no stilts to reach the heights, nor eagles, rails. He left science behind as an impatient warrior on his flying steed leaves behind the heavily burdened footsoldier. To him idealism was not a vague craving for death, but a belief in a life hereafter which was to be won in this life by the serene practice of virtue. Life is as beautiful and as ideal as death. Let us see how he reasoned this out. He tells us that man does not devote all his powers to the study of Nature, only his understanding, which is not the richest, and therefore does not penetrate well into Nature, and man then says: "This is because the axis of man's vision does not coincide with the axis of Nature." [14] Then he tries to explain how all moral and physical truths are contained in each other, any one being in all the others, and says: "They are like the circles of a sphere, which are all comprised in each other, and enter and exit freely without anyone being above another." [15] And thus he speaks: "To a man laboring under calamity the heat of his own fire has sadness in it." [16] "We are not built like a ship, to be tossed, but like a house, to stand." [17] "Cut these words and they would bleed." [18] "To be great is to be misunderstood." [19] "Leonidas consumed one day in dying." [20] "All the facts of natural history, taken by themselves, have no value, but are barren, like a single sex." [21] "That man goes trampling in the mire of dialectics." [22]

His poetry was built out of colossal irregular blocks, like those palaces in Florence. It beats and swells like the sea. Again it may be like a little basket of flowers in a naked child's hand. It is the poetry of patriarchs, primitive men, cyclops. Some of his poems are like budding oak groves. He wrote the only truly poetic verse on this country's great struggle! [23] Other poems are like rivulets of precious stones or like filmy clouds or streaks of lightning. Is it still not clear what his poems are? Sometimes they are like an old man with a spiralling beard, a tormented mane of hair, and fiery glance, singing from a white stone cavern as he leans on an oaken staff; other times they are like a gigantic golden-winged angel, leaping from a high green mount into the abyss. Marvelous old man, at your feet I place my sheaf of fresh palm leaves and my silver sword!

PETER COOPER

HEARTS and flags are at half-mast: Peter
Cooper [1] is dead. This people he leaves behind is a nation of
sons. I was not born in this land — nor did he ever hear my
name — yet I loved him as a father. Had I met him on my way,
I would have kissed his hand. Come May and spring's fragrant
flowers open on their tender stems — not winter's pale, sickly
flowers that grow in hot-houses — I shall pick from some nearby
field a bunch of wild flowers and lay them at the entrance of the
tomb where the body of this loving old man lies, like the cloak
dropped by an angel on his flight to heaven. He died and those
who knew him well, with the approval of the whole city, placed
a lily on his breast. Thus did he descend to his tomb. Oh, marvelous breast on which, after ninety-three years of life on this
earth, a lily now opens! Today life is like a battle in which a
youth in a white tunic struggles in the night with feverish hands
to keep his immaculate garment from being defiled by an army
of crawling, satanical beasts who, dragging their pouchy bellies,
waylay him at every bend of the road. In their human eyes
shines a sinister flame; their gnashing teeth, that would devour
the tunic, distill a slimy liquor. It is well and fitting that the
world should prostrate itself in homage before the dead body
of a man who has passed through such an army and emerged
with his tunic immaculate.

He loved, he founded, he consoled, he practiced the human
Gospel; he brought peace to spiteful hearts, bread to outstretched
hands, nourishment to avid minds, dignity to life, happiness to
himself and glory to his country. He leaves a school [2] where two
thousand workers learn, and many more thousands read and thus
gain peace. No saint has a higher altar in his cathedral than has
Peter Cooper in this school! During his lifetime he dug the

Dated New York, April 19, 1883, published in *La Nación*, Buenos Aires,
June 3, 1883.

ground, felled forests, darned cloth, invented machines for cutting it, machines for rocking children to sleep, to empty out mines, to navigate canals, to keep steam, so rebellious and angry in captivity, under control. The earth, like a bounteous mother, opened her bosom to him. He smelted metals,[3] an exercise that imparts prodigious strength: it seems that new worlds boil in the furnaces, whose glare makes men seem like gods.

He lived serenely, because he lived without sin. His wife was not, like other wives, a harsh amazon who awkwardly leads her horse by the bridle, she was like a wing. He was so gentle he seemed weak; but he had the magnificent energy of gentle men. He wept if he heard a child weep, but he started the first locomotive across the American wilderness.[4] After fashioning a hat for an old neighbor lady with his hatter's art, he sat down and designed a machine to capture and utilize the power of tides.

He attended school fifty-two times and no more. But every year hundreds of men and women leave the school he founded, prepared in arts and sciences, their shield for the battle of life. His parents were very poor. At the age of five Peter Cooper helped his father sell beer. At ten he already made hats; at fifteen if he needed shoes he would make a last with his own hands and then the shoes; later he made carriages and saved money which he gave to his needy father. The English war [5] brought on a scarcity of clothes and of machinery for making them. So he, the poor beer-boy, provided them! With the earnings from the machines and in spite of his constant giving of money (giving was his life), he came to New York to sell spices, across the street from where today he saves souls through his generous Institute. Then he built, bought factories, invented new merchandise, drained swamps, emptied sandbars, broke down mountains, fed thousands of men, discovered things he needed, conquered obstacles, raised colossal steel mills, left his inventions for others to enjoy, bequeathed his property to his children, and raised again new fortunes, he grew like the swelling seas. But his patriarchal, serene hands were always extended over men's tormented heads!

To Peter Cooper there was no merit in doing good, but not to do it was a crime. He would have trembled with fright, as if a tremendous, monstrous hand were about to strike him, had he gone a day without doing a good deed. He considered life a priesthood and selfish wellbeing, an apostasy. He did not rebel against God, angry at feeling Him and not seeing Him, nor did he shake his fist at disdainful Heaven; he lived meekly as one who glimpses supreme delights, and was contented, because he knew the meaning of life. There is only one key that opens the doors of happiness: Love. He who loves does not suffer, even when he suffers, because from the soul devoured by love of mankind enchanting aromas rise, as from a cup where incense burns. He saw that the greatest pleasure comes from doing good and the greatest torture from not being able to do it; that pain when it is pure nourishes, but that impure or base pain, as most human pains are, scourges the soul, as the bundles of barbed wires scourged the buttocks of maddened horses in the barbarian Roman carnival.

And he saw that he who locks himself up within himself lives among lions, while he who emerges from himself and gives himself to others lives among doves. And if scoundrels dig into him an angry tooth, he is pained not by the bite, but by seeing that there are still biting teeth. And he will place his hand on the forehead of him who bites and look into his eyes so tenderly that, beaten, the biter will release his prey.

In brief, Peter Cooper lived assured of a life hereafter, whose dawning already bathed him in light. No worldly pleasure nor orchestral music seemed to him comparable to this music and this delight of his spirit. "Why do you confer upon me this degree of Doctor of Laws?" he once asked the chancellor who handed him the honorary parchment with Latin words with which the university rewarded this man who already held as high a degree from the University of Nature. "If you bestow this upon me because I have preached how to be happy, which is by being good; because I have proved with my long life that giving strength to others increases our own; because my gray hair and my still rosy cheeks are showing that who feeds on young ideas always remains young; because I proclaim that science is no don's hood nor ministry for the initiated, nor privilege of aristocrats of the mind, but man's only way of understanding the laws of life; then I'll take your generous parchment even though I am not a scholar and these Latin words are Greek to me." The man who thus spoke was ninety years old.

He was never strong of body, which he had no need to be,

being strong of soul. When he conceived a goal he never stopped
before he attained it, then he passed on to another. Every natural marvel suggested to him a marvel of the mind. His hand
gave warmth to inventions as the sun warms the spawn of fish.
Whatever he touched he improved. Years back, when the family
ate hard bread, it was he who had to rock the baby's cradle
while his wife minded the kettles. It was then his fertile mind
conceived a little machine that at the same time rocked the
cradle, drove away the flies and started a music-box playing.
He was induced to buy a tract of coast land, generally considered as valueless. He made it productive. A railroad would be a
good thing to carry out minerals from the region, but the land
was too rugged and the engines in those days, like crocodiles of
steel, could not take the curves properly. So he studied their
entrails, and, making them over, created the tubular boiler and
started the first locomotive rolling across America. Produce
brought by rail cost the public too much; it would be sold
cheaper if brought by canals. But horses pulled the barges laden
with foodstuff too slowly along the banks. He conceived a Cyclopean system of chains placed along the banks which moved
the barges one mile in six minutes. It was necessary to carry ore
down a rugged mountain from a high-placed mine to a far-off
depot. The carting down of the full buckets and returning the
empty involved a problem — so he invented a conveyor device
and draped it three miles over the mountain: the buckets were
loaded at the mine and rolled by gravity down the hillside,
dragged along also by the weight of the other buckets being
filled up above, while the light, empty ones naturally returned
to the mine.

One day he heard that Turkey was oppressing Greece and
drowning her in blood. What strange power hides in the thirst
for independence that it makes apostles even of scoundrels and
devastating lions of turtle-doves? Peter Cooper set himself to
contrive an apparatus of destruction, a torpedo, controlled from
the shore by very long wires, as you would a horse by means of
reins, which would destroy the Moslem ship it hit.

He thought it would be a good thing — in order to prevent
the fire of wood from burning the altar on which the fire of
spirit glows — to build his Institute of Arts and Sciences fire-

proof, for which purpose he spent seventy-five thousand dollars
on production machinery, for making steel beams.[6] Sometimes
he seemed like a Satan of Good. When he conquered some ma-
lign force of Nature, a smile full of angelic mischief would spread
over his broad lips. He liked to shut himself up alone among his
crucibles and blowtorches. He did not seek gold, he himself was
gold, instead he sought to wrest from Nature some secret, and
after finding it he would laugh heartily as a player who wins a
difficult match or a child who at last finds the toy his mother
had hidden from him. He tried to produce expensive things
cheaply, so that his friend, the poor man, might enjoy them. He
was forever sitting among his workmen asking if they wanted
better wages, if work was too tiring, or what they would have
him do to reduce their suffering, but no one suffered. What his
genius produced, his hand poured on the pillows of the unfortunate. He felt it was a duty to give away every cent he made.
He considered himself not the owner of his wealth, but its manager. Whenever he had a streak of good fortune in business, he
added a new hall to his Institute. His enterprises brought him
millions, which his charity returned. He was quiet about it,
never accepting prizes, formal recognition, or public praise. He
headed all the great enterprises; thanks to him the telegraph
was improved; the cable broke repeatedly, but he never gave up,
and disbursed enormous sums until it was finally laid.[7] He was
concerned with his private affairs, his school, which he visited
daily, and at the same time with public affairs. Should one have
asked him whether he had children, he would have answered all
workers were his children. He felt their wounds in his own breast.
He begged the wealthy to be merciful, the dissatisfied to be
patient, setting himself as an example and showing them how
his present treasures had come, like ribbons from a magician's
hat, out of that poor bonnet he had sewed, as a boy, for his old
neighbor. He did not believe in the efficacy of wrath, but of
science. He preached that ignorance at times makes justice hateful. He announced that there is no power which can resist cultivated human intelligence. From the harmony of all known laws
and from the imperfection and brutal harshness of present human life, one can infer that man has not yet conceived the soft,
broad laws of life and that the earth holds goods aplenty to

satisfy the desires of all its inhabitants. The straightest way to
the solution of social problems is to study the forces of nature
and how to profit from them. Intellectual intercourse ennobles
men. An ignorant man has not yet begun to be a man. Man
carries all his swords and all his lances behind his forehead.

Peter Cooper was not satisfied to help; he had to redeem.
Charity is a narcotic, not a cure. It dries tears from a cheek, it
does not dry the fountain from which they flow. And Peter
Cooper, who started barefoot on the tearful road, wanted to
strengthen other men's feet for the journey. What does it avail
a man to learn words he doesn't understand, numbers whose
capricious combinations mean no more to the mind than do
some stray bones in a physician's satchel, or geographic boun-
daries that one wing of memory introduces in the brain and the
other carries away? Those who go through schools, which should
be urns brimful with life, in that way can hardly fight life's
battle with such shields and bucklers. Men live by chance, by
other men's bounty, by laboriously acquiring when they are
grown, what they should have learned without labor in their
years of preparation. Since man is born to live, education should
prepare him for living. Schools should teach the use of the
forces which man has for his fight in life. They should be more
like shops than schools. In schools, the pen should be wielded in
the afternoon; the hoe in the morning.

Thus Peter Cooper, who always wished to learn but had no
place to learn, after his sixty-fourth year thought of opening an
industries, arts, and sciences center for those who must live by
them. If one is to be a horseman in the desert should he not
learn to ride? So those who are to live by the earth should learn
about the earth — the living, multiple, throbbing earth. Arches
were erected, spacious floors were laid, stacks were filled with
thousands of books, eminent teachers were engaged, doors were
thrown wide open through which the untrained laborers entered
as if to bathe in waters of redemption. There they go to a class
in chemistry, or wood engraving, or photography, or industrial
design, or mechanics! Men and women come in bustling throngs
to learn together in this noble house the art of living. There, at
the end of the year, they will have in their hands the reins of
Fortune, a degree with which to work in a job the school itself

often obtains for them. Let us enter. What silence! Two thousand men are reading! A little further: what a beautiful sight! Three hundred girls studying! Just look at those spacious corridors, those magnificent halls: there is a rumble of groups waiting for their professors who will come to teach them how to handle certain instruments, to work certain aparatus, or how to move social forces, to store and direct electricity, or to learn how Peter Cooper believes the only worthy religion is that which excludes no one.

Now he is dead! He is dead! He will no longer come every Saturday as he used to, to visit his beloved Institute, leaning on his daughter's arm. Never again will he see the youthful, thankful crowds that awaited him on the steps or hailed him on the street filling the air with cheers and frantic waving of hats. Never again will rough and unceremonious teamsters pull up their carts and wagons, bowing respectfully, to let his carriage pass. Never again will paupers cluster around his carriage sure of receiving some help. Nor will he in full daylight descend from his battered old carriage to help his coachman, with his ninety-three-year-old hands which had made millions, to mend a broken strap with a wooden needle and a string, nor will he ever again, standing on the carriage stirrup, as he once did, speak to the multitude that had gathered to see their benefactor and greet him with loud and prolonged cheers.

The whole city followed his bier. The church where he lay was surrounded by such a thick crowd standing in the rain, that it seemed they could carry the church on their shoulders. Fifteen thousand New Yorkers saw the old man's body in six hours.

The church resembled a basket of flowers, the streets a carpet of bared heads. The Senate, the House of Representatives, the City Administration, the Chambers of Commerce, all have expressed their mourning, proclaiming him father of the nation. All wear black arm-bands.

In the homes, all stand on hearing his name: men, women, children — and servants. Women, seeing the passing funeral procession from their windows, remove their gay, feathered hats as a delicate and uncommon tribute!

WENDELL PHILLIPS

MANY trifling occurrences in the gay city and many congressional squabbles filling newspapers and conversations these days seek in vain expression through my pen.[1] In vain do events weigh upon our memory (where we would rather they were not): a bandit's wife showing off, in a circus before cigarette-smoking and yelling children, the weapon with which her husband had taken so many lives; a murderer who exhibits himself on tour, the friend who killed her husband for a few dollars, and who now reenacts the scene of the murder for the approving pleasure of western crowds, with the same gun and dressed in the same clothes.[2] In vain we hear the din of political or private disputes that sound the way a blade of tin would sound against an angel's sword. Wendell Phillips [3] is dead! That illustrious mouthpiece of the poor; that magnanimous, shining knight of justice and eloquence; that famous orator who faced selfish mobs and made them follow him or, when they shrieked like barbarians, knew how to throttle them; that indefatigable abolitionist of whom John Bright [4] said he had no equal, either among Americans or Britishers, for the pureness of his heart, the majesty of his speech, or the serenity of his character — speaks no more! There is no need to wail over his death, a simple, ordinary event which comes as a reward for leading a clear life, to be awaited calmly and received tenderly. Great men, even those who have found their real greatness within themselves and have cultivated it and used it to the benefit of others, are but vehicles of great forces. They come and go in waves. Their piercing pains, their resplendent martyrdoms, their clusters of sonorous and flaming words, their toilsome merits are, in the presence of eternity, like the white foam that breaks into a mist

Dated New York, February 11, 1884, published in *La Nación*, Buenos Aires, March 28, 1884. Martí wrote another article on Wendell Phillips published in *La América*, New York, March, 1884.

against the rocks or shatters, spreads, and sinks silently in the sand.

It was he who raised to his lips the cup of pleasure and then lowered it, smiling, to walk arm-in-arm with the humble. It was he who soon discovered that life has its plebeians — those who love but themselves and bring all the world to their pillows and their mouths, and its nobles — those who are devoured by a craving to do good, who would quench their neighbors' thirst with their own blood, their hunger with their very heart, who fill the lamp of mankind with the oil of their souls. It was he who, when placed by the accumulation of wealth in an exalted position that inebriates and withers as orgies do, saw through the mountain of death, saw within himself, and was aflame with love, love which is always painful, and avoids contagion. It was he who lifted the wretched out of their wretchedness, claiming for himself as the only worthwhile pay the ever-bitter pleasure of having defended them. It was he who among the general perversion of mental and moral powers found in himself a splendid and broadening intelligence which he held up reverently, as the priest does the host. It was he who was absorbed in helping others and disdained the great advantages that nature's benevolent caprice had showered upon him, because they profited only him. He is now a hero, an apostle, before whom every honest man should stop to kiss his death-cold hand.

It was nearly fifty years ago. The crowd was roaring. Channing,[5] a great orator, had called the people of Boston to a meeting to condemn the murderers of worthy Elijah Lovejoy,[6] a brave advocate of the abolition of slavery, who died beside his printing press. Who said there was no poetry in our times? A certain Austin,[7] a bulldog, Governor of the State, called the Negroes beasts and said such things as only owners of men are good at saying. The meeting, made up of owners, cheered frantically in Austin's honor. Someone had risen, pale and serene, to speak. The air was at once full of booing. There was interference, fist shaking, heckling; the hall was like a strange, snarled trunk putting forth torsos and claws of wild beasts. What a great pleasure it is to face it! Someone was heard saying the young advocate of the slaves was a son of a Mayor of Boston and reluctantly they quieted down. Austin turned pale! The air

was no longer filled with boos but with fiery invectives, with
frightful ghosts! The portraits of the founding fathers seemed
to leave their frames, revengeful, and shake their fists at the
defenders of slavery. There was a new, weak attempt at heckling, but great golden words, a golden orb seemed to fill the hall.
"Hurrah! hurrah!" People embraced each other elated. The
claws changed to wings. Hurrah! Hurrah! Wendell Phillips had
spoken! Oh, word . . . inspired . . . fashioner of wings! [8]

The next day Boston and all the North felt like a mother to
whom a child had been born. Nations tire of their great men, of
seeing them always so high, and in the end lose that loving respect they had for their stature. They also tire of the monotony
and drabness of virtue. Yet there is no deeper joy than to feel
that from the people's ranks has come, and among them lives,
an extraordinary creature. Later they may bite him, stone him,
disfigure him, and abandon him. During his thirty years of abolitionist propaganda Wendell Phillips was scoffed at, insulted on
the streets, and even accused of being a villain and a traitor.

But now he is dead. Arms are presented; flags are at half-
mast; there is mourning from all the pulpits; statues are being
chiseled; all heads are bared in the cold and in the snow when
he passes!

It was an irresistible impulse that aligned him with that
propaganda, then demagogic and almost opprobrious, for he was
Harvard's most eloquent student, in possession of a fortune and
the greater fortune that comes with being born to an old,
respectable family. Where might he not have sat, this portly, cultured gentleman, in whom seemed to shine, as in Mottley,[9] that
austere gracefulness of the good New England stock? What public honors, what handsome profits, what a vast, pleasant reputation, what a comfortable easy life might have been his by simply
following in the footsteps of the powerful, or by merely not joining those who stood in their way? Wendell Phillips had loved
his eloquence because it issued bravely from his mouth as eloquence always should. He could see and hear himself modeling
with his strong hands a more just and generous motherland and
then lighting with the light of his eloquence the statue his hands
had fashioned. Alone in his young lawyer's office he would pon-
der on the meeting of sharp wits in court as in an eager and

dashing fencing match; and he paced up and down continuously as though pushed by winged spirits within him. But one day a mob passed his window pulling the abolitionist Garrison [10] by a rope tied around his neck. It was a well dressed mob. They insulted and struck their prey. They laughed at his plight. Then and there Phillips raised his fists to those scoundrels and never lowered them again

He married Justice. He bartered the ambition of shining by his own natural gifts for the humble glory of sacrificing them for the benefit of others who, while recognizing their glory, would bite the hand that helped them and pay him nothing. He preferred that exquisite satisfaction which lightens and perfumes the soul of those who consecrate themselves to pure justice and to the reconquest of man to the luxury and quiet of Boston life. He found himself alone, alone among fanatics and weaklings, face to face with a human crime and an immense evil, and all his insights and energies concentrated in spite of himself and by mere force of gravity upon the great task, and he acquired, by dint of a powerful imagination, the consistency, impenetrability and height of a mountain. Thus the earth, when it rises at a given point, leaves vast plains around it. In that formidable thirty-year task, Wendell Phillips was just that: and advancing mountain.

The whole universe assumed in his mind the shape of a Negro slave. If the universe had shown signs of favoring slavery, as the mob that had applauded Austin in Faneuil Hall, he would have faced the universe, his glance cutting, dazzling, his word precipitous, flaming. In Wendell Phillips this condensation of forces necessary to oppose successfully a grave, extended evil, at the same time deprived him of the minor talents of adjustment, those petty, bitter talents that great souls seldom acquire. This developed in him from his scanty knowledge of real life, a knowledge which is indispensable if one is to hit upon the laws that govern life. Without that knowledge, discovering the laws of life is as impossible as practicing medicine without having laid eyes on a human body.

An exalted love of sacrifice, of human perfection, of purity was innate in Wendell Phillips. From his schooling, in which he excelled, he derived an impetuous inclination towards the extraordinary. His heroic campaign, since he never had to toil for his bread, sprang from intercourse with the superhuman and the supreme, even before his contact with hard, plodding existence had given him that melancholic and healthy tolerance which tempers the soul without impairing its merits, rather affording it the greatest merit of all, which is to exert wholesome influence through those merits.

The contact with the superhuman alone naturally turns the spirit away from merely human solutions. Whoever has the extraordinary within him, apart from the extraordinary that History, Letters, and Arts add, is in no position to legislate in the field of the ordinary. An eagle cannot trot; and such is life's aim: to make an eagle trot!

Thus this man who raised a prophetic voice, no less vibrant, magnificent, or marvelous than those trumpet blasts that destroyed the walls of Jericho, shook the North American people with a vigor that grew with each new difficulty; stirring whatever depth of generosity and sociability their mercantile, individualistic lives and breath of long, infamous abuse left them. He whose every trait was surprising and loving, ignored at times, perhaps with an intolerance necessary to the success of his campaign, the merits of those who, guided by a better knowledge of the human and the possible, hoped to put an end to slave traffic by less boastful and less violent means. Wendell Phillips would hear of no peace except on perfect, immediate, and extreme terms. Whoever delayed he called a traitor and branded him on the forehead. Since it seemed, according to Calhoun [11] and his followers and against Charles Sumner [12] and the North, that the Constitution of the United States favored slavery or allowed it, Phillips did not hesitate to call the Constitution criminal. "I fail to see," he said, "how a constitution that is static can fit a country that moves on." [13] And since in order to practice his legal profession he was required to swear loyalty to a constitution he considered iniquitous, he did not swear, thereby closing to himself a career which would have been brilliant. He was not among the prudent, who transform, and are necessary, but among the impatient, no less precious, who shake the judicious and whip the selfish who stand in the way of the judicious. His fiery lash cracked over all their heads!

What should not be, should not be. Any deviation from absolute justice, no matter what conditions of the times or reasons might seem to justify it, seemed to him a crime: the higher the one who deviated was, the greater the crime. So Washington owned slaves? Well, he was "a great slaveholder." [14] Henry Clay was "a great sinner." [15] Daniel Webster was "a menagerie of wild beasts and a heretic who had leaned his head on the Delilah lap of slavery." [16] If the villainy of slavery were mentioned in conjunction with anyone dead, he would exhume the culprit, as the bishops did Pope Formosus,[17] sit him on the bench and sentence him. In these unilateral trials, in a grandiose way, a marvelous person with a worm in his side was no longer a marvel: instead of extracting the worm carefully, he preferred to knock down the marvel with a single blow.

There was in him a certain confidence in the purity of his loves, a certain artistic and exquisite finish to his intellectual sacrifice, a certain reliance on the honesty of his purpose, and a certain superior, genuine conception of man against which man himself was not allowed to turn, all of which at times made him harsh in opposing other men, when, in the free exercise of their will, they attacked liberty. Thus the arrogance of his virtue sometimes made the most dedicated champions of justice seem despotic. He conceded to justice unlimited rights, but he also believed that tyranny of virtue was efficacious and natural. Moved by these impulses he would speak in a hollow tone to a public unaccustomed to the absolute, a public which, if it ever declines in the future, be what may its visible magnitude, will decline because of its love for and practice of the concrete.

A people only follows those who set out to lead them and weld them into a unit. A man of high virtue will never mold a people into one. They will hold on to him in the hour of danger, or cross the seas to fetch him, but they will give themselves again, with a minimum of compunction, to the man who shares their puerilities and vices.

Wendell Phillips' only hour of triumph was the fleeting moment when political factors brought at last the solution which rationalized virtue had preached through him. But one could easily see his anger and deep sadness at the tumultuous and mechanical life which a majority of his compatriots led. It pained him sorely to see the country's life centered on money-making. What he had, he gave. He would turn in wrath against the North: "Cotton is choking you! Machines are not going to save you!" [18] Jingling of money is all one hears; there is nothing in the country but squeaking of wheels, market dust, and clinking of dollars. "You have been corrupted by the sordid economy of Franklin's Poor Richard." "Either you uplift your souls or sooner or later you will crumble to earth." [19]

Never did that ardent knight of human dignity, that admirable person consecrated to the highest objectives, purest sufferings, most exquisite satisfactions, that great indefatigable, fluent orator, flatter the masses' passions, not even to insure for his ideas a momentary success. Progress consists in growing and ascending, not in shrinking! Those who court the masses or public passions are as vile as those who search out women to cater to the vices of their cronies and their kings. Such men may be skillful, but they are vile, if not traitors, even if they were born with exceptional gifts, and all the more so if they were so born, for then they are twice traitors: to their motherland and to the spirit of man.

No, court the masses he did not, nor did he ever think a truth and leave it unsaid. His speech was an arsenal or a torrent of clean, sturdy, hard arrows such as those that Norman kings taught their sons to shoot into oak trunks. In his tremendous invectives he used all the resources his language offered, plus his own gift for rounding them out and magnifying them.

He did not discuss: he established. He did not argue: he chastised. He pointed out what was vile, not stopping to prove his claim. His words were serene and lofty like his face; elegant and impassive just as he was. He launched his anathemas surely and quietly. He did not allow himself to be carried away by emotion nor did he try to carry away his public: North Americans do not like to hear displays of passions they do not share. Some of Wendell Phillips' paragraphs are like grand sword duels, some others, which he uttered without scarcely changing his tone, sound like great judgments passed from tall black clouds out of the fiery books of the Prophets. The monstrous and the oceanic appeared everywhere in his eloquence. No other North American orator had the grandeur of ideas, the perfect construction, the harmony and roundness of the phrase — the artistry, in fine — in the measure which he had. A Southern colonel once said: "He is like an infernal machine set to music." "He spoke like a gentleman in a parlor." In the subtlest manner, with a mellow voice, he left a piercing dart in the breast of every slavery sympathizer. But when, because of requirements of his art or of his public, an attitude of greater disdain or wrath became necessary, he would display the holy ire which was always stored within him and convert his eloquence from that fine steel blade into a tremendous, rigorous catapult. A lion's claw, in a glove. He was implacable and fierce like all gentle men who love justice.

GROVER CLEVELAND

GROVER Cleveland,[1] the frank firm, sincere Governor of New York State has now been chosen by the Democratic Party Delegates' Convention as the Party's candidate in the coming November elections for President of the United States. Grover Cleveland is forty-five years old, tall and stocky. He is strong in character, by nature active, impatient, yet disciplined. He is interested in himself and seeks his own advancement, without which there is no success nor reaching high public office, but he will always prefer, as he already has once, to risk his chances of becoming President, rather than flatter the electorate by submitting to a legislative enactment contrary to the express commitments of the State. The danger of democracy lies in the fact that office holders who love the power that affords them fame and well-being, try to retain that power through flattery of the masses who can elevate them or overthrow them with their votes. Grover Cleveland is one of those men who with equal energy will face the wrath of the wealthy who would use him to back their crooked enterprises, or the anger of the turbulent and embittered workmen who cannot see any other justice than that which favors their designs. Labor organizations had threatened to deny him their votes for President if, in the teeth of a state contract preventing it, he did not sanction a legislative enactment reducing from ten to five cents elevated railroad fares at hours which are not the hours for workmen going to and coming from work. But Cleveland, when he saw clearly that the law, which it was his business to uphold, did not favor the workmen's demand, defied labor's wrath and vetoed the bill.

Tammany Hall is the name of a powerful Democratic Party organization in New York. They are like vote-controlling bosses bound by ties as close as in a secret society. At election time

Published in *La América*, New York, July, 1884. It was also published in *La Nación*, Buenos Aires, October 1, 1884.

Tammany Hall holds the city in its fist either by distributing small jobs, or engaging agents who spread certain ideas and stir certain hatreds, or paying for or gaining the good will of highly placed people and neighborhood leaders. And since the self-love which characterizes our time, especially in commercial cities, induces independent voters lamentably to stay away from the polls, Tammany Hall's power grows, because those who alone could balance its influence do nothing to upset it. Since those who serve Tammany have sure jobs in the city government and administration, opportunists and ruffians, who are always a majority, find in serving it an easy reward and pleasant occupation. Since there is nothing more blind nor a greater source of trouble than worry, and it is so easy to stir up the poor classes in these cities that offend them with their show of luxury, Tammany's agents soon gain and hold their influence among the humble and destitute by inflaming the gall and appetite that move them. Therefore, to try to stand in Tammany Hall's way, in this country where everything depends on the vote, is like signing your own political death sentence. Whole districts vote as Tammany commands; Tammany elects senators, governors, the President. Tammany forces them afterwards, as payment for the influence contributed to their election, to appoint to the juiciest public offices the generally corrupt persons it has picked, on the basis of pay or participation in future business. The steed is in the Governor's mansion, but the reins, the spurs, and the whip are in Tammany. Grover Cleveland has risen to the occasion. He has decided to vindicate the democratic institutions threatened by this worm and to pull Tammany out by the roots.

It is this which is significant in the forthcoming elections; not his war against the group of impure Democrats who have accused him and will not vote for him, but the war waged by honest Democrats, whom Cleveland vigorously represents, against the political vices which have been discrediting the virile practices of democracy.

The Republicans have chosen as their candidate a man who sees the country's affairs in a manner no more scrupulous than does Tammany the city's: under Blaine railways and other interests have prospered by repaying with shares or money the influence brought to bear on senators and high public officials,

while Cleveland with his firm and daring vetoes has cut the wings
of all such attempts which sought backing or complicity in his
state's legislature. Blaine believes, to the painful disgust of sensible and loyal North Americans, that there is no shame in using
force if a country has it and that now is the occasion for the
United States to strike with heavy fist all over the face of the
earth as far as it can reach, whereas Cleveland thinks, with the
enthusiastic backing of all the honest people in the Republic,
that whatever nation trespasses on the right, the peace, and the
independence of a neighbor's house, is as a bandit and a ruffian
among nations, and would be branded a criminal and a villain
despite all its imperial strength. As Blaine is on the one side
exhibiting to this country, which has heretofore been the refuge
of human rights and decency when offended throughout the
world, a marked disdain for man and an inclination towards
force and conquest which injure and violate those rights and
that decency, on the other side it was necessary to have a man
who, being discreet, worthy, and intelligent, would retain for
the United States its place as hearth and home for all men, so
that, respected by all nations and in peaceful enjoyment of itself, it might perpetuate this magnificent example of working,
healthy liberty which the United States has been offering. In
view of all this the Democratic Convention chose from among
all the party candidates the one who is more concerned with
managing honestly his own house than meddling in his neighbor's, the man who would not expose to the furies of war and the
clamor of merchants this marvelous temple which rises above
all the world on pillars of prosperous, good men. Whoever has
known how to protect his honor, knows the worth of his neighbor's honor and respects it. The country that has been the home
of the free must not become, no, by God! the dragon on which
conquest rides, nor a new grave for man, such as the despotic,
corrupt countries which have dominated and degraded the Universe have been.

The good people of this country ask of their Presidents brains
and decency; and do not care much for brains if not accompanied by decency. Nature gives man talent as it gives apricots
or nuts, and all are worth about the same, but it does give him
character; this he must build for himself, fostering it and color-

ing it with his own blood and saving it with his own hands from the temptations that sing to him like sirens, from the risks that lure him like snakes. Character is the only thing man can take pride in. Whoever has it, shines. Character should be like marble: white and hard. This is Grover Cleveland's high merit: that in times of corrupt politics he has brought virtue to politics, that he has saved his strong, simple character from temptations and pitfalls. This explains why a large sector of Republicanism also backs his candidacy fervently.

HENRY WARD BEECHER

APPARENTLY, liberty, which is the world's chief joy, can transform even death. Man, who has long been troubled by the presence of the invisible, can now glance upon the world serenely, as though the grave held no fright for him who has spent his life decorously. Rejoicing now dawns in this gigantic crisis: the world emerges more beautiful from each boiling; the practice of liberty leads to a universal, cheerful religion; in vain does diffident reason frown; in vain does doubt, hiding invincible faith with assumed lividity, write her rickety tormented stanzas.

To what else can chastising religions and gloomy governments lead us if not to doubting the efficacy of life? Thus, where reason prevails, faith in the harmony of the universe flourishes.

Man can grow to such stature that he overflows his world and influences the other. Through the strength gained from knowledge he grasps the composition of the invisible and, with the joy of having lived according to law, he reaches its gates sure and happy. As men's circumstances change, so also do literature and philosophy, and also religion which is a part of the latter: heaven always was a copy of mankind and became inhabited by serene, festive, or revengeful images, according to whether the nations who created them lived in peace, by their senses, or in slavery and torment: every shake up in a people's history alters its Olympus. Man's entrance to liberty's happiness and order produces, as a colossal flowering of lilies, a chaste and profound faith in Nature's usefulness and justice. Religions fuse into *the* religion. From the dust of collapsing churches, rises a tranquil and radiant apotheosis; man has outgrown his temples, these and those! The health of liberty prepares for the happiness of death. When one has lived for man, who can do or wish him

Dated New York, March 13, 1887, published in *La Nación*, Buenos Aires, May 26, 1887.

evil? Life must be endured with courage, and death welcomed with a kiss.

Henry Ward Beecher,[1] the great protestant preacher, has just died. In him, a child of his time, the faith in Christ inherited from his people was already tinted by the new glorious heresy. His word, like clouds dissolving at dawn, showed its edges vividly colored by a new light. In him, as in his time and country, rival dogmas, the sickly children of a somber mother, gathered helter-skelter, singing like birds that change their feathers in spring; in him, the prominent son of a free country, life has been a poem and death a house of roses. On the door of his house has not been placed the customary black bow, but a crown. His parishioners embroidered a mantle of white carnations, French roses, and immortelles to cover his coffin. Ministers of all denominations, except Catholic, officiated at his funeral. And his church, whose pulpit he threw open to the persecuted and the slaves, has been covered with roses from floor to ceiling, so that, on entering, one would say the church is one vast song.

Alone man is nothing; whatever he is, his people have placed in him. It avails men nothing to be among those endowed by Nature with exceptional qualities, for they will be mere dust or scourges if they do not become flesh of their people; but if they go along with their people and serve them with arms and voice, they will be uplifted by them as a mountain uplifts the flowers that grow on its summit. Men are products, expressions, reflections; they live to the extent that they coincide with their epoch, or to the extent that they differ markedly from it. What is going on pushes and pervades them; not air alone weighs on their shoulders, but thought. Such are man's great nuptials, his nuptials with his fatherland!

Without the din of his country's battles, without national antecedents and institutions, how would Henry Ward Beecher, a shaky thinker, a plain preacher, a weak and voluble theologian, a rough and forgetful pastor whose preaching in church was frigid, have reached such singular eminence? It matters little that his denomination was more liberal than the rival ones, because men, when they have attained full liberty, need none of their pulpits.

But Beecher, brought up in the beauty and freedom of the

countryside by his parents, who had inherited all the national characteristics, grew, throbbed, and reached his peak with the nation; in his sturdy constitution, which bred in him his disheveled, commanding speech, his country's traits were exemplified, its crime denounced, its fear expressed, its battles and its victories exalted. It was his privilege to be this marvelous thing: a free man living in a great epoch!

He was truly like a harp on which the wind, playfully, rapidly, sets the strings softly quivering, or else strikes upon them with rage and violence, bringing forth sinister sounds. But what would harps be without such winds?

He was wholesome, a good walker, hard-working, crafty, strong; he had built his house with his own hands. From the contemplation of nature he derived a familiar poetry, pleasing and harmonious, and from the ordeals and conflicts of life he drew both daring and caution. In all this he resembled his country, as he did even more in his rebellious spirit, so fitting to countries recently emerged from slavery. He wore, as his countrymen did, a felt hat and calfskin shoes. In his native state he belonged to the party of those who stood against slavery, and when called to a Brooklyn pulpit [2] because of his loquacity, he took with him that local ire which was to become national in scope. He brought to the service of the fiery abolitionist campaign his exuberant health and his undisciplined spirit, his vulgar and picturesque eloquence, his ecclesiastical jargon embellished by a certain natural poetry. In that happy epoch when virtue was a plausible thing, he saw the times grow through deceptive signs, and placed himself in step with the times.

He captured his congregation with the novelty, fragrance, and humor of his sermons; he assailed slavery with his peasant vigor and rudeness; he offered his pulpit to abolitionists that had been stoned by the rabble. The nation soon admired his aggressive and embellished oratory. And when England favored the rebels, the slaveholders, he landed in the heart of England, made her laugh, weep, feel ashamed, follow him enthusiastically in the streets, and proclaim with him the justice of his cause. There he should have died, for he could thereafter render his country no further service! From then on he went down life's hill accused of an odious sin: adultery with a friend's wife, with a sheep in his own flock.[3] For twenty years he has carried that weight, jaded but undaunted. He never again reached the stature he had attained before his sin. One can feign anything except one's own self-esteem. In his tremendous energy or in his sincere contrition he somehow found strength to continue being eloquent when he was no longer honest!

But once the great problem in which he and the nation were united was solved, he was only what one might expect of a man of his wholesome and brilliant nature, hooded in a religious dogma, in a country where faith is not fearsome, a country which takes pleasure in daring and where originality is rare.

His was a verbal power, as others' is factual. There are instinctive words which come upon the world in its hours of growth like hurricanes and landslides: they resound and purify, like the wind; they unconsciously work like insects or the sands in the sea. He was a much better orator than person. He foresaw the future reign of love. He stood up like a lion for human dignity: liberty inflamed his heart. He unintentionally demolished much. He left standing only enough of the dogmas so as not to be expelled from his church as a heretic. He did not establish a creed. He did establish the practice of religions' treating each other as sisters. With this conclave of dogmas he opened the field for the combat which the authoritarian church has come to wage on free thought in its own American home. He offered his pulpit to the adversaries of his theology of love, to a cardinal, or to an atheist. He did not say all a man can say, but he said much more than a pastor alone can say. It was pitiful to see him struggle between his clergyman's hypocrisy and the philosophical conception of the world which had taken hold of his indomitable spirit.

In his later days, scared by selfish interests, he dared not stand up for the poor as he had for the Negroes. But he introduced liberty, charm, and love of Nature into the Christian cult. Through his love of man he gathered together hostile sects that had tormented him with their gibes and gossip. With his oratory, at times golden as the oriole's wings, clear as spring water, melodious as a frond thick with nests, triumphant as dawn's flames, he announced, from the last grandiose temple of Christendom, that the coming and enduring religion is written in the harmony of Nature.

Henry Ward Beecher came from hardy stock: a puritanical midwife, who had brought forth many a Pilgrim's child even before the Mayflower's beams had rotted; brawny fellows who drank cider from kegs held over their mouths as Catalonians drink wine from *porrones;* a blacksmith who, under an oak, made the best hoes in the land; a garrulous innkeeper who spent all day talking religion and politics with his student guests; one Lyman Beecher,[4] his father. In Henry all the aggressive, exalted, nomadic strength of this family of Puritan handicraftsmen comes to a head.

In Lyman's days students bore great names now in the encyclopedia. They all knew Thomas Paine's [5] *The Age of Reason* by heart. Like Paine they frolicked, got drunk, worshiped their fists and their arms, threw Bibles at each other's heads. Lyman, who entered the seminary as pantry boy, emerged an eloquent pastor. His eloquence was the forerunner of that of his son. He composed his sermons while walking in the country and there delivered them, in the disorderly fashion to be expected in one not bred in the exercise and discipline of art, with all the historic strength inherited from his forebears and fostered by his laborious, direct life.

Words bothered and oppressed him until he poured them on his parishioners — apothegms and epigrams — like a tight fistful of hail. He was known as the "Fiddler Pastor," because when he returned from church he was so consumed that he relieved the excitement his sermons produced in him by playing some old tune or gingerly dancing a jig in the parlor of his house, the house of a town pastor earning three hundred dollars a year. The rug on which he danced was of cotton, combed and woven by his wife, and decorated with fringes and boughs, which she herself had painted with paint she fetched from her brother.

Such was Beecher's vehement father. His mother, sitting in the shade of a tree, used to enjoy writing letters to her friends, letters which still smell like flowers. Henry chased butterflies, his blond curls flying behind him; Harriet,[6] the future author of *Uncle Tom's Cabin,* wanted someone to make her a doll. In-

side, in the parlor, the pastors sat talking wrapped in the smoke
of their pipes. Around the windows climbed the fragrant honey-
suckle. Elms and maples moved their tops rhythmically and
sheltered the house. In the orchard apples shone amidst the
thick foliage like drops of blood. Sometimes Henry tired of them
and turned to the imposing pine grove that bordered two neighboring lakes and to the blue, roundheaded mountain which
crowned the distant landscape. At sunset clouds softly changed
into mighty monsters, strange armies, golden roses, or gigantic
chariots. In winter, the pastor, surrounded by his children, would
read from the patriarchs of the English language: Milton, austere as St. John; Shakespeare, whose thoughts were like wreaths
of flowers; the Bible, fragrant as a new forest; or while the children heaped wood for the fire, he would tell them tales about
Cromwell. Ash wood burned incessantly in a colossal Russian
stove in the dining room.

His mother gone, though his stepmother was a good woman,
the child grew rebellious to seclusion and restraint, as behooves
one bred in the freedom of outdoor life. The pine grove attracted
more seductively than books. When they took him to church "he
felt he entered a cave where the sun never shone," but he was
entranced for hours listening to a Negro servant who said his
prayers singing and laughing as though at times he felt the body
of the Lord living within him and at times the health of the
world filling him with happiness. The child had no memory for
words; he showed intelligence only in his repartee, humorous
and wise.

He walked in the valley picking flowers, returning late from
the woods loaded with seeds; he liked to stroll among the rocks
and watch the water meander through them and trace patterns
as fine as thought. How were catechisms and spelling books to
attract this son of an active Puritan and a romantic descendant
of Scottish heroes, who was absorbed in Nature's music, who
compared her shapes and colors, who observed the wisdom of
change, the perpetuity of life, the efficacy of destruction, who
found that he too changed, as leaves and feathers do, with winter,
which strengthens the will, with spring, which loosens wings,
with summer, which torments and fires the blood, with autumn,
the hymn of the earth?

"You ask me for yesterday's prayer?" Beecher once said.
"Send me the song of the oriole trilling in the boughs of my trees
last June, or the iridescent bubbles of foam which in tiny myriads broke on the beach, or the scent of the first violet that
bloomed in May; then, my friends, I shall send you my prayer."
Such was his oratory. He improvised his speeches because he
knew Nature. The vigor of his language led him to love the
English classics; his Puritan ancestry gave him his reforming
impetus; his irrepressible vitality bred his dauntless interest in
public affairs; but that fiery love of freedom and happiness, that
abundance and color of his eloquence came to him from his deep
strolls into the fields and from his mother who, when she bore
him, lived in the garden and was friend to the flowers.

It is necessary that youth be hard. Beecher attended Seminary; never learned Greek; his Latin was scanty; in corporal
exercises he was first: running, swimming, wrestling, ball playing; he was also first in opposing school brutalities: hazing,
drinking, gambling, bullying. His father was a pastor, his friends
were pastors, so they made him a pastor. These inherited callings
spoil men! To this indomitable youth the hood would have been
an unbearable bridle had it not been for the priesthood's vehement spirit among the Puritans and the shrewdness that teaches
it is advisable to follow a trodden path. Woods devour explorers.
Men abandon those who decide to live without flattering them.

Beecher married young, in which he showed nobility. "I'll
marry her, even if I only have for a livelihood the northwest
end of a corncob"; and they went to the village together where
he felled the trees out of which he built his house with the help
of his parishioners and neighbors. He was pastor, sexton, candle
blower; his was a parish of wage earners; he received, as his
father had, three hundred dollars a year. Later, in a more pre-
tentious city, anxiety increased;[7] there, troubles made his wife
grow old; she could not stand the Wild West; she was sick for
eight years. And that eloquent pastor whom they came from all
around to hear; that vigorous defender of the settlers who would
not allow slavery in their state; that minister of the Lord who
had no compunction in calling to arms, as did bishops of yore,
nor in making his listeners laugh with boorish jokes, or cry with
his tender domestic recollections; that brazen preacher who

spoke more of men's rights than he did about church dogmas, worked in his garden to help meet his house expenses, took care of his horse, his cow, and his hog; painted his walls as his mother had the rug; and cooked and washed the dishes!

At last one day a traveler heard him preach and through his recommendation he was summoned to Brooklyn. Brooklyn, in the East! Pastors down there are bookish folk; they don't tell jokes from the pulpit; they don't bellow out hymns with their parishioners; they wear fine shoes and silk hats: what can this red-faced, long-haired pastor do there? But his wife wants to go, so they go. First they had to change their wardrobe, for the one they had was laughable: leg-of-mutton sleeves and ruffled skirts for her; a flowing, imposing frock coat, a cocky hat slanting over one ear, a collar *à la* Byron for him.

The pastor's oratory was laughable. Such gestures, such spicy anecdotes! What violent transitions! What ranting about the ways of squirrels and how birds made love! Why, even about politics he talked! He said: God is served best by being free and taking care that liberty is safeguarded. Some of his paragraphs were like brooklets, others like columns of perfumed smoke. Suddenly he slapped his coat tails or drew a great circle in the air with his arm. And he was heretical! He did not believe in Adam's fall; man was always falling; Divinity was ceaselessly revealing itself; every nest is a new revelation of the Divine; Sundays should be jolly; the world cannot have been made contrary to what its own testimony reveals. Ill will buzzed around his pulpit. Lyman Beecher said: "For God's sake, get my son out of the East! They know too much there!"

Indeed; but there they do not have the driving haughtiness and blissful ignorance of those who thought themselves free from the populous cities. He had already beautified his religion through frank and friendly fellowship, made wholesome by life, perfumed by Nature. He came from the rugged West, where they felled forests, buffaloes, and Indians. The nostalgia for his poor church inspired him with a sincere, deep eloquence: not for a long time had human accents fallen from a pulpit! Beecher began discussing political questions as he had done out West. He was called a clown, a defiler, a heretic. He made them laugh and they applauded. A pastor bringing forth applause! He never took his text from the Old Testament, but spoke of the love of God and man's dignity, using similes taken from Nature. His logic was faltering, his Latin, impossible, his syntax, dubious. He skipped over dogma as though scalded. But in his church birds sang as in spring; eyes wept without pain, men were stirred by virile emotions!

What did it matter if even his parishioners thought his propaganda against slavery exaggerated? They had admired him when, in the face of popular indignation, he had turned over his pulpit to Wendell Phillips, the evangelist of abolition. Who would dare, he told them, stand against God's greatest work: man's thought. And they went, as he advised them, armed with clubs. They came in growing numbers, from all over the country, to hear that famous voice. To those who asked where the church was, policemen would say: "Just follow the crowd."

The pastor's eloquence would rise at times like whirling waves that shatter lacelike. At times it struck hard like his parishioners' clubs. But mostly his speech was as colorful and melodious as a fresh grove on whose low trees climb flowery vines, heavy with red bellflowers, white jasmines, or purple morning glories. Unfortunately, sometimes a coarse joke erupted and it seemed as though a hurdy-gurdy had appeared among the flowers; but then, suddenly, like magic, a childish remembrance would fly about like a dove and, after bringing forth tears, hide in a lilac tree.

Beecher's style flowed like rivulets through the valley, making the sand sparkle, the falling fruit and flowers sway, emerging from shadow to light as clouds moved on, meandering among the shiny boulders, spilling into a thousand channels, dashing into the woody banks and emerging from them more playful and mischievous than before. When the course became deeper, when passion fired his style, the many waters gathered and fell precipitously carrying along flower petals and boulders; then, on reaching a more level path, those waters, which never amounted to a river, would spread again in playful brooklets.

He was no master of the novel word, the abrupt turn of a phrase, the unexpected leap of great orators. He was like a reflection in whose sensitive and rich voice his people manifested itself. He was something of an actor, a mime, a puppet. It was his strength that was gigantic: force in his copious and many-hued words, force to adorn liberty with the frenzied passion of youth. Nothing was beyond attack, except liberty! Then this orator, justly accused of bad taste, would find appropriate examples in the treasury of his impressions from Nature; his blue eyes sparkled as though one could see the ocean in them; this crude-gesturing preacher brought forth without effort sublime harangues. Perhaps it was an unexpected and vibrant note that surged in the air and stayed on high quivering like a bronze-colored pennant, or perhaps a superb blow struck with deadly precision between the eyes.

He did not overload his thought with useless ornaments, but at times his expression was weakened by its very abundance. He wrote many books, induced by commercial interest, which netted him about a million dollars, but he was never a master of the written word. In vain shall we look in his books, in spite of his love of Nature, for Thoreau's sad and piquant expression or Emerson's deep-rooted language. Nor shall we find Nathaniel Hawthorne's warm, limpid, fine prose. But this can well be excused of one who, discovering that love of man is the foundation of all creeds, gave the lie to that other Nathaniel, Nathaniel Ward's fanatic phrase: "Property is the world's greatest impiety." The English language, doubtless, is not indebted to Beecher for any new expression, any unknown or forgotten ingredient, any vigorous grafting. He did not, like Lincoln, illustrate his subject with anecdotes, but with similes. Images were the natural form of his thinking. Man was his book. What he said of Burns can also be said of him, in a lesser degree: "He was a real poet, not bred by schools, but educated without outside help or cultivation." Like Burns, he asked for "a spark of Nature's fire; he wanted no further science."

The Plymouth church was famous in those days when the North, branded on the forehead by Wendell Phillips, encroached upon in its rights, decided at last to protest against slavery. Beecher's eloquence was a flaming scourge; one left the church every Sunday weeping. He showed from his pulpit a ten-year-old slave girl and horror shook the nation. Another day his parishioners freed, with their jewels, a mother and daughter. When a ruffian by the name of Brooks [8] brutally struck the eloquent abolitionist Sumner [9] with the head of his cane, the New York magnates, fearing Beecher, did not invite him to join

them in their protest at a solemn gathering, but he went anyway.
When the public saw him, they gave him the floor, which the
magnates had shirked doing. Forthwith he found historic words
of superb emotion, which are still remembered, as are those
heart-rending words with which he described Lincoln.

Yet, his countrymen's enthusiasm, the way they greeted him
on the street, strewed his pulpit with flowers, the triumphal re-
ceptions in various cities, were little as compared to his glorious
defense of the American Union which he made in England.[10]
The British, who disliked slavery less than they did the prosperity of the United States, were helping the Confederates. The
Union was in danger, this Union which was then considered as
the first successful proof of man's capacity for self-government
without tyrants. No wonder Beecher, defending this cause in his
English debates, found such tremendous impulse. That is what
mountains are made for: to climb them! Whoever has seen bulls
killed, can picture that fight! He spoke under a shower of hisses,
which he would defeat with an unexpected joke. His audience,
mostly made up of ignorant and paid rabble, were soon weeping.
How he could move them with references to their own
misfortunes! How skillfully he would parry off an insolent
interruption! A mortal duel: he, with his facts, his jokes, his
arguments, his wrath, his tears; they, surrounding the rostrum,
frantic, shaking their fists at him, shouting; but always finally
tamed! He fenced, bludgeoned, fulminated. He was unconquer-
able, because his Fatherland was his armor! Great things are
easy! How light are grandiose tasks!

Then came the day of victory and he, who had defended the
justice of the Union in England, was called to proclaim its
victory in God's name, upon those same walls of Fort Sumter
where its banner had first been overthrown. Then came the
bitter days of petty politics, when he, who had helped the nation
rise against the slaveholding South, demanded in vain, in words
that came to earth with their wings broken, that the defeated be
received in the Union with full rights. Then followed the scan-
dalous days when a jealous orator whom he had made famous
and who had married one of his parishioners, accused him of
having defiled the majesty of his old age by stealing his neighbor's wife. This might well have been, since a young woman's

love disturbs old men as though the empty cup of their life were being refilled! He was placed on the bench, to be the nation's laughing stock. They said he had insinuated himself into his lamb's soul; that he the pastor had not "left the man at the door," as a pastor should when visiting; had sucked her mind through mystical witchcraft; had fallen upon Danaë thanks to his divine vestments.[11] The court was like a theatre; one heard things that made one ashamed of living: Tilson, the jealous orator, claimed a hundred thousand dollars for his honor. The Pastor's wife always sat beside him with admirable fortitude. Beecher, dramatically, protested his innocence before God; the plaintiff took pleasure in dragging him in the mud, as a mad dog would his prey. The court neither condemned nor acquitted Beecher, who, exonerated by his church, never stooped his head, either at that time or later. An implacable daily, with Dantesque threats, had in vain demanded he confess. Jovial, buxom Beecher was always the first to arrive at political meetings, at reform gatherings, electoral campaigns, convocations in theatres, feasts. Public opinion, out of gratitude or indifference, went on honoring the man who was privately found guilty.

Perhaps he was guilty; but his guilt was less than his greatness. Great he was for having fiercely chastised his own people when he deemed them wicked or cowardly. To eradicate slavery from his people, he made of his tongue a tower of strength, of his church a barracks, of his son a soldier. He was great because Nature anointed him with the gift of speech, which, though he used it in a calling apt to dwarf and narrow men, he never used to disguise his interests, nor to deceive other men; nor did he ever cut its wings. He was great because, as the sky is reflected upon the sea with its luminaries and its darkness, his country, which is still the best house of liberty, friendly to man and colossal, was reflected in him. He was great because, nurtured at the breasts of a sect, he did not preach the separation of humanity into rival religious groups, but advocated the harmony of all creation in love and happiness, in the order of liberty and the beauty of death. And when he left his church for the last time, while the setting sun colored the portico with dying rays, he walked hand in hand with two poor, smiling children.

GENERAL SHERIDAN

SHERIDAN [1] is dead! His round, close-clipped head weighed on his pillow like a cannon ball. His wife leaned over and shook in vain those shoulders on which never again, except on the day of the funeral, would shine the golden epaulets; within the powerful chest there was a prattling in the veins and arteries as of vapor seeking an outlet; at last it stopped. His wife fell unconscious by the bed where a man had just died who at the age of fifteen earned two dollars a month measuring ribbon in the town store and at thirty-three was Grant's right-hand cavalry general and the scourge of the South's epic army. As death approached, he had no thought of that uphill charge, one evening, against the Confederates, entrenched behind the rocks of Missionary Ridge and how he had, smiling, forced them out of their eagle's nest; nor of the battle of Stone River where his right wing withheld the onslaught of the rebels, proud of having routed the left wing and Rosecrans' [2] center; nor of his noble Rienzi, his jet-black, white-legged, long-tailed steed on which he jumped from Winchester, where he received the news of the army's defeat at Cedar Creek, to the battlefield where the arrival of his black horse seemed to turn the tide; nor of the bloody days when the carmine winter sky reflected its dying rays on mountains of dead bodies, of the grays and the blues: strangling each other, their rifles broken, mixed with knapsacks and gun carriages, some legs protruding in the air, other bodies half buried in the snow — like a mad woman's matted hair; nor of his wild sallies in razed Shenandoah Valley, by the only light of burning farmhouses and granges, in the cold, dismal air, when it was pious to plunge the sword to the hilt and ashes took the place of grass. Of none of these had he thought. "Little Phil! . . . Little Phil! . . ." called those lips more accustomed to

Dated New York, August 18, 1888, published in *La Nación,* Buenos Aires, October 3, 1888.

swearing than to endearment. His hand searched for the head of his six-year-old son. His attractive wife, scion of military fore-bears, trying to catch with her anguished eyes his wayward look, asked "Do you know me? Do you know me? . . ." He searched with his hand for the child's blond head: "Little Phil! . . . Little Phil! . . ." [3]

Only yesterday he was head of the army, with the top rank of general which only Washington, Grant, and Sherman had boasted before. He was peculiarly built: tremendous from the waist up, dwarfish from the waist down. During the war he gained fame as a hero for his impetuous and brilliant attacks, a fame he retained in peacetime because he respected the Re-public. Only yesterday was he acclaimed as he passed the sol-diers whom he had helped pull wagons out of the mud with those same hands with which he would, if need be, whip a coward back into the ranks; only yesterday, at the Philadelphia Cen-tennial of the Constitution, had women strewn the path of their favorite hero with flowers, while children, who had read in their school books the marvelous story of Rienzi, threw wreaths and waved banners in front of his favorite horse, and he passed on, laden with honors, the creator of the cavalry, the enemy of spilling useless blood, the real vanquisher of Lee, the picturesque horseman, the romantic general. He did not bow his head in thanks, nor did his horse prance, nor did he lower his sword except when he passed the President's box. He who receives honors for himself in the presence of the man who symbolizes his country is a traitor! I defended thee, my Fatherland! in the hour of need, but I shall not perturb thee with my ambition in the hour of peace, for thou gavest me my life to defend thee and an opportunity to achieve glory; could I possibly, oh, Father-land! make of my valor a lash and of thee a steed to ride on? Sheridan did not speak thus, for he was not one for fancy words, but thus did he act, which is far better. When he returned from speaking to the President, it seemed as though he returned from another victory.

There never was a more military man, nor one more resolute in battle, more inclined to martial things; he even had that slight disdain which military men often have for those who have not bared their breasts to death as they had. Danger is like an

investiture; those who have seen themselves on the brink of
death acquire a certain majesty. The brotherhood of those who
have risked death together seems to indicate that in death are
to be found the concord and repose we seek in vain in this life.
Of all comrades, fellow-soldiers are the closest; they hate and
are jealous of each other when they wrangle over an expected
prize, but they tacitly stand together with a loyalty that sometimes smacks of crime, when the country menaced by their pre-
ponderance determines to halt them if they seek to turn against
the nation the glory and the privileges received from it. It is
one thing to fight; to govern is another! Sheridan said: "Let the
military, which is the agent of the law, submit to the civil government, which is the law. War does not disqualify for government, but neither is it the proper school for learning the art of
governing. I know how to swear a squadron out of its wits and
to drive an army mad on a gallop, but what do I know about
the nation's composition, the slow and subtle merging of races,
the jealousy and cunning that new countries excite in their ri-
vals, about economic laws, social development, or business
trends? I have read nothing of that on my sabre blade! Boys,
I say, holding up my right arm, that whoever wants me to give
up my quiet glory to jump around in the Presidency of the
Republic like a jack-in-the-box wishes me no well. Hurrah for
law and peace, boys!" [4]

His aggressiveness was apparent in his keen eyes and his
bull-like head.

His body leaned towards the reins. His legs were like threads,
hardly holding up the enormous torso. His shoulders seemed
miles apart and between his chest and his back there was the
proper space for a hero. His spherical, restless, impatient head
protruded from his torso like a turtle's from its shell, and looked
around as if trying to decide where to attack. They say he made
a beautiful sight in battle, when his hair was black and he
weighed a hundred and thirty pounds, as he rode from one group
to another leaning on his horse's neck, cracking his ivory-handled
whip, making up with the glory of his eyes for the shortness of
his legs. "Get after them, boys, until they wear out their boots!" [5]
"Let's see your faces, you rascals, turn around!" [6] "Those are
our tents, boys; we'll sleep in them tonight!" [7] That slip of a

man came and went like a flame from one squadron to another. He galloped up to some high spot to supervise the encounter, and when his piercing eyes espied an unexpected danger at a distance or he foresaw a bitter fight, he spurred his horse into the middle of the fray and communicated his courage to his men. We are here to fight; those who fight are the masters of war! Charge, charge! The only way to win is to attack! It may be all right to retreat, but not as long as you can hold your swords in your teeth! And his soldiers would cheer wildly as they saw his golden epaulets sparkle through the smoke.

The Irish are brave people and he, being of Irish descent, was a born fighter; but not one of those idlers who develop muscles to impress people, but rather like the really brave, who wait to be in the right so as to win by right. When he was five he met opposition from a wild colt, so he crept on him like a cat and started off bareback and reinless! His parents, who were very poor, gave him what education they could (reading and writing) in the village school; enough for him to take a dollar-and-a-half-a-month job as handyman in a store, where every morning the rising sun found him hard at his sweeping! Philip was the talk of the town: he was hard-working, nothing disconcerted him, he was not especially fond of books, yet he was quite a man, nimble at his chores, cautious about entering a quarrel, tremendous once he was in.

There was a vacancy at West Point for his district. Their congressman, a simple man, did not pick a rich man's son, he put up Philip's name. Accomplishment, poor; conduct, worse; good in tactics. What a temper! A class sergeant reprimanded him while in formation and Philip jumped on him with set bayonet; they broke ranks, he threw down his gun and beat up the sergeant, who was two heads taller than he. After a year's punishment he graduated as lieutenant, number thirty-four among fifty-three. They sent him to the new states to deal with frontier ruffians and fight the Indians. He proved to the manner born: knew how to scan the terrain on which to fight, to evaluate everything: trails, brooks, rocks, thickets, tree trunks; whether the ground was sandy or damp; he scented Coquillos and Yakimas;[8] slept with his boots on, always ready to repel the savages. He learned how to forage, to camp, to retreat in

order, to ride fast without tiring the horses, to scout, to turn up
unexpectedly, to sleep in the saddle. Indians are like rivers:
sometimes they seem to travel underground; they disappear at
the foot of an elm and turn up with fresh war paint and plumed
headdresses under your horses hoofs! He learned the Indians'
swiftness, which they learned from the eagle.

When the arrogant South led the business-like North into
war, there he was, pawing like his horse, he who was ultimately
to corral the cadaverous South at Appomattox, when it had no
gold left except that on Lee's sword, nor horses except a few
that had learned to flee, nor wheat except what it had pilfered
from the enemies' granaries. Never was the Southern soldier as
beautiful as when he surrendered at Appomattox, ragged, barefooted, his head bandaged, his beard bloodied, leaning on his
emaciated horse so as not to drop dead of hunger. Sheridan
tarnished his triumph by treating the defeated Louisianans not
with the art of peace, which war does not teach, but with commands and shouts. A soldier's virtue is a ruler's defeat. A people
is not a battle field. In war to command is to destroy; in peace,
it is to construct. There never was an edifice built on bayonets.

At Stone River he commanded not only cavalry but hesitant
Rosecrans' left wing. Bragg pressed on his right pushing the
Federals back at rifle point. The center fell back, before Clay-
burne. But Sheridan, with his trilobite eye, saw forward, backward, sidewise. He shuffled his lines. He closed his formation.
He flew from his vantage point to the flagging troops. The air
was aflame with volleys and curses. Hadn't he learned at West
Point the technique of every arm? Where the infantry fails,
send in your cavalry! He charged from the rear against a pla-
toon about to seize the cannon. That's what cavalry is: the
unexpected. It is always the cavalry that decides a battle, if it
has space to move, and is advanced and withdrawn at the right
time. Three hours of relentless fighting permitted Rosecrans to
place his troops in a position from which the enraged enemy
failed to dislodge them. "General, this is all we have left!"
"What about the three brigadiers?" "Dead, Sir!" [9]

Rosecrans' indecision cost him his command, which Thomas
got because of his determination. Grant at last was placed at
the head of the troops marching against Chattanooga, the heart

of the war. Chattanooga seemed decisive. The Confederates, well armed, held the hill tops; Grant's men awaited the order to scale. It was a clear day; the volley burst like red flowers in puffs of white smoke; the fusilades swept down the hills like the crack of a whip. Suddenly, up went the soldiers braving the rocks! There they went, without awaiting orders, one squadron after another. Sheridan was first to see this assault no general could have held back. He pulled out a flask of whiskey, held it up to the enemy on the brim of the heights, drank it all down, dug his spurs in his steed's loins and galloped up the craggs ahead of his cheering men! Reinforcements arrived to back the mad attack. Bragg slackened. Sheridan led his men up. They seemed taller because they advanced on dead bodies. The Confederates fled downhill. On the highest crest, erect as a stone statue, a short-legged, massive-breasted man pulled his horse to a halt.

There had been a disagreement between Grant and Sheridan on parting. Sheridan was critical of Grant's command, perhaps because he fell victim to those pangs of envy of which not even the noblest are free, perhaps because he was not aware of Grant's real worth, a blindness that eminent men often have for merits analogous to their own. Real greatness is always accompanied by simplicity and generosity, and these two men were great. "All right, I'll make him head of the cavalry," said Grant no sooner had Halleck proposed Sheridan for the post. Lincoln wrote Grant: "I am sending you a man who does not weigh much, but he is the man we need." [10]

War bespeaks greatness, be it eloquence, aggressiveness, resistence, virtue, crime. Grant disturbed people, Sherman astonished them. Only Sheridan dazzled: everyone cheered when Grant made him head of the cavalry.

What anguished months! Jubal Early, the rebel rider, was lord over Shenandoah Valley and every morning his horses kicked dust over Washington. Gold sold at panic prices in the exchanges. Banks closed. Every morning it looked as if Early were going to pick flowers in the White House garden for Jefferson Davis's table. What could be expected of Sheridan's skinny cavalry, a worn-out posse, trained only for sentry or guard duty, a picket here, a squadron there, to escort convoys or watch a

ranch? "You can't chase eagles with nags, damn it!" "I'll show
them now what you can do with cavalry!" True enough. Cavalry
is modern warfare's gerfalcon in that it strikes when least expected, brings the prey back in its claws, is withdrawn at the
hunter's pleasure. Bravery thrives on horseback. There is glory
on horseback. Oh, God, I can't die before leading a good cavalry
charge against the tyrants! . . . Sheridan knew a sword's blade
must be tempered if it is to cut well. A general must first organize, then fight. He overhauled his forces, cut picket service,
called the reserve, ordered a remounting, burned discarded trappings, brushed his horses until they shone: the new metal trimmings sparkled, the capes floated joyfully on men's shoulders.
Soldiers, see to it that your sabres are sharp! While an anxious
nation murmured, he surveyed the land where he would operate,
measured how long it took to climb a hill, how many could hide
in a nook, the roads by which an enemy surprise might come,
from what distance his men must give rein so as to strike when
they were fresh and the Rebels exhausted.

Standing erect in his stirrups he spanned with his eyes the
extent covered by the Northern army which his refurbished cavalry was to protect. Wherever foot-soldiers and cannon go they'll
have horsemen along! If the Rebels spring on the infantry's
throat, the cavalry will appear to grab the Rebels by the nape
of the neck.

This was the occasion of jet-black Rienzi's frantic race.
Sheridan had already beaten Early once. He went to Washington
for a conference. As he paced along on his faithful Rienzi and
meditated on possible new sallies, he suddenly sensed something
wrong. "What is it, General?" "Hang it, can't you smell it in
the air? We are being licked!" In Winchester rumors reached
him of a disaster. "I want twenty men!" The road was full of
cowards. Crook remained behind, beaten. Early was crushing
him! "Turn about face, boys!" "Come on, boys. Who's afraid?"
His beard quivered as did his horse's foamy loins, when he
pulled up reins at Cedar Creek in the mouths of the cannon.
"Where's Crook?" "There!" He dashed to Crook's tent. Gre-
nades burst all around. He heard the report standing, while he
knocked off blades of grass with his whip. Crook's replies were
like bullets. Aides were dispatched with scores of orders. Then

he squatted on the floor and spoke in a hushed voice with his lieutenant. "Sir," said an aide rushing in, "the nineteenth is surrounded!" "Damnation!" He sprang to his feet, lashed off the last blade of grass, shed his cape. They fastened on his general's epaulets; he jumped on the fresh, dappled horse he had ordered and didn't halt his steed until he had lined up in front of his tent the twenty-four pieces the Confederates had just captured, until the panic-stricken foe disappeared up the valley in clouds of black dust.[11]

"He's worth a thousand men!"[12] said one. How he dashed from group to group leaning on his horse's neck! How the soldiers cheered! "Hurrah for Sheridan!"[13] And then he charged. There were tears in his voice, yes, tears: "Boys, go to, don't let them snatch away our honor!" "Go to, boys, this is going to be a good one!" And on he went until he whirled them all out of the valley, dispersed like a stampeded herd. "Damn it all!" he said when he dismounted and caressed, as he would have Phil's head, one of the artillery pieces, "after I'm through with this valley, not a crow will be able to cross it, unless he brings his provisions on his back."[14]

And so he did: not a ration left for men nor forage for the horses. They won't be back marauding! All Shenandoah was on fire: crops, stables, barns, every roof under which a Rebel might take shelter! No one was going to say the North fought with white gloves nor with flourish of hats down to the stirrups as when you dance the quadrille on horseback. "Let nothing remain standing," Grant ordered, "that might encourage the enemy to return; let the army take whatever grain, forage, and beasts it needs and burn the rest."[15]

It was thus the war was ended: with Sherman cutting them in half as he pushed West, Grant hammering at their front and Sheridan picking out their kidney at Shenandoah!

He fought like a bulldog who would rather lose his teeth than let go. One goes to a ball to dance, but to a war to fight! A general must carry his map in his eyes: a battle too well studied is a battle half lost; it should be half studied, but the other half improvised. My map is the battlefield; my inkwell, my stirrup!

He had the knack of improvisation and of meeting the foe's

sudden changes with new plans. He would train his soldiers to
pay attention to the smallest trifles, so that they could meet any
surprise in the pinch of battle. The soldier is my son, he used to
say. It is the soldier who wins battles! "Careful there with that
wounded man! Carry him softly across your horse's croup!" [16]
As long as the campaign lasted he was in his boots and with his
whip in his hand, as though he expected an attack at any moment. No sooner had he repelled one attack than he was making
ready for the next. Food for his men and for his horses were his
greatest concern. Though later in Washington at banquets he
developed a taste for famous broths and dainty dishes, at war
he was so frugal that once after a charge at Chattanooga he
exchanged a quail with bread and honey which he was to have
for supper for some oysters and crackers. He was as prudent in
the preparation of his plans as he was speedy in their execution.
He discovered that the best way to have his men respect him
was never to expose them unnecessarily and to fight at their
head. "Never afraid?" asked Dana, the director of the *Sun*,
after Cedar Creek. "Whoever says he is never afraid is a liar!
As for me, I can say I'm scared as the devil and if I could I'd
start running; bravery is nothing but the power of will over
mind." But it sufficed to look into those eyes, now turned bovine
by the easy living of his last years, to know there was an un-
extinguishable flame in that broad, cavern-like chest! He cursed
worse than a Spaniard. At times he was brutal. But if he ever
offended a brave officer in the lines without cause, he, the Major
General, would apologize to him in the lines with his hat in
his hand.

2

NOTABLE EVENTS

THE CHARLESTON EARTHQUAKE

CHARLESTON has been destroyed by an earthquake. There is nothing but ruins where once stood a city spreading like a basket of fruit between the sandy waters of two rivers, merging inland into beautiful villages surrounded by magnolia trees, orange trees, and gardens.

Since the war, the defeated whites and the now tolerated Negroes have lived there in languid concord. Trees do not shed their leaves there. There one can see the ocean from vine-draped balconies. There, in the bay, almost hidden by the sand, stands Fort Sumter on whose walls the bullet struck that first called North and South to war. There the unfortunate travelers of the barge "Puig" were received kindly.

Streets run straight towards both rivers; an avenue of trees borders the city on the water front. A multitude of ships alongside the wharves load cotton for Europe and India. King Street is the business center; the rich hotels are on Meeting Street. The garrulous, tightly packed Negroes occupy a crowded neighborhood. The rest of the city abounds in beautiful residences, not built shoulder to shoulder like these immodest and slavish houses in the cold North, but with that noble detachment which contributes so much to the poetry and decorum of life. The smallest house has its rose bushes and its square patio with a lawn and sunflowers and orange trees at the door.

Brightly colored rugs and ornaments contrasting with the white walls, are hung out in the morning on the veranda along the upper floor gallery by smiling Negresses with red or blue bandannas covering their heads. The dust of defeat has dimmed the brick-red color of opulent residences. They live with courage in their soul and light in their minds in this peaceful, black-eyed town.

Dated New York, September 10, 1886, published in *La Nación*, Buenos Aires, October 14 and 15, 1886.

But today trains have to stop outside of the city on the twisted, broken, sunken, torn-up rails; towers have toppled; the population has been a week on their knees; Negroes and their former masters have slept under the same tent and partaken of the same bread of compassion, in front of the ruined houses, the fallen walls, the grilles wrenched from their stone supports, the broken columns!

Charleston's fifty thousand inhabitants, taken by surprise in the evening by the earthquake which shook their homes like straw nests, are still living in the streets and squares, in wagons, under tents, under huts built with their own clothes. Eight million dollars turned to dust in twenty-five seconds. There have been sixty killed, some by falling walls, others by fright, and in the same tremendous hour many children were born.

Calamities such as this coming from the bowels of the earth must be envisioned from the high heavens! Thus looked upon, earthquakes, with all their fearful accouterments of human suffering, are but an adjustment of the crust of the earth over its shrinking entrails to maintain the equilibrium of creation. Man, with all the majesty of his grief, with all the impact of his judgment, with all the flutter of wings that goes on within his skull, is but one of those shimmering bubbles that dance and stumble blindly on a ray of the sun! Poor warrior of the air, arrayed in gold, always knocked to earth by an invisible enemy, always getting on his feet, stunned by the blow but ready to fight again, his hands never quite enough to wipe from his eyes the streams of his own blood! But he feels himself rising as the bubble on the sunbeam rises! He feels within himself all the joys and lights, all the tempests and sufferings of nature which he tries to uplift! All this majesty lay prone to earth in the hour of horror of the Charleston earthquake.

It was about six in the evening. Our good brothers who make the newspapers were working at their composing stands like golden bees; in the churches the worshipers, who in Charleston, a place of scanty science and abundant imagination, are plentiful, were finishing their prayers; doors were being closed and many sought in love or rest strength with which to fight the following day's battle; Charleston reposed while the suffocating, stilled air could hardly sustain the scent of roses. The misfortune awaiting the town traveled faster than light!

This Charleston earth softly sloping to the sea had never quaked before. The town stretches on alluvial ground along the coast. There never were volcanoes, big or small, vapor spouts, ground disturbances, or *solfataras;* the only vapors rising were aromatic ones, the aroma of orange trees always filled with white blossoms. Nor had the shallow waters of her coast of yellowish sands ever been beaten by those mighty breakers, dark like gorges, which the ocean sends against the shores when its bottom is deranged, broken, or raised, and out of the abyss rises the tremendous force that swells and curves the waves and dashes them like voracious mountains on the beach. In that lordly peace of southern cities night was just taking its leave when a rumble was heard like that of a heavy object being dragged hurriedly along.

To tell the story is to see it. The rumble swelled: lamps and windows shook . . . underground there was a sound like the rolling of heavy artillery. Printers left their type on the composing boxes, clergymen left their cassocks and fled, women ran out onto the streets forgetting their children, men shuttled desperately from one tumbling wall to the next. What was this terrible hand that grasped the city by the waist and shook it in the air, disjointing it?

Floors surged, walls cracked, houses swayed from side to side; half-naked people kissed the earth: Oh, Lord! Oh, dearest Lord! cried suffocated voices. A whole porch collapsed! Courage fled, minds became crazed. Then it subsided, waned, stopped. The dust raised by the crumbling buildings hovered above the trees, above the housetops.

Desperate parents availed themselves of the truce to look for their children. A beautiful young mother removed the rubble from her own door. Brothers and husbands dragged out or carried out fainted women. A poor wretch who threw himself out of a window crawled on his stomach screaming painfully, his arms and legs broken. An old lady started trembling, and died. Another, dying of fright, was left alone to her spasms. The weak gas jets, scarcely perceivable in the thick air, lighted the per-

plexed crowds which ran to and fro praying, crying out to
Jesus, shaking their arms towards heaven. Suddenly, great fires
rose out of the shadows, bathing the scene in a red glare and
moving heavily their tongues of flame.

The new light shining on every face showed that they had
just seen death. About some faces reason seemed to flow stripped
to tatters, about others it seemed to wander blindly groping for
a foothold. The flames spread like a panoply, the fire rose. Then
— how can words describe what then was seen? Again the muffled rumble was heard; people circled around as though seeking
the best exit; then fled in all directions; the swell from below
grew and expanded; each thought a tiger was upon him.

Some fell on their knees, others face down; old gentlemen
were carried by their loyal servants. Great crevices rent the
earth; walls waved like wind-blown flags; the cornices of buildings facing each other touched on high; the people's horror was
increased by that of beasts: horses, unable to shake themselves
away from their wagons, threw them over; another horse bent
his fore-legs, another sniffed the ground, still another's eyes
shone red in the flames' glare, his body trembling like a reed in
a storm. What dreadful tremor in the earth's entrails was calling
to battle?

Then, when the second wave was over, when souls could hold
no more fear, when the cries of dying people, as though they
had hands, pushed their way out of the rubbish, when the
trembling horses were tied down as though they were wild elephants, when falling walls had dragged down with them telegraph poles and wires, when the wounded shook off the bricks
and lumber that cut off their flight, when the wretched women,
with the marvelous sight of love, descried in the shadow their
tumbled-down houses, when fright sparkled the Negroes' tempestuous imagination, a clamor began to spread over that carpet
of prone bodies, which seemed to rise from unfathomed depths
rending the air with dart-like wings, a cry that soared over their
heads and made it seem as though it were raining tears.

The few brave ones still standing, very few indeed, struggled
in vain to quench that growing clamor which pierced their flesh:
fifty thousand humans coaxing God at once with the most insane
flatteries fear can breed!

The bravest put out fires, raised the fallen, dropped those who had no further reason to be lifted, carried away the horror-stricken aged. No one knew the time: all watches had stopped at the first quake.

Morning revealed the disaster.

Gradually by the day's early light appeared bodies strewn along the streets, mountains of rubbish, walls crumbled to dust, porches cut in slices, iron grilles and posts warped and twisted, houses folded over their foundations, towers upset and the tallest church spire held on only by a thin iron thread.

The sun began to warm all hearts. The dead were taken to the cemetery where Calhoun,[1] the great orator, now lies silent, as do Gadsden,[2] Rutledge,[3] Pinckney.[4] Doctors took care of the sick. A priest gave confession to the fearful. Leaves of doors and Venetian blinds served as stretchers.

Rubbish was piled high on the sidewalks. Some entered houses requesting sheets and blankets with which to put up tents. Negroes frantically reached out for the ice that wagons were distributing. Many houses still smoked. A sulphur-smelling sand had oozed from the crannies of the freshly-cracked earth.

Everyone was astir. Some prepared straw beds, others put a baby to sleep on a pillow and shaded it with a parasol. Here a group ran from a collapsing wall; there a fence fell on two old men who did not have time to escape it. Tears streamed down a bearded man's cheeks as he kissed his old father's body he held in his arms. It seems many babies had been born during the night. Under a blue tent one mother had given birth to twins.

The city's best buildings have either collapsed or are out of plumb: St. Michael's, the church of resounding bells; St. Phillip's the one with the lofty tower; Hibernian Hall, where speeches bristling like bayonets were once delivered; the Guard House . . .

A one-armed man with a thick, black mustache, drawn face, and eyes aflame with joy approached a group of men sitting dejectedly on a broken pediment: ". . . it hasn't fallen, boys; it hasn't fallen!" What had not fallen was the Court House where the spirited McGrath,[5] on hearing the first shot fired by the federalists on Fort Sumter, shed his judge's gown swearing to give the South all his blood, which he did!

Among the homes, what desolation! Not a sound wall re-

mained in the city, nor unrent roof. Many porches, their over-
hanging roofs unsupported by columns, look like faces without
jaws. Some lamps had been nailed into walls or looked like
spiders smashed on the floor; statues had descended from their
pedestals; water from tanks on the roof-tops had drizzled
through wall cracks and flooded the houses; in front even the
withered jasmines on the branches and the stooping, faded roses
seemed to take their share of the damage.

The first two days the city's anguish was great. No one returned home. No business or trade was transacted. One tremor
followed another, though each less violent than the previous. It
was like a religious jubilee: the arrogant whites, when fear grew,
humbly joined the frantic Negroes in the improvised hymns;
many a Negro girl hung to a white woman's skirts as she passed
by and weepingly implored her to take her with her — for thus
does habit convert crime itself into goodness and invest it with
poetry. Thus these creatures, conceived in misery by parents
whose spirit had been frozen in slavery, still conceded a supernatural power to the race which wielded that power against their
elders! Which gives us the measure of the goodness and humility
of this race which only the wicked can disfigure and disdain, because the greater its shame, the greater our obligation to pardon
it!

Groups of Negroes went out into the country in search of
produce, only to return horrified at what they had seen. Within
a radius of twenty miles inland the ground was everywhere
parched and cracked; there were bottomless crevices two feet
wide; out of many new wells came a fine, white sand mixed with
water, or sand alone, spilled over the edges of the well as if from
ant holes, or water mixed with blue mud, or little mounds of
mud topped with little mounds of sand, as if under the crust of
the earth there was mud first and sand deeper down. The new
water tasted like sulphur and iron.

A hundred acre reservoir suddenly dried up when the first
quake came and was now full of dead fish. A dam had broken,
the water sweeping everything before it.

Trains could not reach Charleston because the rails had been
lifted or had snapped or wound around raised ties.

At the time of the first quake a locomotive was speeding on

proudly when it suddenly jumped, shook the trailing cars like beads of a rosary and plunged with its dead engineer into the crevice that opened across the road. Another which followed whistling merrily, was lifted in the air and dropped into a nearby reservoir where it lies under forty feet of water.

In all the frightened towns in the area people have taken up their abode in trees. Country folk fill the churches and listen in dread to the words of ire the stupid pastors visit upon their heads. The hymns and prayers in country churches can be heard for miles. The town of Summerville, where it seems this rupture of the earth had its center, was razed to the ground.

In Columbia people held on to the walls as though they were sea-sick. In Abberville the quake caused the bells to ring, now a wild alarm, now a plaintive knell. In Savannah the fright was so great that women were known to jump out of windows with their babes in their arms, and right now a column of smoke can be seen coming up out of the sea a few meters from the coast.

That night the woods were filled with city people who, fleeing from their shaken dwellings, took refuge among the trees, and gathered in the darkness to kneel and sing out their praises to the Lord, imploring His mercy. The earth also shook and was rent in Illinois, Kentucky, Missouri, and Ohio. A man who was being initiated in a Masonic lodge stampeded out to the street with a rope around his waist. A Cherokee Indian who was brutally beating his poor wife, on feeling the ground move under his feet, fell on his knees and swore to the Lord he would never punish her again.

A strange spectacle awaited those who at last, jumping over crevices and wells, succeeded in bringing to Charleston money and tents! They arrived at night. The streets were lined with wagons like western caravans. In the squares, which are small, families slept under tents improvised from blankets, towels, or even woolen clothes. There were purple, red, yellow tents; white and blue tents with red stripes.

The most dangerous walls had already been demolished. Booths, reminiscent of those of fairs, had been set up around the ice wagons, fire engines, ambulances. Wild screams came from afar, from the suburbs. When women met they embraced and wept, and their weeping was the language of gratitude to Heaven.

They knelt in silence, prayed, and went their separate ways consoled.

Certain pilgrims come and go with their tents on their backs, sit a while, then march on, then stop and sing. They do not seem to find a sure place for their rags and their fear. They are Negroes, Negroes in whom is reborn, in wailing hymns and terrible dances, the primeval fear with which the phenomena of nature filled their emotional ancestors. It is as though fearful birds, unperceived by other men, had lighted on their heads and plucked at them and furiously lashed at their backs with their wings.

From the moment one had eyes to see in that night's horror, it became apparent that a strange nature began to surge out of the blurred memory of those Negroes and show on their faces: it was the constricted race; it was the Africa of their parents and grandparents; it was that sign of ownership which every nature stamps on its man and which, regardless of accidents and human violations, lives its life and finds its way!

Every race brings with it into the world its mandate and it must be left its right of way, lest the harmony of the universe be disturbed, so that it may employ its strength and fulfill its mission with all the decorum and fruitfulness of its natural independence. Can anyone believe it possible, without incurring a logical punishment, to interrupt the spiritual harmony of the world by closing the way to one of its races, under pretext of a superiority which is but a degree in time?

It seems as though a black sun illumined those men from Africa! Their blood is fire; their passion like biting; their eyes flames, and everything in their nature has the energy of Africa's venoms, the enduring potency of her balms. The Negro has a great native goodness, which neither the martyrdom of slavery has perverted, nor his virile fierceness obscured. But he, more than the men of any other race, lives in such an intimate communion with nature, that he seems more capable than other men of shuddering and rejoicing with her changes.

In his fright and his joy there is something supernatural and marvelous which cannot be found in other primitive races. His movements and his glance bring to mind the majesty of the lion. In his affection there is such a sweet loyalty that we do not think of dogs but of doves; and his passions are so clear, tenacious, and intense that they resemble the sun's rays.

Those deformed creatures whom whip and fear have perhaps spared only in order that they might transmit to their offspring, conceived in the gloomy, tormented nights of slavery, the beastlike emotions of instinct and a vague reflection of their impetuous, free nature, are but a miserable parody of those other superb specimens.

But not even slavery, capable of putting out the sun itself, can completely extinguish the spirit of a race. Thus was it seen rising in these quiet souls when the greatest fright of their lives shook within their veins the inherited sediment of jungle winds, swaying bamboos, rustling reeds! Thus lived again in these Negroes — mostly born in America and educated in American ways — that fear with all its melancholic barbarism, violent and ingenuous like all the fears of their fiery race, the fear of the changes of ravaging nature, which creates among plants the hemlock, among animals, the lion!

Having been taught the Bible, they utter their fright in the Bible's prophetic tongue. The Negroes' horror reached its extremity from the very start of the earthquake.

The greatest love of these disconsolate creatures in all of what they know of Christianity is Jesus, because they see him whipped and meek like themselves. Jesus is theirs, and in their prayers they call him "Jesus, my Master," "my sweet Jesus," "my blessed Christ." They implored Him on their knees, beating their heads and their thighs as spires and columns came crashing down. "This Sodum and Gemorrah" they cried trembling. "Mount Horeb is opening up; it sure is!" And they wept, and opened their arms, and swayed to and fro, and begged not to be left alone until "the judgment was over."

They came and went dragging their children about crazily. When the poor elders of their caste appeared, the elders held sacred by all men but the white men, they prostrated themselves around them in great groups, listened to them on their knees with heads bowed to the ground, repeated together convulsively their mysterious exhortations, which derived from the vigor and candor of their nature and the divine character of old age such sacerdotal strength that even the white folks, the cultured white

folks, rapturously joined the music of their distressed souls to
that tender and ridiculous dialect.

Some six Negro children, in the night's saddest hour, rolled
in a tumble on the ground, possessed with the racial frenzy in
the garb of religion. They actually crawled. In their song an un-
utterable anxiety trembled. Their eyes were bathed in tears.
"They're the little angels, the little angels, knocking on the
door!" [6] In a low voice they repeated singing the same stanza
they had sung out loud. Then came the refrain, heavy with
prayer, incisive, desperate: "Oh! Tell Noah to hurry and build
his ark, and build his ark, and build his ark!" The elders' prayers are not joined sentences, but the short phrases proper of
genuine emotions and simple races.

Their contortions have the monotony, the strength, the wear-
iness of their dances. The surrounding group invented a rhythm
after each phrase which seemed to them musical and appropriate
to the mood of the occasion, and, with no previous agreement,
all joined in. It is this that imparted a singular power of conviction and a positive charm to these grotesque prayers, at times
so purely poetic: "Oh Lord touch not, oh Lord touch not again
my city!"

"Birds got their nests. Lord, leave us our nests!" And the
whole group, their faces touching the ground, repeated with a
heart-breaking anguish: "Leave us our nests!"

In front of a tent we see a Negress whose extreme old age
gives her a fantastic appearance. Her lips move, but we do not
hear her words. She sways her body incessantly back and forth.
Many blacks and whites surround her visibly anxious until the
old woman takes up the hymn "Oh let me go, Jacob, let me go!"
The crowd joins her singing, swaying like her, raising their hands
to heaven, clapping to express their ecstasy. One man falls to
the ground imploring mercy. He is the first convert. Several
women, bearing a lamp, kneel around him and hold his hand. He
shudders, stammers, sings out a prayer. His muscles become taut,
he contracts his hands. A veil of blissful death seems to be drawn
over his face. He lies fainted in front of the tent. Others follow.
There is a similar scene before each tent. When dawn comes the
singing and the swaying still continue. In the sinful neighbor-

hoods the beasts which abound in all races indulge, under the pretext of religion, in the most abominable orgies.

Then, after seven and a half days of praying, people began to return to their homes. The women returned first, giving courage to their husbands. Women are easily alarmed, but are first in resignation. The mayor is again living with his family in what remains standing of his sumptuous residence. Trains loaded with bales of cotton ran again on the repaired tracks. Strangers stream into the city once consecrated by bravery in war, now by catastrophy. The town floats a nation-wide ten million dollar loan to reconstruct damaged buildings and replace the ones fallen to earth.

Stock exchanges, theatres, newspapers, banks send their help in money. Many tents, left empty by their occupants, are folded up and removed from gardens and squares where the government had pitched them. The earth continues to quake as though it has not yet settled definitely on its new foundations. What could have been the cause of this shaking of the earth?

Could it be that, as the earth's entrails shrank by the slow loss of heat which they incessantly let out through hot springs and lavas, the outer shell contracted, adjusting itself to a changed and reduced interior that sucked it in? The earth then, when it can no longer resist the tension, shrinks, waves, cracks, one lip of a fissure overlapping the other with a terrific clatter, and the successive tremors caused by the adjacent rocks giving in and pushing the ground up and sideways, until the echo of the clatter subsides.

But there are no volcanos in the vast area where the earthquake was felt, and the sulphuric fumes and vapors that escape through holes and cracks in the surface are those that naturally abound, because of its geologic formation, in this low and sandy Atlantic coastal plain. Could it be that in the sea's far-off bosom, because of a similar gradual cooling of the fiery core, the bottom, too extended to cover the weakened dome, began to undulate and snapped as would a body that contracts violently and then, closing over the broken edge with an enormous impetus, made all the foundations shake, sending the movement surging with a roar to the surface of the waves? But then in that case a monstrous wave would have advanced, wrinkling the face of the sea, and chastised the land with its great jaws, unleashing its wrath on the gallant town that breeds flowers and black-eyed belles on that shore's uncertain sands.

Or perhaps the coast's inclined plain, formed of fragmentary rock, loaded with the rivers' secular residues, broke off violently, yielding at last to the weight of the gneiss that descended from the Alleghanies, then slid along the granitic foundation which three thousand feet below sustains the plain on the seaside, the weight of the highest detached rocks compressing the lower levels, thereby swelling the surface and shaking the cities with each undulatory impact! Such is the general belief: that the Atlantic coastal plain, soft and unsettled, yielding to the weight of sediments deposited upon it by rivers in the course of centuries, slid on its granitic berth toward the sea.

Thus simply did the earth follow its law of formation, swallowing men and snatching from them their homes as winds snatch leaves, with the majesty that becomes Nature's acts of creation and pain!

Wounded man strives to stanch the flow of blood that blinds his eyes, while he feels for the sword hanging from his side to combat the eternal foe; he goes on dancing in the wind, an atom on his way, forever rising, like a scaling warrior, up the sun's beams!

Charleston lives again, though her agony is not yet over, nor has the ground ceased to rumble under her swaying houses. The relatives and friends of the dead find that work reconstructs in the soul the roots that death has pulled out. The humble Negroes, once the fires that burnt in their eyes in the hour of fear have been spent, return to their tame chores and their abundant progeny. The spirited young shake from the mended porches the dust of roses.

And in the public square seem to laugh, one to each side of their mother, the twins born under a blue tent in the very hour of desolation.

DEDICATION
OF THE STATUE OF LIBERTY

FOR him who enjoys thee not, Liberty, it is diffi-
cult to speak of thee. His anger is as great as that of a wild beast
forced to bend his knees before his tamer. He knows the depths
of hell while glancing up toward the man who lives arrogantly
in the sun. He bites the air as a hyena bites the bars of his cage.
Spirit writhes within his body as though it were poisoned.

The wretched man who lives without liberty feels that only
a garment made of mud from the streets would befit him. Those
who have thee, oh Liberty! know thee not. Those who have thee
not should not speak of thee but conquer thee.

But rise, oh insect, for the city swarms with eagles! Walk or
at least crawl: look around, even if your eyes fill with shame.
Like a smitten lackey, squirm among the hosts of brilliant lords.
Walk, though you feel the flesh stripped off your body! Ah! if
they only knew how you wept, they would pick you up, and you
too, dying, would know how to lift you arms toward eternity!

Arise, oh insect, for the city is like an ode! Souls ring out
like well-tuned instruments. If it is dark and there is no sun in
the sky, it is because all light is in the souls; it flowers within
men's breasts.

Liberty, it is thine hour of arrival! The whole world, pulling
the victorious chariot, has brought thee to these shores. Here
thou art like the poet's dream, as great as space, spanning heaven
and earth!

That noise we hear — it is triumph resting.

That darkness we see — it is not the rainy day, nor gloomy
October; it is the dust, tinted by death, thy chariot has raised
up in its wake.

Dated New York, October 29, 1886, published in *La Nación*, Buenos
Aires, January 1, 1887.

I can see them with drawn swords, holding their heads in their hands, their limbs a formless pile of bones, their bodies girded with flames, the stream of life oozing out of their broken foreheads like wings. Tunics, armor, scrolls of parchment, shields, books gather resplendently at thy feet, and thou commandest at last over the cities of interests and the phalanxes of war, oh aroma of the world! Oh goddess, daughter of man!

Man grows. Behold he has outgrown churches and chosen the sky as the only temple worthy of sheltering his deity! But thou, oh marvelous one! growest with man; and armies, the whole city, the emblazoned ships about to exalt thee approach thy mist-veiled feet, like variegated shells dashed on the rocks by the somber sea when the fiend of tempest, wrapped in lightning, rides across the sky on a black cloud.

Thou hast done well, Liberty, in revealing thyself to the world on a dark day, for thou canst not yet be satisfied with thyself! Now you, my feastless heart, sing of the feast!

It was yesterday, October 28, that the United States solemnly accepted the Statue of Liberty which the people of France have donated to them in memory of the 4th of July, 1776, when they declared their independence from England, won with the help of French blood. It was a raw day: the air was ashy, the streets muddy, the rain relentless; but seldom was man's rejoicing so great.

One felt a peaceful joy as though a balm soothed one's soul. From brows to which light is not lacking, light seemed to shine more brightly, and that fair instinct of human decency which illumines the dullest faces emerged even from opaque spirits, like a wave's surge.

The emotion was immense. The movement resembled a mountain chain. Not an empty spot remained on the streets. The two rivers seemed like solid land. The steamers, pearly in the fog, manoeuvred crowded from wheel to wheel. Brooklyn Bridge groaned under its load of people. New York and its suburbs, as though invited to a wedding, had risen early. Among the happy crowds that filled the streets there were none as beautiful — not the workmen forgetful of their troubles, nor the women, nor the children — as those old men who had come from the country with their flying cravats and greatcoats to salute, in the com-

memorative statue, the heroic spirit of the Marquis de Lafayette,[1] whom they as children has greeted with waving hands and
boughs, because he loved Washington and helped him make this
country free.

A grain of poetry suffices to season a century. Who can forget
that beautiful friendship? Washington was the graver and older
of the two. There was scarcely a down on Lafayette's upper lip.
But they shared, under different appearances, the same blind
determination and capacity of ascent common to all great per-
sonalities. That noble child had left wife and king to help the
humble troops that in America were pushing the English king
to the sea and phrasing in sublime words the teachings of the
Encyclopedists' words through which the human race announced
its coming of age with no less clatter than that which had accompanied the revelation of its infancy on Mount Sinai.

That blond hero kept company with the dawn. His strong
soul preferred marching men to the iniquitous pomp with which
his monarch paraded shining opalescently on the shoulders of
his hungry vassals like a saint carried on a litter by barefoot
porters. His king persecuted him, England persecuted him, but
his wife helped him.

God pity the heroic heart whose noble enterprises found no
welcome at home! He left his house and regal wealth, armed his
ship, wrote from his ship: "The happiness of America is inti-
mately bound up with the happiness of Humanity. She is going
to become a cherished and safe asylum of virtue, of tolerance,
of equality and of peaceful liberty." [2] How great his soul, ready
to give up all the privileges of fortune to follow a handful of
poorly clad rebels on their march through the snow! He jumped
off his ship, flew to the Continental Congress: "I wish to serve
America as a volunteer and without pay." [3] Sometimes things
happen on earth that shed a heavenly splendor over it.

Manhood seemed to have matured within that youthful
body. He proved to be a generals' general. As he clutched his
wound with the one hand, with the other he commanded his
fleeing soldiers to turn about and win. With a flash of his sword
he mustered a column that a traitor had dispersed.

If his soldiers were on foot, he was on foot. If the Republic
had no money, he who was offering her his life, advanced his

fortune. Behold a man who glittered as though he were all gold!
When his fame restored to him his king's affection, he realized
France's hatred towards England could be helpful in chasing
the exhausted English out of America.

The Continental Congress girded on him a sword of honor
and wrote to the king of France: "We recommend this noble
man to Your Majesty's notice, as one whom we know to be wise
in counsel, gallant in the field, and patient under the hardships
of war." [4] He borrowed the wings of the sea. France, the van-
guard of nations, bedecked herself with roses to receive her hero.

"It is a wonder Lafayette is not taking with him to his America the furniture of Versailles," [5] exclaimed the French Minister,
as Lafayette crossed the ocean with France's help to the newborn
republic, with Rochambeau's [6] army and De Grasse's [7] navy.

Even Washington was at the time despairing of victory. But
French noblemen and American farmers closed against Cornwallis [8] and routed him at Yorktown.

Thus did the United States assure with France's help the independence they had learned to wish for in terms of French
thinking. The prestige of a heroic deed is such that this svelte
marquis has sufficed to keep united during a century two nations
that differ in spiritual warmth, in the idea of life, and in the
very concept of liberty — egotistical and selfish in the United
States, and generous and expansive in France. Blessed be the
country that radiates its light!

Let us follow the throngs that fill the streets, coming from
every direction. It is the day of the unveiling of the monument
consecrating the friendship between Washington and Lafayette.
People of all tongues are present at the ceremony.

The rejoicing is to be found among the common people. Banners flourish in men's hearts; few on men's houses. The emblazoned grandstand where the procession is to pass awaits the President of the Republic, the delegates from France, the diplomatic
corps, the state governors, the army generals.

Sidewalks, portals, balconies, roofs begin to seethe with a
joyous mass of people. Many fill the wharves to await the naval
procession. The war ships, the fleet of steamers, the prattling tug-
boats which will carry the invited guests to Bedloe's Island,

where the statue stands waiting on her cyclopean pedestal, her face covered by the French flag. But most gather along the route of the grand parade.

Here comes a band. Here comes a fire brigade with its ancient fire engine raised on stilts. The firemen wear black trousers and red shirts. The crowds make room for a group of deliriously happy Frenchmen. Then comes another group in beautiful uniforms garnished with gold braids, full, striped trousers, plumed cap, fierce mustachios, slender figures, bubbling palaver, and very black eyes: they are a company of Italian volunteers. From around a corner juts the elevated railroad. Up above, a crowded train; down below policemen branching out to their beats, their blue frock coats well buttoned up with gilt buttons. The rain fails to wipe out everyone's smiles.

Now the crowds step back onto the sidewalks, as the mounted police advance pushing against them with their horses' haunches. A woman crosses the street, her oilcloth coat filled with commemorative medals bearing on one side the monument, on the other the sculptor Bartholdi's [9] pleasing likeness. There goes an anxious-looking man making notes as he walks.

But what about France? Here there is not much talk of France, nor of Lafayette. Little do they know of him. No one is aware of the fact that a magnificent gift of the modern French people to the American people is being celebrated.

There is another statue of Lafayette in Union Square: also the work of Bartholdi, a gift of France. Only the men of letters and the old men with the cravats remember the admirable marquis. There is a new life boiling in the enormous cauldron. This country where each man lives and toils for himself has really not much love for that other country which has fertilized every human seed with its blood.

"France — says one ingrate — only helped us because her king was an enemy of England." "France — ruminates another in his corner — gives us the Statue of Liberty so that we will let her finish the Panama Canal in peace."

"It is Laboulaye [10] — says another — who gave us the statue. He would apply English brakes to French liberty. Even as Jefferson learned from the Encyclopedists the principles of the Declaration of Independence, so did Laboulaye and Henri Martin [11] try to take to France the methods of government the United States had inherited from the Magna Carta."

Not so at the Dedication: A small man (Lesseps),[12] who would fit in the hollow of the Statue of Liberty's hand, started to speak. His voice was so firm and fresh that the illustrious gathering, fascinated, enraptured, hailed that human monument with an interminable cheer. Compared to this man, accustomed to severing continents in order to join the seas, what was all that clatter, the clamor of machines, the cannonade from the ships, the monument which towered above him? Why, he even provoked laughter there in front of the statue with his first words! "That steam, American citizens, which has done so much good to the world, at this moment I find very obnoxious and harmful."

Marvelous old man! Americans do not like him because he is doing in spite of them what they have not had the courage to do. But with his first words he won them over. Then he read his speech written in his own hand on big, white, loose sheets of paper. He spoke familiarly or gave familiar form to graver matters. From the way he phrases his sentences we can see how it has been easy for him to reshape the earth. Within his every idea, no bigger than a nutshell, is contained a mountain.

As he speaks he moves incessantly; he turns to every side so as to face everyone. When he utters some phrases he drives them home with a movement of his head. He speaks a martial French, resonant like bronze. His favorite gesture is to raise his arm rapidly. He knows the land should be trodden victoriously. His voice as he talks on grows stronger instead of weaker. His short phrases are wavy and pointed like pennants. He was invited by the American government as the foremost Frenchman of his time.

"I have hastened to come," he says as he lays his hand on the flag of France draped in front of the rostrum, "the idea of erecting the Statue of Liberty does honor to those who conceived it as it likewise does to those who with understanding have received it." [13] To him France is the mother of nations and with exceptional skill he mentions without contradiction the opinion expressed by Hepworth Dixon: [14] "An English historian, Hepworth Dixon, in his book *New America*, after having said of your

constitution that it is not a product of the soil, and that it does
not emanate from the English ideas, adds it can on the contrary
be regarded as an exotic plant born in the atmosphere of
France."

He does not deal in symbols but in objects. Things exist, in
his opinion, according to what they are good for. The Statue of
Liberty leads him to his Panama Canal. "You like men who dare
and persevere. I say, like you, 'Go ahead!' We understand each
other when I use that term!"

"Yes, indeed, it was Laboulaye who inspired Bartholdi. It
was his idea: Go, he said, and propose to the United States the
construction, jointly with us, of a superb monument in commemoration of their independence. Yes, the statue was to signify the
prudent Frenchmen's admiration of the peaceful practices of American liberty." [15]

Thus (says he) was born the idea which grew like the stream-
let that swells along its course from the mountain top until at
last it reaches the sea. On the grandstand sit the delegates from
France, the sculptor, the orator, the journalist, the general, the
admiral, and this man who joins the seas and cleaves the land.
French tunes flitter over the city; French flags flap against balconies and wave on the tops of buildings. But what livens all
eyes and gladdens all souls is not the gift of a generous land,
received perhaps with insufficient enthusiasm, but the brimming
over of human pleasure on seeing the instinct of our own majesty, which resides in the marrow of our bones and constitutes
the root and glory of our life, rise with stupendous firmness, a
symbol of captivating beauty.

Behold, they all reveal the exhilaration of being reborn! Is
not this nation in spite of its rawness, the hospitable home of the
oppressed? The voices that impel and counsel come from within,
from deeper than the will. Flags are reflected on faces, heart-
strings are plucked by a sweet love, a superior sense of sovereignty brings to countenances a look of peace, nay of beauty.
And all these luckless Irishmen, Poles, Italians, Bohemians,
Germans redeemed from oppression or misery, hail the monument to Liberty because they feel that through it they themselves are uplifted and restored.

Behold how they run towards the wharves from which the

statue can be seen, elated as shipwrecked people who descry a hopeful sail! These are the humblest, those who fear the main streets and the clean people: pale tobacco workers, humpbacked stevedores, Italian women with their colored shawls. They do not run brutally, disorderly as on ordinary holidays, but in friendly equable groups. They come from the east side, the west side, the congested alleys of the poor neighborhoods. Sweethearts act like married couples, husbands offer their arms to their wives, mothers drag their young along. They question each other, encourage each other; cram into the positions from where they think they will see better.

In the meantime, among the crowd's hurrahs, the lavishly decorated gun carriages roll along the broad streets; buildings seem to speak and hail each other with their flags; the elevated trains, like an aerial, diciplined, steaming cavalry seem to stop, paw, unload their riders on the beach; the steamers restlessly test the ties that hold them to their moorings, and out there, in the distance, wrapped in smoke, the enormous statue rises, greeted by all the incense burners on earth, crowned with clouds, like a mountain.

The greatest celebration is at Madison Square where, facing the impious monument of Farragut which commemorates the North Americans' inglorious victory over Mexico, rises the grandstand bedecked with United States and French flags from where the President is to watch the parade. He has not yet arrived, but everyone is anxious. The brown helmets of policemen protrude above the dark mass. Tricolored festoons hang from house fronts.

The stand is like a bunch of roses on a black background. Now and then a murmur spreads over the nearby groups as though their collective soul had suddenly been enriched, for Lesseps has walked up, and then come: Spuller, Gambetta's [16] friend, with his steely eyes and powerful head; bold Jaurès who gloriously led twelve thousand soldiers, closely pursued by the Germans, out of the battle of Mamers; Pellisier who although wounded at Nogent-sur-Marne applied his pale hand to the wheels of his cannon; Lieutenant Ney who, when his Frenchmen fled in panic from a trench on fire, opened his arms, steadied his feet firmly on the ground, his face embellished by the bronze-hued glare, pushed the cowards through the hellish mouth and then followed; Laussédat, the grey-haired Colonel who with youthful hands built barriers against the Prussian arms; Bureaux de Pussy who kept his great-grandfather Lafayette's sword from falling to the enemy, Deschamps, the Mayor of Paris, who three times fell prisoner to the Germans and three times got away; Villegente, the young naval officer like a figure out of a Neuville painting; Caubert, lawyer and soldier, who wanted to organize a legion of lawyers and judges to hold Prussia back; Bigot, Meunier, Desmons, Hielard, and Giroud, who have served the Fatherland bravely with purse or pen; and Bartholdi the creator of the statue, who planted on the buttress of Fort Belfort his sublime lion and cast in silver for Gambetta that pathetic, cursing Alsace, whose eyes, melancholy as great men's eyes are, reveal all the sadness of the standard-bearer dying on his Alsace's bosom, and all the faith of the child by her side in whom the Motherland is reborn.

Familiarity with what is enormous cannot but engender light. The habit of conquering matter imparts to sculptors' faces an air of triumph and rebellion. The very capacity to admire what is great makes one great, much more so to model it, caress it, give wings to it, to extract from our mind the idea which, by means of our arms, our deep glances, our loving strokes, gradually curves and illumines the marble or the bronze.

This creator of mountains was born a free soul in the Alsatian city of Colmar, stolen from him later by the German foe, and in his eyes, inured to the sight of Egyptian colossi, liberty's beauty and grandeur took on the gigantic proportions and eminent majesty to which the Fatherland rises in the minds of those who live bereft of her. Bartholdi wrought his sovereign statue out of all his Fatherland's hopes.

Never did man create anything of real beauty without deep suffering. That is why the statue advances as though to step onto the promised land; that is why she bows her head and there is a widow's expression on her face; that is why she stretches her arm, as though to command and to guide, fiercely toward the sky.

Alsace! Alsace! cries every inch of her. The sorrowing virgin has come more to ask for a French Alsace than to light the way for world liberty.

Smiles and thoughts are but an abominable disguise, a tombstone when one lives without a Fatherland or when a part of it falls prey to the enemy's clutch. An atmosphere of drunkenness perturbs judgment, shackles words, quenches verses, and then whatever a nation's minds produce is deformed and empty, unless it express the soul's craving. Who feels more deeply the absence of a good than he who has possessed it and lost it? From the vehemence of sorrows stems the greatness of their representation.

There is Bartholdi, greeted lovingly by his comrades as he takes his place on the grandstand. A vague sadness veils his face; in his eyes shines a chaste grief; he walks as in a daze; looks where there is nothing to see; his unruly locks falling across his forehead bring to mind cypresses and shattered banners.

And there are the deputies: all have been chosen from those who fought most bravely in the war in which Alsace was lost to France.

Over there sits Spuller, Gambetta's friend. At the reception given by the French Circle of Harmony in honor of their compatriots there had been vague talk full of compliments, talk of historic brotherhood, of generous abstractions. Then Spuller appeared, a veritable lion. At first his speech was like a prayer, he spoke slowly, sadly as one burdened with some pain. Over the august, tearful silence he gradually draped his flaming words; when he drew them to a close the whole audience sprang to its feet; Spuller was sheathed in an invisible flag; the air seemed to vibrate like a smitten sword: Alsace! Alsace!

Now Spuller moves with bowed head, as always do those who are preparing to charge.

The French delegates gathered on that grandstand together with President Cleveland and the country's personages surrounding him watched the gala parade with which New York celebrated the dedication of the statue: rivers of bayonets, miles of red shirts, gray, blue, and green militiamen, a spot of white naval caps, a miniature model of the Monitor on a truck led by a boy in navy uniform.

The artillery in its blue uniforms passes by; the police, marching heavily; the cavalry, with their yellow lapels; on either hand the sidewalks black with people. The "hurrah!"

raised at the foot of Central Park passed on from mouth to mouth and died amid the rumble of the Battery. Then pass Columbia University students wearing their square caps; then carriages bearing invalids, veterans, and judges; and then Negro groups. Bands are heard; an anthem follows them all the way.

The gallant 7th Regiment militia gets an applause from the grandstand; the 22nd Regiment militiamen are handsome in their campaign capes; two German girls who came with one company hand the President two baskets of flowers; almost speechless, a child dressed in blue presents Lesseps with a silk banner for Bartholdi; the golden clarion notes of the "Marseillaise" fly over the procession; the President salutes bareheaded the tattered flags; as they pass the grandstand each company dips its colors and each French militia officer kisses the hilt of his sword. There are frantic cheers from the stand, sidewalks, and balconies when armless sleeves, bullet riddled flags, wooden legs pass by.

An old man in a dove-colored cloak drags himself along. Everyone wants to shake his hand. There was a time in his youth when he was a volunteer and pulled a fire engine as bravely as now he drags his old bones. He had broken his arms catching in them a child in flames, and his legs trying to protect an old man from a falling wall. He is followed by firemen dressed as in days of old and pulling their engines by means of ropes. Just as the oldest engine of all, lovingly cared for, brightly polished and laden with flowers, comes shaking on its fragile wheels behind the young red-coats, one of the formidable new engines dashes through the crowd to put out a fire nearby. It leaves the air stricken and warm in its wake. The smoke is black, the horses black. It knocks down carts, runs over people. Puffs of sparks redden its smokey mane. Then the hook-and-ladder wagon flies by followed by the enormous pumper as noisy as the artillery.

A bell sounding like an order is heard and the masses respectfully step aside to allow the passage of an ambulance with a wounded person. The regiments can still be heard far away. The golden clarion notes of the "Marseillaise" still hover over the city.

Then, when the hour came to draw away the flag that veiled the statue's face, everyone's heart swelled and it seemed as though the sky had become covered with a canopy of eagle

wings. People rushed to the boats as impatiently as would bride-
grooms. Even the steamers, dressed to look like great wreaths,
seemed to smile, chatter, and bustle about as merrily as girls at
a wedding feast.

Everyone's thoughts were uplifted by a deep feeling of respect as though the festival of liberty evoked all those who have
died in its quest. Over our heads a ghostly battle was being
waged! Oh, the lances, the shields, the statuesque dead, the
superb agonies! One fighter's shadow alone was as great as a
public square. They stood up straight, stretched out their arms,
glanced down on men as if they were creating them, and then
vanished.

The brightness which suddenly cleaved the dark atmosphere
was not from the rays of the sun, but caused by clefts between
the shields through which the splendor of the battle pierced the
mist. They fought, they fell, they died singing. Such is the
triumphal hymn which, better than the sound of bells and cannon, becomes this statue made, rather than of bronze, of all the
sunshine and poetry in the human soul.

From the time the parade was over, until dusk brought an
end to the celebrations on the island where the monument stands,
New York City and its bay were like one great cannon volley,
a ringing of bells, a column of smoke. . . .

In her presence eyes once again know what tears are. It was
as though souls opened and flew to take refuge among the folds
of her tunic, to whisper in her ear, to perch on her shoulders, to
die like butterflies in her light. She seemed alive, wrapped in
clouds of smoke, crowned by a vague brightness, truly like an
altar with steamers kneeling at her feet! Not even Rhodes'
Apollo,[17] with the urn of fire on his head and the dart of light
in his hand, was higher; nor Phidias' all gold-and-ivory Jupiter,[18]
son of the age when men were still women; nor the Hindus'
statue of Sumnat,[19] inlaid with precious stones like their fancy;
nor the two thirsty statues at Thebes,[20] captive as the desert
soul on their chiseled pedestals; nor the four colossi guarding
by the mouth of a cavern the temple at Ipsambul.[21] She is greater
than the Saint Charles Borromeo in crude bronze on the hill at
Arona [22] by the lake; greater than the Virgin at Puy,[23] a low-
flighted conception on the mount overlooking the hamlet; greater
than the Cheruscian Arminius [24] who rises over the Teutoburg

gate summoning with his sword the German tribesmen to route
Varus' legions; greater than the Niederwald *Germania*,[25] a sterile armored beauty who opens not her arms; greater than
Schwanthaler's *Bavaria*,[26] who proudly crowns herself on the
Munich plain, with a lion at her feet; over and above the
churches of all creeds and all the buildings of men. She rises
from out of a star-shaped pedestal, "Liberty Enlightening the
World," without any lion or sword. She is made of all the art
there is in the Universe, even as Liberty is made of all the
sufferings of mankind.

She has Moses' Tablets of the Law, Minerva's uplifted arm,
Apollo's flaming torch, the Sphinx's mysterious expression, Christianity's airy diadem. Even as mountains rise out of the depths
of the earth, so has this statue, "an immense idea in an immense
form," sprung from the soul of man's brave aspiration.

Man's soul is peace, light, and purity. Simply clad, liberty
seeks heaven as its natural abode. Girdles are painful to liberty;
it disdains crowns that hide its forehead; it loves nakedness as
symbolic of nature; liberty stands pure in the light from which
it was born.

Thus the tunic and the peplum become Liberty as a protection against unlove and impure desire. Sadness also becomes her,
that sadness which will only leave her eyes when all men love
each other. It is right that she be barefoot, as one who only feels
life in her heart. The diadem made of the fire of her thoughts
emerges naturally from her temples, and even as a mountain
ends in its peak so does the statue taper to the torch above in a
condensation of light.

At the foot of the statue, the grandstand built for the occasion from fresh pine trees and adorned with virgin flags seemed
as small as a poppy. The more favored guests occupied the
platform in front of the stand. The whole island was like one
human being.

How the people roared when their President, who had come
up as they had from the worker's bench, stepped into the official
launch to go and accept the image in which every man seems to
see himself redeemed and uplifted! Only an earthquake is comparable to such an explosion.

The rumble of cannons smothered out the clamor of men.
The steam compressed in the boilers of factories and ships es-

caped in unison with a mad, stirring, wild jubilation. At times
it seemed as though the soul of the Indian charged across the
sky yelling its war cry; or that churches knelt, their belfries
bent over, their bells pealing; or that from the steamers' chimneys came, now weak, now strident, the cock's crow, the symbol
of victory.

At times what was enormous became childlike: steam rushed
in the boilers; lighters frolicked through the fog; the crowds on
the steamers nagged the bands; stokers, garbed in gold by the
glare of the fire, poked coal into the furnaces; through puffs of
smoke one could see sailors standing on the yards of navy vessels.

At the grandstand the Commander-in-Chief of the American
Army called in vain for silence waving his black three-cornered
hat. Nor did the Reverend Storrs'[27] prayer, lost in the confusion, quiet the bustle. But Lesseps did conquer it, Lesseps with
his eighty-year-old head bare in the rain. The magnificent spectacle was unforgettable. The great old man had not simply stood
but jumped to his feet.

Oh, benevolent old man! Before he sits down, rewarded by
the applause even of his opponents, astounded and won over,
let thanks reach him from us "down there," from the America
which has not yet had her fiesta, because he remembered our
peoples and pronounced our forgotten name on that historic day
when America consecrated Liberty, for who have better known
how to die for her than we? Or loved her more?

"Until we meet again at Panama, where the thirty-eight stars
of North America will soon float at the side of the banners of
the independent States of South America, and will form in the
New World, for the benefit of all mankind, the peaceful and
prolific alliance of the Franco-Latin and the Anglo-Saxon races!"

Good old serpent charmer! Lucid soul who sees the greatness
of our hearts under our blood-stained garments! The other
America loves you because you spoke of liberty as though she
were your daughter!

Before Senator Evarts[28] got up to offer the statue to the
President of the United States on behalf of the American Com-
mission, the audience, stirred by Lesseps' words, insisted on
greeting Bartholdi, who, with becoming modesty, stood and
gratefully acknowledged the tribute from his seat. Senator Evarts' speeches are characterized by noble language and lofty

content, and his eloquence, deft and genuine, reaches the heart because it is born of the heart.

But his voice faded when he read from narrow sheets his speech depicting France's generosity in phrases like ribbons and pompons. After Lesseps he seemed a stooping reed: his head is all forehead; his inspiration finds difficulty in shining through his lean, parched face; he is dressed in a frock coat with turned up collar and a black cap on his head.

Before he concluded his speech someone mistakenly thought the expected moment had arrived when the banner covering the face of the statue would be drawn and the Navy, the ships, the city broke out in a unanimous din that seemed to ascend to high heaven from a shield of resounding bronze. Astounding pomp! Sublime majesty! Never did a people incline with greater reverence before any altar! Men at the foot of the pedestal, stunned by their own smallness, looked at each other as if they had fallen from above. Far away the cannon boomed, masts disappeared in the smoke, the growing clamor spread through the air. In the distance the statue seemed like a huge mother among the clouds.

President Cleveland seemed entirely worthy of speaking in her presence. His style too has marrow, his accent is sincere, his voice warm, clear, and powerful. He suggests more than he explains. He said such broad, lofty things as sound well before a monument. His left hand rested on the rostrum rail, his right he sank under the lapel of his frock coat. His glance had that challenge which becomes honest winners.

Shall we not forgive for being haughty one who knows he is surrounded by enemies because he is pure? His mind is a compensation for his overflowing fleshiness. He looks what he is, kind and strong. Lesseps glanced upon him affectionately as if wanting to make friends.

He too, like Lesseps, bared his head to speak. His words brought forth applause not so much for the pompous phrase and commanding gesture, as for their vibrating tone and sound sense. If the statue could be melted into words, they would say the same: "This token of the love and esteem of the French people proves the kinship between republics and assures us that we have a firm ally across the Atlantic in our efforts to recommend to all men the excellence of a government built on the will of the people." "We are not here today to bow our heads before the image of a war-like and fearful god, full of wrath and vengeance, but to contemplate joyfully our own goddess guarding the gates of America, greater than all those the ancients worshiped, a goddess who instead of wielding the bolts of terror and death, raises to heaven the beacon that lights the way to man's emancipation." The long applause that rewarded this honest man came from loving hearts.

Then Chauncey Depew,[29] "the silver orator," began the main oration. It must have been good when he was able to hold untiringly the public's attention at a late hour.

Who is Chauncey Depew? All that talent can be without generosity. Railroads are his business, millions his figures, emperors his public, the Vanderbilts his friends and Maecenas. Men are of little concern to him, railroads of much. He has a preying eye, a broad, haughty brow, a hooked nose, a thin, narrow upper lip, a long, pointed, close-shaven chin. He is idolized here because his speech is brilliant and harmonious, his will aggressive and sharp, his judgment keen and sure. On this occasion his fresh, versatile style did not sparkle as it often does in his much praised after-dinner talks, nor did he present a point with irrefutable logic as when he pleads a case as lawyer and railroad executive, nor had he adversaries to brow-beat mercilessly as he is reputed doing at the malignant, fearful performances of political meetings. Instead, he told in fiery phrases the generous life of him who, not satisfied with having helped Washington found his nation, returned — blessed be the Marquis de Lafayette! — to ask the North American Congress to free "his Negro brothers."

In ardent paragraphs he described the friendly talks between Lafayette and Washington at the latter's modest Mount Vernon home and the speech with which the Marquis, "purified by battles and privations," took leave of the American Congress in which he saw "an immense temple of liberty, a lesson to all the oppressors and a hope to all the oppressed of the world." [30]

The year of 1793 did not appall him, nor the dungeon at Olmütz tame him, nor Napoleon's victory convince him. To one who really feels liberty in his heart, what are persecutions more than challenges, or unjust empires more than soap bubbles? It is such men of instinct that guide the world. They act first and reason after. Thought corrects their errors, but lacks the virtue of sudden action. They feel and push. Thus by the will of nature it is written that things should be in the history of man!

Chauncey Depew looked like a magistrate when, shaking his arm and a trembling forefinger over his head covered with a silk cap, he summarized admirably the benefits man enjoys in this land founded on liberty; and with all the fire of a charger that feels his loins sorely spurred, he transformed his hidden fear into bravery, rose up in the name of free institutions to attack the fanatics who, under their protection, would seek to defeat them, and having learned the lesson of the social problem spreading over the United States, this "silver-worded" gentleman humbled the pride for which he is noted and drew out inspired strains to utter as his own the very phrases which are the gospel of the workers' revolution.

Oh, Liberty, how convincing is thy shadow: those who hate thee or use thee bow before thy commanding gesture!

Then a bishop appeared on the rostrum. He raised an age-bitten hand; all around the men of genius and of power stood up. There was a magnificent silence while he blessed in the name of God the redeeming statue. Guided by the bishop the audience intoned a slow, soft hymn, a mystic doxology. A sign from the top of the torch indicated the ceremony was over.

Streams of people, fearful of grim night, rushed to the narrow wharves, without concern for age or rank. Bands were heard vaguely as though lulled by the evening twilight.

The weight of joy rather than the weight of people seemed to load down the ships. Cannon smoke covered the official launch that carried the President back to the city. High above, the astonished birds circled fearfully around the statue as though it were the top of a new mountain. Men felt their hearts were firmer within their breasts.

When, among shadows, the last boats left the shores of the island, now transformed into an altar, a crystal-clear voice breathed out a popular melody which passed from ship to ship. Garlands of lights, reddening the sky's canopy, shone from the cornices of buildings. A song, at once soft and formidable, spread at the statue's feet and along the river. A united people, pressed together on the sterns of ships, gazing toward the island, with an unction fortified by night, sang: "Farewell, my only love!"

CENTENNIAL COMMEMORATION
OF THE CONSTITUTION

WHY should I, on this overcast day, try to describe the festivities with which the United States celebrate the anniversary of the Constitution which has brought glory to them? Philadelphia, which witnessed in 1778 that treacherous *meschianza*,[1] when the Philadelphia belles in Moorish costumes danced in mirrored halls with British officers uniformed in black and gold or white and red silk, on occasion of the gala farewell to Sir William Howe,[2] has now commemorated, with historical pageants, great pomp, mass meetings, and solemn prayers, the day when men, brought up in freedom, reconciling in a prudent code their stubborn differences, set up a government worthy of that freedom. Nations are uplifted by such festivities, and even we miserable men who yearn for freedom and find it unpalatable in a foreign land, felt as it were a freshness of dawn, a heroic bliss, when Philadelphia emerged from the blackness of night that luminous morning, bedecked with flags. Philadelphia is always beautiful, but it is more so when, viewed from the tower of its new Town Hall, it reveals to us its conglomeration of red buildings girded by its clear, quiet river, against a uniformly blue sky whose majesty is enhanced by the rich, emerald-green plains. On this occasion the marble and brick city took on a graciousness that seemed to reflect a wedding day's ineffable well-being. Men, who not even in the presence of death quench their enmities, forgot them to commemorate the form of government to which they owe their happiness; a commemoration which springs not out of egoism, but because of the divine pleasure with which men, still troubled and confused, hail whatever promotes and

Dated New York, September 28, 1887, published in *La Nación*, Buenos Aires, November 13, 1887. It also appeared in the Mexico City *El Partido Liberal*. There are a few divergencies between the two publications.

hallows their own persons. Houses seemed to be speaking. At dawn, beautiful Quaker maidens hung the last garlands and streamers, while old men were first on the streets. Life has its golden hours when a sun seems to rise within us and, like an advancing army, send glory bubbling through our veins. One breaks out in laughter or weeping, feeling enough strength in one's breast to overthrow a fortress.

One hundred years ago, when men wore plush trousers, silk frocks, and neckbanded waistcoats, Philadelphia experienced the same frenzies, discords, and strifes which Latins in their ignorance and their sickly inordinate admiration [3] consider the exclusive heritage of our race. There were as many conflicting opinions as there were buckles on men's shoes at the assembly summoned by the weakling Congress in order to unite under one really effective government the thirteen disconnected and jealous states which, out of excessive love for their own sovereignty, cancelled through their rebellion or their indifference the national measures adopted by the federal Congress, powerless under the Articles of 1781 to enforce its recommendations. Congress became the object of popular derision. Each state, whether rich and populous as Virginia or feeble and insignificant like Rhode Island, had one vote. The Nation was as flimsy as air, yet the states, under pretext of poverty, withheld their support. There seemed to be no way of getting the states to comply with the sickly bills Congress passed in the hope of tying together through equitable trade the old colonies disunited by jealousy and rivalry in production. New England, already becoming industrialized, disregarded the laws destined to favor the agricultural South. The latter aspired to free trade with Europe, which would be detrimental to the maritime East, hoping to obtain a monopoly of sea traffic. There was no common currency — an idea favored by some, opposed by others. No one state could live alone, yet enticed by the idea of a useless sovereignty they did not agree on fixing by law the union so indispensable to their existence. The sole visible sign of the nation was Congress, which only succeeded in evidencing its inefficiency. Superior men, few as always, anxiously recommended to their countrymen the advisability of establishing a new live government capable of putting an end to the recent discord which menaced the Union and availed the states nothing, only benefiting the blameful politicians who pompously displayed their own passions. Each state had some false shepherd, more concerned with being a boss in his corner than a secondary figure in a great republic. Prominent men, overshadowed at times by unworthy rivalries, coincided through the inevitable brotherhood of greatness, in the desire of promoting a glorious nation before apparently hostile interests prevailed over virtue. Hamilton [4] with the peculiar martial composure of his wisdom, under the pen name of Phosyon, demonstrated the necessity of joining the states under one strong government. At that time writers used ancient names: Phosyon declared, Publius explained, Pacificus debated with Helvidius. There were Honestuses, Camilluses, Leonidases. Rome and Greece reigned supreme, as in France. Youths poured themselves into Plutarch's [5] molds in the hope of resembling his heroes. Madison [6] had on his fingertips the debates of the Agora, Cleon's [7] speeches, Lycia's [8] laws. But Washington did not learn from parchments, rather from life, from politics. He entreated in his letters, urged in his speeches, propagandized in his trips; he was as concerned with the union of the states as he would have been with that of his children. Franklin likewise signed his unblemished name, as free of powder and pretense as his venerable head, at the foot of those wise epistles with which his amiable influence illumined men's minds in favor of the Constitution and which penetrated caressingly into men's hearts.

At last Congress authorized the revision of the useless Articles of Confederation. The Mercantile Convention called by New York to remedy commercial disorder turned into the much wanted National Convention to decide upon new bases and functions for the government. Since William Penn in 1698; since d'Avenant and Livingstone, about whom Bancroft [9] has not wished to write; since a Virginian's pamphlet on the Government of British Establishments; since Lord Stairs and Daniel Coxe, who wanted to arm the united colonies against France; since Franklin's Albany Plan, which took advantage in favor of the colonies of the Frenchmen's hatred for and fear of England; since the Congress of 1775, proclaiming the liberty of the states, had placed in Jefferson's hand the pen with which he was to write on a lady's desk the Declaration of Independence, and had adopted, on the motion of Franklin himself, the articles of the first Confederation; since then the States had not gathered together naturally as the members of a single body. A drawing of those days depicting a serpent cut in three pieces read "Union or Death."

There they had met, the dignitaries, the learned, the businessmen, the merchants, some wearing black or green cloth coats, others in velvet breeches and lace collars and cuffs. They had been sent by the states, displeased with the disrepute and impotence into which the federal government had fallen, to devise a manner of strengthening the Union without the loss of sovereignty of any of its parts. There they all were: slavists and abolitionists, rice planters, ship builders, manufacturers, nationalists and provincialists, typical orators and practical organizers. Impetuous Hamilton was there, whose elegance concealed his valor, whose graciousness covered a multitude of talents and a sagacious, untiring disposition; a man cautious in deed and in words, born of a Scotsman and a French woman, precocious as one born in the tropics, the builder of a fortune, an upperclass, brilliant, splendorous man, accused of wanting a monarchic form of government; one not without blame, who later died of a bullet shot. The wise counselor Madison was there, a man of letters, of history, a clear, persuasive expositor, endowed with such sure judgement that he could discern originality amidst a mountain of empty rhetoric; yet capable of hating Washington. There was Martin,[10] whose form was as fleeting as his babbling; prominent at the time, sure of shallow applause, he would dazzle the populace for hours with his travesty of grandiloquence; he would burst forth with studied apostrophes; he was the instrument of the passions he served. When he had finished, everyone asked: "What did he say?"

There was Morris, Gouverneur Morris,[11] whose mind seemed never to have known childhood, a subtle knower of men's motives, a cold clever pilot in debate, a creator of opportune formulas, the counselor of kings and republics; refined in his apparel, his treaties, and his madrigals. And there was Paterson,[12] wayward and fruitful, the defender of states or of petty claims; a weapon the born enemies of greatness always had at hand, made for the purpose of dividing as those incapable of founding always are; the stubborn advocate of New Jersey's absolute sovereignty of the states plan. There was dramatic, showy Randolph,[13] more inclined to declaim than to meditate; lacking the character which would have given his brave impulses permanent beauty; the agile defender of Virginia's plan for an energetic national government; a regrettable minister. There was the wealthy merchant Gorham,[14] who liked to draw his arguments from reality, an irate enemy of slavery, concerning which, as likewise Rufus King,[15] he was intransigent: "What is to be tomorrow, let it be today. What manner of Republic is this, borne on the shoulders of slaves, like the English *meschianza,* where Negroes marched with rings around their necks?" There were the makers of deep phrases and the judicially minded arbitrators: Ellsworth [16] and Rutledge,[17] who with Gorham, Randolf, and James Wilson [18] drafted the Constitution; Roger Sherman,[19] first a shoemaker, then a lawyer, a judge, a signer of the Bill of Rights, of the Declaration of Independence, of the Articles of Confederation; Johnson,[20] a university man, honored abroad, even by the British; James Wilson, who learned from D'Aguésseau [21] and Montesquieu,[22] and on whose arm Franklin leaned.

It is a new, superficial fashion to suppose that accidents of education and climate change the essences of men, identical everywhere, except for what the accumulated life of generations stamps or fails to stamp upon them. Corn speaks the same tongue as meat. The blond man hates, cheats, and boasts the same as the dark man. The North American becomes impassioned, exalted, rebellious, confused, corrupt even as the Hispanic American does. Witness this Convention! Each had his plan. One called his neighbor a demagogue, who retorted by calling the former a Monarchist. Of the thirteen states, three refused to attend. Of three New York delegates, two walked out of the Convention infuriated. One state had no funds to pay its delegates' traveling expenses. The small states called the large states tyrannical. "We shall rise against the Union." "Rebel!" "Rather than yield to the Virginia plan we will submit to a foreign despot!" There were hundreds of speeches: Madison alone delivered 198. The disorder reached such a point and the sessions closed so heatedly that Franklin, who was less cordially respected than he should have been, proposed opening each day with a prayer. General scuffles were sometimes imminent, and only avoided by referring the contentious questions to *ad hoc* committees, where interests were counterbalanced, phrases stretched or shrunk, the wounds of desire healed with the balm of flattery. When fury again broke loose, Franklin would exclaim "My God!" and lock himself up on a Sunday to write a prudent speech full of witty apologues. But what calmed and convinced the assembly was not the speech itself, but the fact that the old man had put so much of his soul into it that his voice had failed him and he had had to hand his paper over to Wilson to read as he himself dropped into his chair. After this the speeches became moderate and timid. It was in vain that a few parricides, tiring of justice as had the Greeks, made fun of the "great names!"

That debate, natural under the political conditions that originated it, was fruitful because of its very violence. Sincerity is never to be feared, only what is hidden is to be dreaded.

The health of the republic needs this combat in which one learns respect, this fire which concocts good ideas and dissipates vain ones, this airing which brings to light the apostles and the scoundrels. These impassioned debates serve to adjust conflicting rights, to nullify artificial theories in the face of reality, to trim down grandiose, proud ideals so as to make them compatible with opposing interests. The thirteen states, having to live together despite hostilities, having to create a national government without losing their own sovereignty, after fighting desperately for their extreme aspirations, decided to compromise them on the basis of facts. "All want something, all expect something of our Convention," wrote Washington to a friend "but as long as there is so much fiery fighting for the absolute sovereignty of the states, as long as local aims and special interests, weighing excessively in each, do not yield to a higher conception of politics, the incompatibility between the laws of the various states and their disrespect for the general government will hold this great country back in weakness, impotence, and a lamentable condition." [23]

That mad struggle of each state for its peculiar interest, that fear of small states of losing their independence if they joined the larger ones, that aversion of each state to risking its special wealth or submitting its institutions, even the inhuman one of slavery, to the conveniences of all, kept the Constitutional Convention in heated battle and jeopardized the success of its

discussions right up to the last moment. Yet, while these conflicts hindered the immediate triumph of generous ideals, they
succeeded in finding, with precise originality in view of the nation's dual character as several and as one, the only live form
which could preserve with prospects of improvement and on the
basis of reality, the indestructible and diverse elements opposed
to a purer union. But the tremendous war which was finally indispensable three quarters of a century later to settle the dispute
between the rival sections, a war which would have had the same
results and been less bloody at the beginning of the Union,
shows us that, while there may be compromise in matters of
mere distrust, pride, or interests, no compromise is possible nor
has ever been sanctioned by history if it curtails or twists the
essence of human nature. Justice admits no delay, and he who
demurs in its fulfillment turns it against himself. It is political
experience that shows us this is so, not mere sentiment. In these
times of aboveboard policies it is no longer possible to be ashamed
of being honest. Blackguards have made it fashionable to mock
those who resist being blackguards. But only virtuous politics
is useful and lasting.

There was deep rancor among the constituents. Some wanted
a strong national government, others opposed it; some favored
an unblemished and absolute equality of the states within the
Union, others upheld the primacy of men's natural rights over
those of abstract statehood. Some sought forced trade between
the states of the Union, others resisted any obligation that might
hamper free trade with foreign countries. The small states accused the large ones of seeking their absorption and insisted, in
order to maintain a fictitious equality, in assigning to all states
the same number of votes in the national government. The large
states claimed it was inadmissible that three million people of
one state should have the same number of votes as two hundred
thousand of another. The slave states, anxious to make their
Negroes count as men in order to increase their representation,
insisted on having them recognized as factors of production, and
on being allowed to import them from Africa free of duty, to
which the free states objected, seeing in the unlimited importa-
tion of slaves and in Negro representation the danger of the
slave states controlling, by this false and inhuman expedient,

the government of a nation constituted for the triumph of humanity. The coastal states, wishing to keep their boats active, wanted the government to be authorized to avoid the predominance of the British flag in American waters, to which the agricultural states were opposed, fearing that an American shipping monopoly might bring about an unavoidable rise in the price of the indigo or the rice they sold to Europe. How could the distance between the champions of representation by states and the advocates of the personal vote be shortened? How was it possible to conciliate the northern and eastern states, which were in favor of free votes exclusively, with the western states, desirous of having slavery for their agriculture, and with the southern states who threatened to secede from the Union if slave representation was denied? How to reconcile the East, thriving to favor its merchant marine, with the South, which resisted its domination?

Such were the conflicts during the four painful months the Convention lasted. There were insults, threats of secession, duels, shaking of fists. All the rest counted little: whether there should be three branches of government or one supreme body, at once judicial and legislative; whether the Executive should be unipersonal or of three men, temporal or for life, elected by the people or by the Legislature; whether the legislative branch should be composed of one or two chambers; whether the members of the lower house were eligible at the age of twenty-five or of thirty; whether senators were to serve nine, seven, or five years, or as long as they were well-behaved. But though these debates were often heated, especially those on the Presidency, none brought about tempests like those that shook the Convention when vital interests clashed or the question of the sovereignty of states was raised. There were three major battles and three compromises. As none could defeat the other, discussions were put an end to by the reciprocal recognition of vital interests.

First was the battle on sovereignty of the states, maintained by New Jersey's plan and opposed by Virginia's. Small states abhorred even the word "national." Virginia would not have representation by states; New Jersey rejected personal representation; the small states argued that the Convention had no right to create a new union, but only to reform the previous one; the large states denied the possibility of their collusion, since their interests were different: "It is the small ones who confabulate." "The large states will drown us!" "Can we accept having equal representation in the nation's government when we contribute larger sums to its support, when quotas are fixed on the basis of population, the self-same population of the contributing states to which the vote is denied?" [24] Then, in the quiet of an examination committee, Franklin, with his jokes and down-to-earth examples, contributed to the first adjustment which led to all the others. The really new idea of the Constitution of the United States was there suggested by the special composition of the different political entities to which it was to be applied: in order to reserve for personal representation, i.e. for the states which might suffer thereby, the decisive vote on matters pertaining to the Treasury, a two-chamber Congress was devised, one representing the people (one vote for every forty thousand) and another representing the states. Both would jointly discuss the laws of the nation. This adjustment has lived one hundred years and as the states are real entities and the difference between the Senate and the House of Representatives in the right to vote the budget, which the latter retains, is based on a real difference in the population, an equilibrium is maintained in the states' representation in this noble government, while the local laws of states, fashioned on their respective peculiarities and customs, facilitate the government's task relieving it of matters that do not touch upon or involve the nation and allowing ample dispersion of vanities and ambitions which, when concentrated, are a constant menace to a republic.

No sooner had personal representation been agreed upon in the calm of smoldering passions, when rage broke out again and states shifted their battle positions the moment the South demanded representation for the Negroes. "Why this demand if in the South Negroes are persons only for the purpose of bearing immoderately upon the states that do not have the stain of slavery?" [25] The fight was no longer between the small states and the large, but between the free states and the slave states. One would give Negroes a full vote, others three-fifths of a vote. The South held that slavery which contributed to the nation's wealth should be represented in its government. "So for being inhuman and lazy," retorted the free states, "you are to have a greater representation than we who are humane and industrious?" Morris, a free state representative, moved that the state quota in the federal expense budget should be fixed according to the number of representatives. "If you pretend to keep us from demanding the Negroes' representation by threatening to levy a higher quota on us for having them, I shall walk out of this Convention!" said the member from North Carolina. As three other states were already absent, the retirement of North Carolina would have rendered the Convention inoperative according to the very Articles of Confederation under which it had convened. It therefore became necessary to yield. King and Gorham would not yield. "This Convention cannot make us accomplices to inhumanity!" But the Congress did yield. "The Gorham issue is not a question of humanity; the point is that if Carolina retires, Union, which is indispensable to us, becomes impossible." [26] So the next adjustment was reached; the free states and the slave states reconciled their differences: the number of representatives was to be determined by the states' direct quota and both representation and quota by population, evaluating the Negroes at three-fifths of their number. The compromise passed by a majority of one. One hundred years have elapsed and this adjustment has not survived, having been born as it was not of what is real and permanent, but of a capricious sharing of power on the unnatural and transitory basis of crime. How fatal this concession of fear to avarice was is evidenced by the stifled and growing hostility that millions of ignorant, emancipated Negroes, who but for this disgraceful compromise would not have been born, show towards their former, still brutal owners.

It was not without threats that the small states, who were anxious to annul the concessions just made, were induced to attend further debates. Fearful of new defeats, they believed the Convention's debates should be closed and the findings submitted to Congress. The blazing August sun already shone when, in an impressive silence, one of those silences that seem to give birth to light, the delegates, seated in their high-backed chairs, received the draft of the Constitution printed with broad margins and in spaced lines and indeed quite different, save for the essential adjustments, from the text that after wild discussions,

announcements of secession, and rude insults, was to be eventually signed in solemn order by those who had proved finally
capable of sacrificing their pride to the commonweal.

Only scanty notes exist of the lively debates in which, after
many of the real issues had been settled, the learned displayed
their knowledge of facts, the demagogues rang feigned alarms
and the friends of man held fast, unabashed, when liberty, so
essential to man's happiness, was attacked. The names of the
branches of government were erased; the Executive became
"President," the Chamber of States became the "Senate," and
the chamber elected by the total population, the "House of
Representatives." The President was denied the title of "Excel-
lency." The draft gave him a seven-year term which was cut to
four; it forbade reelection, but it was subsequently decided that
the President might be reelected without limitation; the draft
did not require him to be native born, while the approved Constitution did. During these discussions and others there was a
bitter fight between the small states which would curtail the
functions of the national government, of which they were jealous, and the advocates of a strong federal government. With
these, unfortunately, joined forces those who, exaggerating their
just desires, rather than seeing in Union greater strength for
weak states, denied the common people's capacity for government and would have liked it reserved, as among the British, for
a superior caste of the "well born."

But it was not until the question of the authority of Congress
over commerce and navigation was brought up and the hostile
interests of the various states again came into play, that confusion in the debates was once more complete. The South wanted
to be allowed to bring in slaves from Africa without having to
pay duty, on the ground that they produced wealth and were
essential to the agricultural states. The East, opposing such a
concession, became exasperated by the South's reluctance to invest Congress with the power to protect the national merchant
marine by means of a prohibiting law: "If British ships are not
barred from our waters, our shipping industry will be ruined,"
said the East. "If the East's ships are given a monopoly of the
sea," said the South, "freights to Europe will increase so that
we will not be able to export our products." "Either we are
allowed to import slaves duty-free or we leave the Union," said

South Carolina and Georgia. "We leave the Union," said the
East, "if Congress is not authorized to guard the ships we live
on against foreign competition." [27] A third adjustment reconciled their interests: slaves could be introduced duty-free until
1808; Congress would have the right to legislate on ocean and
river trade. Thus, thanks to bargaining (not always dignified),
the adjustment of conflicting interests, mutual, painful submis-
sions, there was drawn up the Constitution which Gladstone [28]
believed to be "The most marvelous work the human mind has
ever wrought at a given moment."

At last they are ready to sign. Washington, who never exhib-
ited that familiarity to which courters of the masses are inclined,
seems transformed and differentiated from the rest even before
the eyes of those who love him not. Secretary Jackson [29] hands
him the pen he has just dipped in a silver ink well. Yet opposing
projects are still being suggested, a new Constitution already
demanded, amendments proposed. Franklin, in his paternalistic
manner, in his always harkened-to and humble tone, calls for
prudence. Morris hits upon the sought-for formula. Washington
is the first to sign the document drawn up "by the consent of
the states," exclaiming "I feared we would not come to this
without blood." The delegates sign in the geographical order of
their states. Sixteen refuse to sign. Franklin approaches the
presidential table on whose canopy a sun is painted. "I often
wondered," said he, "whether this sun was rising or setting;
now I see it is a rising sun." [30] As late as two years afterward
one stubborn state remained unwilling to enter "The good ship
Constitution" and take shelter under its "new roof." [31]

The bloodshed Washington feared did come. To postpone is
not to solve. When there is an evil, nothing is gained by permit-
ting it to accumulate. Crime, nay the crime of allowing crime,
always brings blood. But the Constitution of the United States,
prospering in spite of crime, teaches the world that only the
forms of government that are born within a nation take root in
it, and that even as the Articles of Confederation fell into disuse
and ridicule because they were false imitations of the Greek
leagues, likewise foreign purple can rot a cloth ill-fitted to receive it, and needing perhaps no other colors than those the
native sun will shed upon it.

These last days Philadelphia has proved herself worthy of

the event commemorated. She had arches built at her entrances, stands along her sidewalks, flag ornaments placed in every window. Her squares were turned into coliseums. The President and his wife came. The state governors came. At a jolly banquet the journalists acclaimed Cleveland who, at another banquet urged merchants to sacrifice at times, as a tribute to the Constitution, their local or immediate interest to the interest of the Republic. But it was neither the military parade nor the speeches which imparted novelty and significance to the event, but the pageant which showed industries as they were a hundred years ago, wretched, rustic, on donkeyback, and as they now are.

Thousands of men marched in the parade. It was as the usual thing: crowds, flags, much cheering, bands. The President, seated in a beautifully carved mahogany armchair watched the parade from his grandstand. Heading the parade marched Sheridan, the peace-loving General, who, during the war with the South, led his cavalry with the speed and flash of his sword-blade. The President's wife, dressed in black, watched from a balcony. The Marines marched by with their white trousers, blue shirts, and red hats; then the Pennsylvania Militia, victorious and imposing like an avalanche, all powerful men; then, amidst loud applause, the orphan Cadets. From one court comes much applause: a fountain surrounded by beautiful plants separates two sun-drenched groups: in one there are uniforms, epaulets, and plumes, in the other, invalids' beds. When the veterans march by, the President rises. Gradually the horse tails, the shining butts of rifles, the musical strains, and the cannon disappear in the distance.

The speech-making ceremony the next day was also under a scorching sun. The grandstand was full of dignitaries. Distinguished families and guests sat in sumptuous boxes. The crowd was so thick one could not pass a rose leaf between two persons. A Protestant bishop in a black silk tunic, a purple stole and a square-crowned cap gave the invocation. Unfortunately the President failed to find the grandiose words that the commemoration of such an extraordinary human event required.

The speaker of the day, Judge Miller,[32] after helping himself to two glasses full of refreshment and drinking them down, greeted his public and read an inopportune though reasonable diatribe, against those who, incapacitated by a European monarchial education to understand the order of liberty, came here offering to serve this country but really to menace it. In closing, Cardinal Gibbons,[33] dressed in red, besought God's blessings upon the Republic.

But the greatest event occurred the day of the pageant, which took nine hours in passing. It showed the century: its cradle, its ending. Not all we call new is new — in science, industry, literature, politics — but never have men advanced more in a hundred years, because never was liberty so real. A great painting representing the Republic led the parade. It showed in one hand farming implements of a century ago, in the other those of today. Many floats followed displaying plows with pompous names, whereby the manufacturers availed themselves of the patriotic event to advertise their ware: "The king of the West," "The Pride of the East," "The Sovereign." Behind a farmer sowing seed out of a bag comes a mechanical planter, which all cheer, and a steam horse proud and puffing. On one float we see typesetters composing letters in forms, melting types, while an imp all in red — the printer's devil, the errand boy — in rapid succession, tries to help, mixes up all the type, misplaces things, gets beaten, jumps, flees. On a mule rides a Negro with wheat for the mill, as in yesteryears, followed by heaps of modern barrels of flour. An old-fashioned saw which could scarcely strip a hundred and fifty feet a day, precedes a whizzing machine that turns out three thousand feet an hour. Then come canal boats, complete houses, the house where Washington stopped at Valley Forge. On a golden eagle's back rode many knights in armor, then loricas open, their helmets on their knees or at their feet. Following floats on which rode Indian children from the Carlisle school,[34] writing, drawing, sewing, assembling wood, there came, as a symbol of the Indians of old, a group of Pawnees,[35] in their war paint, on their ponies. A Negro stripped to his waist as in the days of slavery, planting cotton, preceded a carriage in which rode the city's prosperous Negro industrialists. Forty beautiful horses pulled a locomotive, not as beautiful as they! Closing the pageant came Washington's coach, empty, since no one else can deservedly occupy it.

CENTENNIAL OF WASHINGTON'S INAUGURATION: THE BALL

THE sumptuous Centennial of Washington's inauguration begins tonight. . . . What neither rich nor poor tire of speaking about is the famous ball: about the people of lineage's great concern lest the ball get out of hand and become a public affair; about the steps one has to climb and the dollars to pay in order to obtain from certain frowning gentlemen an admission ticket engraved in gold with a medallion of Washington in the center; about the representatives and senators of the State of New York finally coming to the ball, among whom it seems there is an accomplice of bandits, a good talker who is in the pay of gamblers and murderers; about the squabbles there have been among the men and women of the "four hundred," the higher-ups, the cream of the cream because the committee will only allow to dance in the honor cotillion those who can prove without a shadow of a doubt that they are direct descendents of the families who danced at the Frenchman Moustier's [1] the historical counterdance on occasion of the first inauguration, when Washington, swordless and dressed in velvet, stepped forth to do the step-and-chain to the tune of violins with that disdainful, coquettish Sally Carry who, when he was young, had turned him down to marry a certain Lord Fairfax.[2] There had been much gossip at the time; there was still more now; for no matter how far the rich draw out their geneologies it never reaches a hundred years; there is always a branch broken by a trader like Astor,[3] or a boatman like Vanderbilt,[4] or a spice-vendor like Peter Cooper.[5] This is the reason why a certain slighted millionaire [6] has already chosen to depart for his castles in England rather than bite his lips at the ball, seeing from his box "badly dressed

Part of an article dated New York, April 18, 1889, published in *El Partido Liberal*, Mexico City, 1889.

paupers," "with silver-mounted stones" pirouette among the Adamses and Jays, the Hamiltons and Fishes, the Lewises and Gerrys, the Morrises and Kings, as though to come from the founders of a nation constituted a greater merit than to profit therefrom and enjoy ivory bathtubs, onyx bedrooms, and golden dining rooms.

3

LIFE IN THE U.S.A.

THE GREAT "BUFFALO BILL"

"BUFFALO Bill" we read printed in large colored letters on every corner, wooden fence, sign post, deadend wall in New York. Sandwich-men — that is what they are called — walk along the streets, stuffed between two large boards which fall front and back, and sway as does the untroubled fellow who carries them, while the crowds laugh and read the bright letters shining in the sun: "The Great Buffalo Bill."

"Buffalo Bill" [1] is the nickname of a western hero. He has lived many years in the wilderness among rough miners, and buffaloes less fearful than the miners. He knows how to chase buffaloes and tumble them and how to approach them, stun them, mock them, confound them, and lasso them. He knows how to dazzle ruffians and make them recognize him as boss; because no sooner does one of these jump on Buffalo Bill wielding a knife, than he falls with Buffalo Bill's knife between the ribs, or if Buffalo Bill is shot at, his bullet meets the other in mid air and bounces back against the aggressor, for Buffalo Bill is such a crack-shooter, that he can shoot at a flying bullet, stop it and disintegrate it. He knows all there is to know about Indians, their customs, tricks, ways of fighting, and like them, he can see in the dark and can tell by putting his ear to the ground how many enemies are approaching, how far away they are and if on foot or horseback. As to fighting, he would just as soon shoot it out in a saloon with troublesome cowboys who are not satisfied if they haven't buried, with boots and spurs on, some neighboring cowboy or unwary traveler, as with howling, agile Indians who, leaning against their mounts' necks, flourishing their deadly rifles, swarm down fiercely upon the white man, himself forced to take shelter under his horse's belly or behind a nearby tree. All such terrors and victories can be read in Buffalo Bill's clear,

Published in *La América,* New York, July, 1884, and in *La Nación,* Buenos Aires, October 1, 1884.

melancholic, sparkling eyes. Women love him; they find him
handsome and desirable. Never is he to be found alone on the
streets. He is always accompanied by a beautiful woman. Boys
gaze upon him as though he were a Sun god, high and brilliant,
who charms them with his skill and pluck. His brown, greying
hair hangs long over his powerful shoulders. He wears a wide
brimmed, white felt hat, and boots.

Now he is cashing in on his reputation and tours the United
States at the head of a large troup of cowboys, Indian sharp-
shooters, horses, bucks, stags, and buffaloes. Either in the afternoon, by sunlight, or in the evening, by electric light, in a tent
as spacious as a prairie, they put on a show presenting all the
scenes full of risk and romance that have made the West famous.
In real, live tableaux he presents to wide-eyed New Yorkers the
marvels and dangers of that restless, wild life. We can see the
cowboys approaching with their leather trousers fringed at the
seam, their short jackets, neckerchiefs, dashing Mexican som-
breros, flung rather than seated on their spirited steeds, their
lariats rolled on the saddle horns ready to be whirled in the air,
their guns, with which they settle their smallest disagreements,
ready to be drawn from their crude holsters. The brave rascals
— homeless, childless — look upon death as though it were a mug
of beer: they give it or take it: they bury their victims or, with
a bullet in their breast, they roll up in their blanket to die.

Then the cowboys move on after showing off their persons
and tricks, and the Indians appear close behind a white traveler
who seems unaware of being followed. The Indians advance
single-file, facing front, at a slow gait, holding back their restless ponies, which the moment the wild men cease to rein them
in, will charge against the white enemy as though it were up to
them to avenge their riders' people. One would say men's grievances had steeped into the earth in such a manner that everything that sprouted from that earth brought those grievances
back to life again! Thus the Indian pony is, like its master,
slender and nervous, crafty and resentful. Like an arrow come
to life, this pony is a weapon that does not seem invented cas-
ually by the men who use it, but is the expression, concretion,
and symbol of the race's physical and spiritual traits, and of the
episodes of its history. The slender Indians come, singing a

dragging, monotonous, piercing song that penetrates the soul and saddens it. It is a song as of something which is departing to sink dolefully into the bosom of the earth. When it is over it continues vibrating in our ear like a twig on which a pigeon has just died.

Suddenly there is smoke all around; the plaintive wail is followed by a diabolical outburst of cries. The ponies charge, the heads of the Indians on a level with the ponies' heads. If one could swing a great knife under the horses hoofs, not one hoof would be touched. Screaming and shooting, in a cloud of dust reddened now and then by powder flashes, they fall upon the white man who kneels and empties all his cartridges like grapeshot. While loading he uses both hands and holds his gun between his teeth. The Indians shoot between their horses' ears or under their bellies. They are like ghosts through whom bullets pass without harming them. The white man, who is Buffalo Bill, runs out of ammunition; by the way he sways it seems he is badly wounded. The Indians encircle him as vultures would an eagle still alive. He embraces the neck of his horse, which he has used as a parapet, and dies.

The war cries now become cries of victory. You would not say they had killed one white man but all of them. It's just a circus show for the benefit of Easterners, but this is so deep-rooted in their souls that the show seems real. They take him away hanging across the saddle of a horse belonging to an Indian fallen in the fray. Off they go elated, yelling, when, amid screams and lashing of whips, there appears a stage coach full of white men, and drawn by small mules with many bells on their harness. The fight is on! The old coach becomes a barricade, the coach box a castle's battlement, every window a loophole for firing. The savages, in vain try to defend their dead prey. Again there is smoke, flashes, bullets, powder everywhere; at last the ponies stampede away and the brave avengers carry the traveler's body to the stagecoach. The public applauds frantically. This much we have advanced since Rome; then the throngs applauded the gladiator who slew, now they applaud those who save. The whip crack, music is heard, hymns rumble, and the rickety statgecoach disappears in a thick cloud of dust.

Thus Buffalo Bill's men represent the scenes which are still being enacted out West. A horseman appears flying. A shot is heard. He undoes the pouches, hanging against the horse's rump, disengages both feet from the stirrups and, as he rides past another horse already saddled which a man holds by the bridle, he jumps on its back with his leather bags and continues on his way on a fresh mount, while they blanket and revive the tired one. Such was postal service in yesteryear; before railways, men did the work of railways.

Or again it is a herd of buffaloes, charging with their muzzles sweeping the ground. The cowboys on their horses swiftly surround them, dazzle them with their shouts, lasso them with their skillful lariats around the horns or by whatever leg the public chooses, or tumble them or ride them in spite of the beasts' efforts to shake the riders off. And sometimes a very able cowboy will lasso the beast by the horns, speed up on his mount so that the rope will slacken; then, with a jerk, he will make a noose in the air, land it on the animal's muzzle and, with a strong wrench, fasten it there like a halter.

The show comes to an end amidst thousands of shots, as the sharp-shooters break clay pigeons in the air, and choruses of hurrays that die down as the crowds board the trains homeward-bound; then the electric lights, shedding their brightness on the empty circus, mimic one of those magnificent spectacles that surely take place in the very bowels of Nature.

CONEY ISLAND

NOTHING in the history of mankind has ever equalled the marvelous prosperity of the United States. Time will tell whether deep roots are lacking here; whether the ties of sacrifice and common sorrow that bind some people together are stronger than those of common interests; whether this colossal nation carries in its entrails ferocious, tremendous elements; whether a lack of that femininity which is the origin of the artistic sense and the complement of nationality, hardens and corrupts the heart of this wonderful country.

For the present, the fact is that never has a happier, a jollier, a better equipped, more compact, more jovial, and more frenzied multitude living anywhere on earth, while engaged in useful labors, created and enjoyed greater wealth, nor covered rivers and seas with more gaily dressed ships, nor overflown lovely shores, gigantic wharves, and brilliant, fantastic promenades with more bustling order, more childlike glee.

United States' newspapers are full of hyperbolic descriptions of the unusual beauty and singular attraction of one of these summer resorts, with crowds of people, numerous luxurious hotels, crossed by an elevated railroad, studded with gardens, kiosks, small theatres, saloons, circuses, tents, a multitude of carriages, picturesque assemblies, vending wagons, stands, and fountains.

French newspapers echo its fame. From all over the Union come legions of fearless ladies and country beaux to admire the splendid scenery, lavish wealth, blinding variety, Herculean push, and surprising aspect of famous Coney Island, an island which four years ago was nothing but an abandoned heap of earth and is now an ample place for rest, seclusion, or entertainment for the one hundred thousand New Yorkers who visit its shores daily.

Published in *La Pluma*, Bogotá, December 3, 1881.

It is composed of four hamlets joined by carriage, tram, and steam railroads. One is *Manhattan Beach,* where, in the dining room of one hotel, four thousand people can comfortably sit at the same time; another, *Rockaway,* has arisen, as Minerva arose with lance and helmet, armed with steamers, squares, piers, murmuring orchestras, hotels big as cities, nay, as nations; still another, less important, takes its name from its hotel, the vast, heavy *Brighton.* But the most attractive place on the island is neither far off Rockaway, nor monotonous Brighton, nor aristocratic, stuffy Manhattan Beach, but *Cable,* smiling Cable with its elevator, higher than Trinity Church steeple in New York, twice as high as the steeples of our Cathedral, to the top of which people are carried in a tiny, fragile cage to a dizzy height; Cable, with its two iron piers projecting on elegant piles three blocks into the sea, its *Sea Beach Palace,* now only a hotel, but which in the Philadelphia Fair was the famous Agricultural Building, transported to New York and reassembled as if by magic, without a piece missing, on the shores of Coney Island; Cable, with its fifty cent museums where human monsters, freakish fish, bearded ladies, melancholy dwarfs, and rickety elephants, bally-hooed as the biggest elephants in the world, are shown; Cable with its one hundred orchestras, its lively dances, its battalions of baby carriages, its gigantic cow being perpetually milked, its fresh cider at twenty-five cents a glass, its countless couples of loving pilgrims which bring back to our lips García Gutiérrez's tender cries;

> In pairs they go
> Over the hillocks
> The crested larks,
> The turtle-doves; . . .[1]

Cable, where families resort in search of wholesome, invigorating sea breezes instead of New York's foul and nauseating air; where poor mothers, as they open great lunch baskets with provisions for the whole family press against their breasts their unfortunate babes who seem consumed, emaciated, gnawed by that terrible summer sickness which mows down children as a sickle does wheat, *infantum cholera.*

Steamers come and go, trains whistle and smoke, leave and

arrive emptying their serpent belly-full of people on the shore. Women wear rented blue-flannel suits and coarse straw hats which they tie under their chins; men in still simpler suits lead them to the sea, while barefooted children at the water's edge await the roaring breakers and run back when the waves are about to wet them, disguising their fear with laughter. Then, relieved of the smoldering heat of an hour ago, they charge, tirelessly, against the enemy, or, like marine butterflies, they brave the fresh waves, play at filling each other's pails with shovelfuls of burning sand, or, after bathing — imitating in this the behavior of grown-up people of both sexes who do not heed the censure and surprise of those who feel as we do in our countries — they lie on the sand and allow themselves to be buried, patted down, kneaded into the burning sand. This practice, considered a wholesome exercise, lends itself to a certain superficial, vulgar, and boisterous intimacy to which these prosperous people seem so inclined.

But the most surprising thing there is not the way they go bathing, nor the children's cadaverous faces, nor the odd headresses and incomprehensible attire of those girls noted for their extravagance, their eccentricity, and their disordinate inclination to merry-making, nor the spooners, nor the bathing booths, nor the operas that are sung at café tables in the guise of *Edgar* and *Romeo,* and *Lucia* and *Juliet,* nor the grimaces and screams of Negro minstrels, surely not like the Scotch minstrels, alas!, nor the majestic beach, nor the soft, serene sun. The surprising thing there is the size, the quantity, the sudden outburst of human activity, that immense valve of pleasure open to an immense people, those diningrooms which, seen from afar, look like bivouacked armies, those roads which, from two miles away, do not seem like roads but like carpets of heads, that daily out-pouring of a portentous people upon a portentous beach, that mobility, that change of form, that fighting spirit, that push, that feverish rivalry of wealth, that monumental appearance of the whole place which makes a bathing establishment worthy of competing with the majesty of the country that supports it, the sea that caresses it and the sky that crowns it, that swelling tide, that dumbfounding, overwhelming, steady, frenzied expansiveness, and that simplicity in the marvelous; *that* is the surprising thing.

Other peoples — we among them — live devoured by a sublime inner demon who pushes us tirelessly on in search of an
ideal of love or glory. When we hold the measure of the ideal
we were after, delighted as though we were holding an eagle, a
new quest makes us restless, a new ambition spurs us, a new
aspiration heads us toward a new vehement desire, and out of
the captive eagle emerges a rebel, free butterfly, daring us to
follow it, chaining us to her circuitous flight.

Not so these tranquil souls, only disturbed by the craving of
owning a fortune. Our eyes scan the reverberating beaches, we go
in and out of those halls as vast as pampas,[2] we climb to the
peak of those colossal structures as tall as mountains. Prome-
naders in comfortable chairs by the seaside fill their lungs with
that bracing, benign air. But a melancholy sadness, as it were,
takes hold of the men of our Latin American countries who live
here, for they seek each other in vain and no matter how much
first impressions may have lured their senses, charmed their eyes,
dazzled and puzzled their reason, they are finally possessed by
the anguish of solitude, while the homesickness for a superior
spiritual world invades them and grieves them. They feel like
stray sheep without their mothers or their shepherd. Tears may
or may not flow to their eyes, but their astounded souls break
in bitter weeping, because this great land is devoid of spirit.

What a bustle! What flow of money! What facilities for
pleasure! What absolute absence of all sadness or visible poverty! Everything is in the open air: the noisy groups, the vast
dining halls, that peculiar courtship of North Americans into
which enter almost none of the elements which make up the
modest, tender, exalted love found in our lands. The theatre, the
photographic studio, the bathing booths; everything in the open.
Some get weighed, for to North Americans to weigh a pound
more or less is a matter of positive joy or real grief; for fifty
cents, others receive from a stout German woman an envelope
containing their fortune; still others, with incomprehensible delight, drink certain unsavory mineral waters out of tall, narrow
glasses like mortar shells.

Some ride in roomy carriages from Manhattan to Brighton
at the soft twilight time. One fellow shores his boat, in which he
had been rowing with his smiling girl friend, who holds on to

his shoulder as she jumps, frolicking like a child, onto the bustling beach. A group of people admire an artist who cuts silhouettes out of black paper of whoever wishes to have this kind of portrait of himself and glues them on white cards. Another group watch a woman in a tiny shop less than a yard wide and praise her skill at fashioning strange flowers out of fish skins. Others laugh uproariously when one fellow succeeds in hitting a Negro on the nose with a ball, a poor Negro who, for a miserable wage, sticks his head out of a hole in a cloth and is busied day and night eluding with grotesque movements the balls pitched at him. Bearded, venerable citizens ride gravely on wooden tigers, hippogriffs, sphinxes, and boa constrictors that turn like horses around a central pole where a band of would-be musicians play unharmonious sonatas. The less well-to-do eat crabs and oysters on the beach or pies and meats on tables that some large hotels offer free for such purpose. The wealthier people lavish large sums on fuchsine infusions passed off as wine and on strange, massive dishes which our palates, fond of the artistic and light, would certainly reject. To these people eating is a matter of quantity; to ours, of quality.

And this lavishing, this bustle, these crowds, this astounding ant hill lasts from June to October, from morning till midnight, without respite, without interruption, without change.

What a beautiful spectacle at night! True enough, a thinking man is surprised at seeing so many married women without their husbands and so many mothers strolling by the humid seaside, concerned with their pleasure, and heedless of the piercing wind that might harm the squalid constitution of the babies they hold against their shoulder.

But no city offers a more splendid view than Cable Beach by night. More lights shine at night than heads could be seen by day. When descried from a distance offshore the four towns shine in the darkness as though the stars of heaven had suddenly gathered and fallen to the sea.

The electric lights that bathe with magic brightness the approaches to the hotels, the lawns, the concert pavilions, even the beach whose every grain of sand can be counted, seem from afar like restless sprites, like blithe, diabolic spirits romping about the sickly gas jets, the garlands of red lanterns, the Chinese globes, the Venetian chandeliers. One can read everywhere, as though it were day: newspapers, billboards, announcements, letters. All is heavenly: the orchestras, the dances, the clamor, the rumble of the waves, the noise of men, the ringing of laughter, the air's caresses, the loud calls, the rapid trains, the stately carriages, until the time comes to return home. Then, as a monster emptying its entrails into the hungry gullet of another monster, the colossal, crushed, compact crowds rush to catch the trains, which, bursting under their weight, seem to pant in their ride through solitude, until they deliver their motley load onto gigantic ships. These latter, livened by harps and violins, take the exhausted tourists to the piers of New York and distribute them in the thousand cars and along the thousand tracks that like veins of steel traverse the sleeping city.

THE THIRTEEN CLUB

TODAY'S papers are saying more about the eccentricities of The Thirteen Club than about protectionist Kelly's[1] death . . . They write more about the Club's thirteen coffins and thirteen candles than they do about the delay of the United States in recognizing Brazil's new government[2] . . . more about the thirteen plates, the thirteen wines, the thirteen toasts, the thirteen chairs, the thirteen tables . . . than about a presidential candidate's shameful defence of Harrison's Senator friend who, in a letter, ordered the purchase of Indiana's "floating" votes[3] . . .

It is of The Thirteen Club and its great yearly banquet everyone speaks today: that the menu will be printed on a drawing of a tombstone and the wine list on that of a coffin; that the guests will be seated thirteen minutes after the appointed hour; that the club will be lighted by as many candles as it has members, who are numerous and famous, not because of the adequacy of the illumination, but because the club was founded to dispel anxieties and to fight against foolish fears, and since the first clubhouse had come tumbling down and the fall of a wall in the second had cut off the gas, they had lit "the candles of life" and seeing they did not go out, continued using them.

Proud Conkling,[4] who died when he saw himself beaten in his personal useless politics, was among the thirteen founders. Barnum,[5] the mischievous octogenarian, was another; another was Ingersoll,[6] who believed in honesty and poetry as the only religion. They disinter strange legends: in the times of the first English kings, was it not the bard who sat in the thirteenth seat among the twenty-four dignitaries gathered around the festive board? Knighthood is now the vogue because of the fact that,

Dated New York, January 13, 1890, published in *La Nación,* Buenos Aires, March 12, 1890.

not counting Don Quixote, no book has been better written on it, nor given it a worse thrashing, with more efficacy and novelty than a book written by the humorist Mark Twain with his man-of-nature strength, with foresight and indignation.[7]

ELECTIONEERING

STATE and municipal elections have just been held. Their importance has been to awaken the public to self-consciousness and self-sufficiency and to rescue it from the bold political bosses who once disposed of the people's votes as of their personal property. Many positions were to be filled: those of state senators, members of the federal Congress, high state officials, Attorney General, Public Treasurer . . . In Brooklyn, a Democratic city, the mayorship was at stake . . . In New York, all eyes are turned toward the close, interesting contest between a millionaire and a laborer. In Brooklyn, apart from personal circumstances that added amenity and color to the fight, the issue involved was electoral freedom. In New York a tall, imposing, slender, stylish man, named Astor [1] ran for Representative to the federal Congress against a stocky, broad-shouldered, jovial, plain, humble man: Roswell Flower.[2] In Brooklyn, the Mayor, who during his term of office has shown intelligence and integrity but proved to be like wax in the hands of a formidable boss who controlled the city's political organizations, ran for re-election against a young, charitable, just, impetuous, wealthy man: good Seth Low.[3]

The Flower vs. Astor contest is worth noting. All of them follow the same pattern; but this one was livelier, more throbbing, more revealing of the spirit and practices of this people than any other. Astor is a grand gentleman turned to politics, who owns palaces and has dreams of glory, whose greatest asset is that of not considering riches as the right to idleness. He is poor in years, not in millions. He is a state Senator. He is a member of and hopes to be a representative of that singular aristocracy of fortune, who, to gain their passports to society try to hide the only credentials that count: those of a humble origin.

Fragments from an article dated New York, November 12, 1881, published in *La Opinión Nacional*, Caracas, November 26, 1881.

First-generation rich look back fondly upon the times when they
were store clerks, stable hands, wool-combers, poor errand boys,
cow herders. But the second-generation rich, who galantly mount
the steeds their fathers once led by the bridle, consider as an
unbecoming stain in the newly rich the very thing in which their
parents took the most pride: being self-made. To a man already
rich, one who is in the process of becoming rich is a base and
despicable being. There is an abysmal difference between those
who are wealthy through inheritance — thin, pale, with the appearance of a long flute, as is the fashion among the British gen-
try — and those whose power stems from work — healthy, chaste,
resolute, robust, and extremely clean, with that sober, solid,
American cleanliness.

A political aristocracy, born of an aristocracy of wealth, dom-
inates newspapers, wins elections, and prevails at meetings over
that proud caste who ill conceal the impatience with which they
await the hour when the number of their followers will allow
them to lay their heavy hand upon the sacred book of the Fatherland and reform in favor of a privileged few the Magna
Charta of generous liberty under which these vulgar strong men
amassed the fortune they would now employ in wounding it
gravely. Astor backs and is backed by such. The friends of what
is here called "strong government" are his friends. Gruff Grant [4]
and supercilious Conkling [5] are for him. It is axiomatic for him
that his family, his millionaire family, should be represented in
the Union's Congress, as were the branches of state in the old
Spanish Cortes. It is like an inopportune attempt to introduce
England's aristocratic system, where young noblemen learn the
art of government as an unshirkable duty and an unforsakable
right.

Candidate Astor, modest like the first generation rich, still
keeps his rimless hat and his wornout shoes as trophies. He now
rides in a carriage, but he remembers when he walked barefoot.
"I know what simple food tastes like," he said magnificently a
few days ago, "that simple food brought from home in a tin can
over which the workman so avidly leans at noon." Roswell
Flower has the magnetism, the impetus, the fragrance, the at-
tractiveness of a new force. He is now the director of a bank
where he is loved. He had once stretched out his arms in vain

asking for a job. He speaks the truth, disdains hypocrites, loves the unfortunate. He has the pride of his humbleness, the only healthy pride there is. During his electoral campaign, his sole weapon has been his history. "Workmen will vote for me because I have been a workman: for many years I never saw my feet free of wounds and bruises. Young men will vote for me, because it must be a matter of rejoicing for them to see a man whose life proves one can reach the highest ranks from the lowliest beginning." Workmen and young men did vote for him, as did his Democratic partisans and his Republican adversaries. His district during the week preceding the election was worth seeing.

Great placards read in black letters: "Vote for Astor." Other, yet no smaller, placards announced in red, green, and blue letters: "Roswell Flower." Posts, fences, piles of bricks, dead-end walls were all covered with immense signs. Every hotel was a boiling-pot, every bar an electoral office. Carriages full of election officials drove up and down the streets of the district, and newly won, volunteer followers turned diligently to work for the Democratic candidate's triumph. Astor's election office was like a great telegraph exchange or a general's headquarters on a battlefield. One could constantly hear the rattle of closing envelopes, folding letters, scratching pens. Messengers collided with each other as they dashed in and out. The district voters and politicians swarmed around like butterflies on a honey-laden flower. And every butterfly's service was weighed, appraised, and paid for. There were whisperings, passages in and out of secret doors, mysterious shakings of hands, malicious smiles. Some made a sad exit, but seemed relieved; others were jolly, but appeared weighed down with new responsibilities. The election of a representative to Congress has cost no less than $16,000 to the candidate or his party. Astor's campaign has cost him $80,000. He paid his clerks two hundred dollars a day. Forty thousand circulars were mailed to his electorate. Whole cartloads of circulars and letters left his political office. There were one hundred and five districts in his precinct and each received one hundred dollars for petty expenses. Large numbers of people offered themselves as influential among voters: the useless were separated from the useful and the useful given a fifty-dollar gratuity every day for their services. Fountains of champagne, beer, and whiskey

spouted in every bar or tap room when the candidate visited
them. He was accompanied by an electoral cabinet made up of
proven molders, seducers, and violators of popular suffrage. Avid
reporters followed him closely in the rain, along slushy streets.
Into his last footstep quickly fell one of their feet, and no sooner
had he uttered a word or dropped a coin on a barroom counter
when they resounded immediately on a newspaper's composing
table. Journalists followed him like gadflies and they lost this
gadfly war.

It is customary for candidates to visit taverns, to win friends,
mingle with the voters, dazzle them with a cordial phrase, an
opportune promise, a tone of intimacy or a sparkling chat, to
capture voting bar owners with their lavishness and induce them
to influence other voters. In such ovens had elections here been
traditionally baked. Around these wooden counters bargaining
went on over the price of votes, and in shady corners full of
smoke small groups whispered mysteriously. There vote seekers
degraded themselves by speaking lewd trivialities, improper
complacencies, or unbecoming familiarities. There a relatively
impecunious candidate would approach a group of tramps, who
greeted him uproariously, and say, "What will you gentlemen
have? Beer?" There another, who is now ambassador in Europe,
once when the bartender was otherwise occupied took off his
coat, turned the beer barrel tap, served his friends, clicked
glasses, shook hands, and won them all with his friendliness.
There would mighty Astor enter with his chamois gloves, his
humble countenance, his affable smile. He treated the hangers-on
to champagne, expensive wines, and rare liquors, nothing less.
He threw on the counter heavy twenty-dollar gold coins and
didn't wait for the change. There are eighty breweries in the
city; he visited almost every one. His guests drank their fill, but
he only touched the glass to his lips. He might cultivate one beer
merchant by talking to him readily in the language of his beloved
Vaterland; but another certain German would receive him rudely,
while still another denied the millionaire his vote face to face
after having received quantities of the latter's good money for
his own bad beer. He once attended a low-class dance, strewed
the counter with brilliant coins so all the dancers could drink
abundantly, and danced with the humblest girls. Now he de-

fended some action of his in the Senate, now he apologized for opposing some useful bill, offering to back it in the future. Oh, wretched glory, debaser of those that seek her fleeting favors, lowering them to such manner of behavior! On the other hand was Seth Low's reaction in Brooklyn: "Not a cent shall I pay to be elected!" "Nor shall I buy others beer I don't drink, nor buy votes which do not honor me."

And Roswell Flower did not engage in what they call "personal campaigning" or "barroom campaigning" . . . Astor's agents paid for a glass of Seltzer water with five-dollar coins leaving the barman the change "to treat the boys when they came." Roswell Flower, however, turned down a group of Democrats who demanded a small cash compensation, and if anyone mentioned the possibility of purchasing a few Republican votes he would reply bravely: "I don't expect to lose, but I would rather lose than owe my victory to the purchase of Republican votes. I want to come out of this campaign clean." "My opponent has more wealth and longer legs than I, but my loyal Democratic voters will make up for that. I started life as a poor boy of the people, the people will give me their votes; the honest ones of the Republicans will give me their votes." . . . At nightfall, a sad young man, seated in a presidential arm chair at the head of a broad table, feverishly shook a nervous, bejeweled hand. It was Astor who, surrounded by his humbled henchmen, kept receiving in telegrams and letters news of his inglorious, complete defeat.

Flower won by more than two thousand votes in a district where previous polls had given Astor's Republicans the same margin over Flower's Democrats. It was normal that in the City of Labor a working man should be elected. The future laws of a good and strong people were not to spring from the bottom of beer kegs or the will of a few purchasable tramps and paupers. He sits uneasily who sits on paid shoulders, for paid men, once they have squandered the pay received, or when they wish to serve another master, or recover their self-esteem, are apt to shake off the riders who pay them.

And the press, that new queen, that lovable, powerful queen, whom Flower has thanked most graciously, was a deadly weapon against the millionaire. Not because of an unhealthy hatred of wealth, but a virile repugnance of seeing it so basely used. Cultured newspapers protested and complained of the attempts at taking advantage of uncultured people. Such a purchase of men wounded their dignity as men. . . .

And thus the newspaper reports of this campaign have been like rapiers, darts, tongues of accusation, piercing swords, war axes. The defeated millionaire has reaped this harsh and merciless lesson out of his ignorance of and disrespect for men. . . .

But the same (press) which chastised the corrupt millionaire has raised unto heaven a virtuous man amidst hymns of victory. Seth Low, heir to the biggest fortune in Brooklyn, elected its mayor by a landslide, has been praised, defended, congratulated. His followers staged a lively campaign. Brooklynites packed the meeting halls to listen to the virtuous young man, who made six to eight speeches every night, full of honest thought, delivered calmly in plain language; indeed not a torrential, slashing, serpentine style like Beecher's,[6] but colloquial, serene, ungarnished, concerned with what was being said rather than with the manner it was being said. Democrats and Republicans alike have elected Seth Low out of hatred of the political pressure exerted in the city by a Democrat boss and out of respect for Low's unusual qualities. He is one of those rich who could well lose their wealth without losing the love they have won. . . . He inherited his fortune from his father, his resigned, humble, industrious, charitable nature from his mother. He believes a rich man should not be a gilded parasite born with a golden spoon in his mouth, but a lively creature, a harp that sings when stirred by a human wind, a useful fighter in life's vast and complicated jousting field. He now makes ready to occupy his high seat and from it to work for the public weal, free suffrage, practical schools, rapid communications, and to do nothing but what involves fear of God and of self, but never fear of other men's censure.

THE ORIGIN
OF THE REPUBLICAN PARTY

THERE never was a political party of more glorious birth than the Republican Party of the United States, because none was conceived with more disinterested purposes nor more noble hopes.

This country's Constitution was tainted by an original sin: it had compromised with the slavery of a race. The Republican Party was formed to clean up that stain. It was made up not only of the best among the living; it may be said to have been formed also by the illustrious dead. The shadows of Washington, Jefferson, Franklin, Hamilton presided over its sessions; the great ancestors of North American liberty participated in spirit in the task of remolding by which the pure gold was to be separated from the dross.

One historian has pointed out that the seeds of slavery and of liberty fell upon this continent's soil at one and the same time. The Mayflower brought the Pilgrims to Plymouth in 1620, and also in 1620 a Dutch boat landed twenty African slaves in Virginia. There never was a more extraordinary parallelism. On the one hand, social discipline, dignifying the citizens' obedience by depriving public authority of all undue force; on the other the Negro traffic, degrading labor, vilifying property, placing piracy among the country's fundamental institutions. Thus did the United States start life.

The Declaration of Independence contains these memorable words: "We hold these truths to be self-evident, that all men are created equal." The Declaration of Independence was the genuine expression of the spirit that moved the heroes and the preachers of liberty, the spirit that fought at Bunker Hill and

Dated New York, October 20, 1884, published in *La Nación*, Buenos Aires, November 6, 1884.

162MARTÍ ON THE U.S.A.

triumphed at Yorktown. The Constitution, on the other hand, was but a pact, *an agreement with Hell,* as Wendell Phillips was to call it later.

The resolution to establish the Union and, later, to maintain it prevailed over the generous hatred with which the northern and eastern states looked upon the infamous institution. Those who at any cost, even at the cost of their lives, wanted to erase the ominous stain, had to confront and fight the prudence of that patriotism which placed the Union over and above all ideas and sentiments. In the South they called them criminals; in the North, fanatics. In the South, the slave owners brought them to trial and thence to the scaffold; in the North, businessmen and statesmen considered them turbulent, dangerous people who were to be put down, and whom they were willing to turn over as peace offerings to the southerners on whom they could wreak their vengeance. The Union, thus considered, meant nothing more than material aggrandizement: vast cotton plantations, great cane fields, great tobacco lands, gigantic distilleries. In order that the Union be something more than that, one cold, snowy night, the night of January 6, 1832, twelve men of good will met in a Boston church and signed the antislavery party charter. They were as poor and humble as the twelve Gallileans, and the Gospel they were to sow in their compatriots' cold hearts was doubtless the same their grandparents had come to America to be able to read freely upon her virgin soil. The purpose of their magnificent campaign was to raise that Gospel over the heads of slaves in token of protection and over the slave-dealers' whips as anathema. For enthusiastically proclaiming this Gospel, Garrison [1] was dragged through the streets and insulted, but finally it all was to lead to the laurels of Gettysburg, to Lincoln's emancipation proclamation, to the defeat and utter wrecking of the titanic power which had been thriving on Negro blood, to the Thirteenth Amendment of the Constitution of the United States, which Washington would have wanted to sign, that charter of liberty of five million helots, of rehabilitation and cleansing of thirty million citizens.

The history of this propaganda would be interesting to trace, if the nature of this article allowed. It would be an act of piety and justice to pay tribute on the tombstone which lies by the roadside of great human memories and holds martyrs and heroes, and to repeat the sublime words of orators and poets who gave moving expression to the sighs of the unfortunate and the indignation of the just and which, in Whittier's Pindaric stanzas, in Bryant's [2] majestic chants, in that unforgettable novel which illumined the inside workings of slavery,[3] in those newspaper columns of Greeley,[4] in the voices of Beecher or Channing [5] ringing from the pulpit, in those gloomy legislative sessions where an Adams [6] or a Sumner [7] spread the starry highness of their lofty speech and the gleam of their spirit upon vulgar debates, to repeat the sublime words, in fine, which in all those deeds of powerful fancy and purest emotion shine with the classic beauty never lacking in the sincere and enthusiastic revelation of human ideals.

It was necessary to fight everywhere: in meetings, in the press, in books, in church, in the Capitol, in swarming streets, and in home conversations. Two inimical spirits, two currents of conflicting ideas stirred this immense country and shook its institutions, violently striving to control them forever. The first words against the Union came forth in pain and shame out of the ranks of the generous. *King Cotton,* as slavery was then sarcastically called, seemed at the time too strong to dream of dethroning him while maintaining the Union. "Since Union is infamy, *delenda est Carthago!*" — cried Wendell Phillips [8] — "thank God it is a long time since I have ceased to consider myself a citizen of the United States." [9] The most ardent, indeed, would have nothing to do with politics. We cannot, they argued, without swearing to defend the Constitution, and such an oath would be sacrilegious. We will have no Union with slave traders. This democracy is not a model to the world but a scandal. To purify ourselves of the ignominy which it throws upon us and upon our children it is necessary that we break all alliance with crime, that we *strike down the national authority which protects it and the national church that gives it its blessing.*

As the propaganda grew, the electric shocks between opinions became even more frequent, both in public and in private life. The clamor of contrasting passions, the harsh, inflamed, biting language in which adversaries addressed each other could be heard in hotel lobbies or among the seats of Congress. Slavery had its high priests as later it was to have its martyrs; it had its psalms, its prayers, its interpretations of the Bible. At first even the Southerners called it a "necessary evil." Later, in the heat of the contest, the justification of slavery became dogma. To the Southerner any attack against slavery spelled menace to his property, ignoring his rights, attempting to exert federal tyranny, and lastly an outrage, incredibly enough, an outrage to his religious faith. The Southerner believed in slavery as he believed in God.

After several fragmentary organizations which led the way as trials, the Republican Party was founded. In the wake of the fiery ranks of tempestuous precursors came the calm men, the men of serenity, of political tact, of sound sense tantamount to genius, to convert into reality and plant on solid ground the ideas of dreamers and prophets. Thus it must be if justice and beauty are to conquer in this world. Everlasting praise and thanks be to those who with feverish hands, made unsteady by their inspiration and enthusiasm, break the urns of society or art in which their ideas could live; but let us bless the laws of Nature for placing by their side, perhaps on a lower level, the men who are capable of channeling the seething torrent, even though curtailing its volume, so that the multitudes may drink of it. Garrison and Wendell Phillips had wanted to untie the Union; Abraham Lincoln came to consolidate it.

The Republican Party did not hoist the banner of abolition. To others fell the eminent, noble task of presenting the redeeming idea to the people's conscience. It had been proclaimed by apostles and poets: "let us no longer be content," said Whittier in splendid verses, "let us no longer be resigned to speak the truth in whispers or cowardly murmurs; let us speak out with clarionlike tongue." [10] A necessary, sublime imprudence. But the men who were to fight in the polls, who preferred slow victory to heroic defeat, who had the vocation and the gift for political contest, chose another ground and other arms for the definitive battle. As public opinion stood, and given the resources and situation of the two factions into which the country was split, abolition as a political program was out of the question. The Republican Party went only so far as to reject the concessions the North, intimidated by the South's energy, had made to it.

These commitments made the abyss opened by the Constitution unspannable. It was as though the free lands were yielding before the irresistible invasion of slavery. Each successive legislature, because of the South's energy and the North's business fears, opened new markets to the iniquitous trade and cast the venomous shadow of servitude upon a new stretch of land. These commitments made possible what the North had always opposed: the spread of the gangrene. Soon, if the Republican Party did not prevent it, it would no longer be possible to repeat Daniel Webster's words with regard to Ohio: "The Ordinance of 1787 stamped upon the very land, when it was still a wilderness, the impossibility of its being trodden upon by slaves." [11]

In 1860 Abraham Lincoln, that most quiet and serene enemy of slavery, one of those men called providential because they meet every requirement of their allotted ministry, gained power by two million votes and carried with him to the White House the flag of the Republican Party. I need not recall the South's ire, the breach of the pact, Buchanan's [12] miserable behavior, Europe's rejoicing over the Colossus' falling apart, the many extraordinary vicissitudes of war. On January 1st, 1863, the President of the United States, in use of a faculty the most authoritative interpretation of Constitutional Law recognized in him, in punishment of the rebels, and by virtue of the supreme dictates of war, proclaimed the emancipation of Southern slaves. The image of the Cabinet meeting in which Lincoln, standing, read to his Secretaries the proclamation he himself had written in that style which history cannot alter, which says things once and forever, has been preserved by painting, poetry, and oratory. "I am aware of your impatience," he said, "I would have wanted this to be done before, but I waited for the opportune moment;" and then, in an almost imperceptible voice, he added: "When Lee was driven out of Maryland, I promised God the slaves would be emancipated."

It is known that the abolitionists did not consider their task finished. The bills and the institutions of welfare and learning with which they tried to lift the browbeaten race as high as possible are notable. Some years after the war an eyewitness tells of an old Negress kneeling on the street in front of a Republican school in the South. Asked what she was doing there, she replied: "It is too late for me to go in, but I am praying for those who founded this house in which it is possible for my grandchildren to learn."

The Republican Party, therefore, in the first period of its existence, wise in council, relentless in war, strong and great in speech and in deed, accomplished one of humanity's most heroic sagas, opened in the sky of history a patch of blue. Shadows no longer obscured the incomparable stars on the country's flag, which the Party vigorously uplifted, and now that, under its broad folds, the only race banished from civilization could live under the Law, it was possible to write on the Constitution's first page as upon imperishable granite a North American tribune's eloquent dictum: "Union and Liberty, one and inseparable, now and forever."

HEATED CAMPAIGNING

WHEN August girds the ripening fields, heated passions line up for the Autumn elections which, being local, are fought tooth and nail, with formidable hatred. Debates here are like boxing matches — in public and without gloves. In our countries, if we heard what here is calmly heard, our garments would soon be bloodied. This has been somewhat corrected, but only in the cities, even as the parlor of a house is often kept tidier than the bedrooms.

In the hinterland states votes are bought and sold the same as in New York, but the language and accusations heard are shockingly bold and malicious. One governor pays fifty dollars for each vote in the convention to nominate the party candidate. Another offers to pardon the inmates of a penitentiary and smuggles his own secretary to them at night to obtain their written statements under oath to the effect that during the Democratic government they were obliged to skin the Irish or Negroes who died in prison "and make walking sticks out of strips of their skin." A lie? Ohio's Republican governor goes from platform to platform reading the sworn statement.

"That's not all," he adds. "The Democratic governor employed a warden who received money from the prisoners . . . in exchange for better treatment and an easy job." "That's a lie!" cries someone from the public benches. . . . Two hours later he makes another speech. His statements seem more formidable than those about the warden and the skinning of dead prisoners. "Democrats have committed every manner of fraud in the Ohio elections: non-voters have registered as voters; the same voters have voted twice; ballots which were never cast have turned up in boxes; Republican ballots have vanished; vote counters have been guilty of disloyalty and perjury. Everybody knows this in

Fragments from an article dated New York, October 3, 1886, published in *La Nación*, Buenos Aires, November 7, 1886.

Ohio. Such and such an election was a farce, an outright bur-
glary. And those judges! When we went to court, there was always a Democratic judge willing to confirm the fraud."

The truth is these were no imaginings of Foraker.[1] It was
thus that the Republicans snatched the presidency from Tilden.[2]
It was the way that Blaine's [3] friends tried to rob the presidency
from Cleveland in the last campaign. It is exactly how local
elections are often perverted here by false lists and ballot jug-
gling.

Concerning the language used, here is an example. Governor
Foraker in one of his speeches spoke thus: "All Democratic employees are a bunch of good-for-nothings, brazen, shameless
scoundrels who rob and plunder right and left from the day they
take office to the day they are kicked out to where they should
be, where they can wait until they are sent, as they ought to be,
to serve the state, not as employees, but in the penitentiary." [4]

Such is the case in Ohio. In Connecticut, where elections for
governor are also about to be held, the candidate is accused of
having bought the Republican Convention votes.

Is the accuser a Democrat, a nobody, one of those paid
barking or hand-licking dogs? No, the accusations are brought
in a very detailed pamphlet, by a Republican of high standing
in his city.[5]

All this wrangling appears to stem from deep divisions within
the (Republican) Party. When they work together everything
seems sacred to them; when they are divided by their commitments to or sympathies towards rival bosses, they denounce
their own acts as crimes of their partners of yesterday.

Neither charity nor white-glove attitudes come natural here.
Blaine attacks his enemies without charity, without gloves, the
same as they attack him. Even the unruly gray locks on his
forehead are indicative of the implacable passion of Blaine's
politics. His exceptional aggressiveness dazzles and wins even
his enemies in this aggressive, fighting country. His versatility,
his catholicity, the genuine power of his speech charm men who
mostly lack these gifts. Blaine's very defects: the skill with
which he sells his political influence, the calm with which he
meets the gravest proven accusations, his stubborn determination to place himself by every means over and above whomever

stands in his way, his apparent lack of scruples or shame in committing and hiding public faults are as mirrors in which masses of people see themselves reflected and pardoned, for they see in the public sinner who triumphs the sanction of this country's boundless love of success.

And then he has the gift of seeing in what direction the people's passion flows at a given moment, and, with a tiger leap, places himself at the head of the passing trend. Nothing discourages him. Such astounding capacity for survival, such ardent, indomitable faith in himself and in his fortune, win him the admiration and control of the great mass of a country made up of men who see in life itself a challenge for conquest . . .

The elections this year for governor of the state of Connecticut are but an episode of Blaine's drama. No sooner had he fallen, defeated by Cleveland, when he picked himself up out of the dust, wiping the sweat off his brow, with a terrifying speech on his lips, and blandished his candidacy once again.

There was a cold shiver up the spines of those Republicans who, through honesty or envy, had helped in his defeat. His bold tenacity induced his friends to stay by his side just when, figuring that he was through, they were ready to abandon him. After his defeat he has not lost a single friend. He has gleefully watched the Democrats' hapless discussions, their incapacity to vote together on the silver, the tariff, and the civil service issues, the interested masses' resistance to backing Cleveland's reform policy upon which his greatness rests, the Secretary of State's complicity in a proven telephone venture, the mistake committed by Secretary Bayard [6] in the Mexican question.

He fights to the death; so do his enemies fight him. That is why an outstanding Republican, hostile to Blaine, accuses the Republican Blainist candidate for the governorship of Connecticut of corruption and bribery. Governorships lead to the presidency. So a glance at these elections is a way of beginning to study the presidential elections of 1888.

When Blaine was chosen his Party's candidate in the last elections, the purest and most respected of his copartisans left him, and were generally praised for so doing; they proved the evident charges against his personal and political integrity and, without resigning from the Party, worked for Cleveland's election as "Independents" . . . preferring for head of the nation a clean adversary rather than a guilty copartisan.

Now, for 1888, the situation seems to be the same. As things look today, Blaine can count within his Party on more votes and raises more enthusiasm than stern Edmunds,[7] loquacious Logan,[8] or cautious Sherman.[9] And the "pure Republicans" seem inclined to keep the Democrats in government rather than turn the reins of power over to a guilty politician who, as they see it, disgraces the Republican Party.

Though Blaine has carried on in Maine brilliant assaults against the Temperance Party, so strong in that Puritanical section, it is not there that the autumn campaign has been surprising, nor in Connecticut, where one Democrat has proved to another that he has bought the nominating convention dollar upon dollar, and is using church influence to have confirmed on election day that affront to popular suffrage, nor even in Ohio, where none less than the governor assures us that they made walking sticks out of Irishmen's and Negroes' skins in the state penitentiary.

An extraordinary thing has been happening in Tennessee where two brothers,[10] one a Democrat, the other a Republican, are campaigning together throughout the state as rival candidates for the governorship, making speeches for their respective parties from the same platform.

They speak from the same stage; sleep under the same roof. Each demands of his friends normal respect for his brother. They discuss heatedly and unreservedly the merits and shortcomings of their parties; masses welcome them; processions follow them; they speak in theatres, woods, caves; they are escorted by horse-guards. After each debate they are deluged with flowers. Democratic girls, all dressed in white with a white rose pinned to their bosoms, come from their villages to greet their candidate "Bob" Taylor. Throughout the campaign "Alf" and "Bob" have not separated for a single day. It is said that there never was in Tennessee a more brilliant debate, and that it has dulled the usual brutal edge of political campaigning, because of the respect with which the brothers treat each other, notwithstanding their frankness.

They both play the fiddle and — oh, the simpleheartedness

of young nations! — one night, after a discussion, someone brought each a violin to the stage, whereupon the two brothers, sitting on twin chairs, carried on their debate musically. Yesterday, after his speech, Bob was presented with a violin made of tuberoses.

Both brothers, sons of a quiet Protestant minister, are very eloquent. Alf, the Republican, short and stocky, has a large head, full of facts and good sense. Bob, the Democrat, is tall, magnetic, his hands hold what they touch, his eyes make friends, his loquacity is aggressive and sparkling. Alf shoots off his phrases with a sharpshooter's accuracy: he aims, caresses his target, covers it with his glance, hits where it hurts, but he does not thrill. Bob looks as though his feathers were all ruffled under his dress coat, catches his brother's words on the wing as would a fighting cock. . . . When a good argument of his brother catches up with him, he lets it go by, as though conceding he had scored a point, but then and there he pounces upon him with some laughable flight of fancy and kills with jokes, which always go over well with ignorant audiences, the arguments he was not able to destroy otherwise.

Once a ruffian in the Democratic section yelled some offense against Alf. Bob got up, advanced towards the public, which in Tennessee is not noted for its softness: "Whoever insults my brother insults me!" There were no further offenses.

Thus, night after night, in town after town, they go on discussing free trade, which Bob wants and Alf doesn't, Blair's project,[11] which Bob opposes because he does not think that Negroes, who are free citizens of a state, should be educated with funds of the nation, with federal alms as it were.

They are always surrounded by eager partisans who pick up their witticisms and make slogans out of them . . . An old farmer comes up to Bob. "I'm entitled to shake your hand, because I have brought into this world thirty good Democrats, seven sons and twenty-two grandsons." "You haven't lived in vain, my good man." "No wonder there are so many Democrats in Tennessee," grumbled Alf.

The Republican women wear red scarfs, the Democrat, white. The opponents' friends form separate ranks as they wait for them at the stations, sometimes on horseback to escort them to a nearby park or grove spacious enough to hold the multitude, sometimes on foot to follow them from the depot to the City Hall or the theatre.

Whether on horseback or on foot, the two processions advance separately along the streets, those of one wearing white roses or ribbons in their buttonholes, those of the other with red roses, dahlias, or ribbons. Women present them with banners, standards, flowers, fruit. Men vie with each other for the honor of putting them up in their homes.

A Democrat gentleman, who is host to both candidates, asks his wife as they go to the table, "Whose arm will you take?" "Both," she replies, and advances on the arms of her two guests amid general applause.

That same night ten thousand Democrats gathered under the balconies of the house to serenade Bob. The street seethed with flags, torches, flowers, fireworks. Bob, surprised, stepped out on the balcony. The crowd suddenly realized they might be unwillingly hurting his feelings if the serenade proved humiliating to his brother, so they cried out asking the two brothers to appear on the balcony! It sounded like a hymn.

But what is really like a hymn is the energy, the love, the contagious faith with which the workers of New York, for the first time united in a serious political effort, are trying to elect as mayor of this workmen's city one of the wholesomest, boldest, cleanest thinkers who today contemplate the complex entrails of this new Universe: Henry George.[12]

He, with his Socratic forehead, seems to shed light on this apostolic campaign. Clergymen help him; also reformers who are as good as clergymen.

Many Latin Americans help him by word or deed. The purely political parties do not hide their fear at the advent of this new force; and it so happens that this city, born of facts and capable of facts, receives with respect the candidacy of this honest innovator.

We will witness attentively this baptism of a new way of life.

WOMEN'S SUFFRAGE IN KANSAS

THE Kansas State Legislature, by exception now controlled by the Republican Party, sought a broader electoral base to favor that Party against the Democrats who had always defeated it, so they decided to grant the vote to "native born" women. This condition made the measure necessarily advantageous to the former, because while it excluded the naturalized citizens who were mostly Democrats, it enrolled the Negro women who look upon the Republicans as their liberators and would gladly grasp the opportunity of meeting face to face at the polls their mistresses of twenty-five years ago. Kansas, as the rest of the South, is Democratic.

Helen Congar . . . was the soul of the reform. . . . She knew her men. . . . She said to them: "Pass in your Republican legislature this bill which I myself drafted, granting women the vote, and when election time comes I will get your Republican candidates elected."

Helen Congar kept her word. The experienced Party organizations had nothing on the women's organizations. Boards were established in every city. They visited beer saloons and houses of ill repute. They drafted a code of ethics: "Let there be posted a list of all husbands who leave their homes at night to slobber over saloon bars. . . . We want husbands we can respect, not brutes. Let us publish the names of those who frequent sinful places." . . . Hatred, slavery's inevitable aftermath, poisoned the contest. . . . And so they began to discredit Helen Congar, to question her morals. . . . "What about your own morals," she retorted in one of her speeches. "These Negro women of mine wash and iron, but their men are their men. Their houses

Fragments from an article dated New York, April 10, 1887, published in *El Partido Liberal,* Mexico City, and in *La Nación,* Buenos Aires, May 21, 1887 don't have two doors: one for the husband who foots the bills and another for some handsome officer!"

Polls opened at daybreak. . . . This time, two lines are formed: one for men, one for women. There is not much talking, because they fear each other. There are many sour faces because anger brings out all the soul's filth. Carriages hired by the Republicans come and go with their loads of Negroes. They are ladies, why shouldn't they be driven in carriages? They all wear their best Sunday finery. The "mistresses," arriving in their own carriages, take their places in line behind their handmaids. "Ha! Miranda," yells out a frolicsome Negro to his wife standing in the other line, "are you voting Democratic?" — "No, Republican!" — "Well, then, let's go home: your vote cancels mine. Your arm, Miranda!" So happily they walk away arm in arm. But Miranda comes back alone and votes Republican.

Two grand ladies approach a Negress to buy her vote. Some men interfere; words are soon backed by fists, voters scatter like corn in the wind . . . A great applause is heard: a mulatto woman by the name of Stevens has just passed. She had made a public speech flanked by two judges and some high-class ladies, for indeed not all turn their backs on the humble; some even take pleasure in giving them a hand!

THE CHINESE IN THE U.S.A.

AS the railroads' assets have shrunk and they have found themselves with less goods to carry and a too lively competition on the part of rival carriers soliciting to transport that same scanty available cargo, they have had to reduce freight charges and cut the number of men they employ on the lines, in the shops, and in their mines. They have cut wages; reduced coal extraction. To this general conflict another specific conflict has been added.

Chinese have been flowing in torrentially through ill-guarded ports, despite the legislation which practically prohibits their entering the United States. By means of some ruse or other, or through bribery, the American officials themselves help them get around the law. In San Francisco Chinese merchants have it all over German and American merchants.

The Chinaman has no wife, lives on a pittance, dresses cheaply, works hard. He sticks to his customs, but abides by the law of the land. He rarely defends himself, never attacks. He is crafty and because of his sobriety and sharpness he wins over the European workman.

He is not endearing: a people with no women cannot be; a man deserves esteem not for what he does for himself, but for what he gives of himself. A married man induces respect. The man who resists helping another life, displeases. Woman is man's nobility.

But as a worker the Chinaman is frugal, cheap, and efficient. As he lives differently from the white worker, consumes less, and is not concerned to the same extent with the latter's problems — needs, wages, strikes, he is satisfied with what he earns, which at least covers his bare requirements, and avoids intercourse with white workers and knows that they hate him.

From an article dated New York, September 19, 1885, published in *La Nación,* Buenos Aires, October 23, 1885.

Whatever step white labor takes, the Chinaman stands in the way: if the white man is not available, there is always the Chinaman.

The Chinaman is also astute and as he will do anything for pay, no sooner does he hear of an opportunity for gain — a soft pit in a mine, a desirable privilege — than he manages to grasp it, which aggravates the white worker, limited as he is by special conditions, who perhaps failed to see the opportunity the Chinaman saw.

Since he is tame and meek, though no less skilled and vigorous than workers of other races, the employers are happy to have him. On arrival at a mine the Chinese raise their houses, eating place, laundry, store, theatre, and with less money live comfortably, which makes the European miner bitter and jealous.

Then, one day, there is smoke coming from the mine. It has happened in so many places! There has been a fight way down in a pit: four Chinamen are killed.

Their panic-stricken comrades leave their work and sound the alarm. All the Chinese gather in their living quarters. The whole mine suspends work. The white workers summon those of the vicinity and armed with rifles, revolvers, axes, and knives march against the Chinese quarter, and order them to leave the mine within the hour. The poor devils obey without protest and have scarcely time to pick up their belongings.

A few minutes elapse and the white miners start shooting at the Chinese, who, in great fright, leave their houses screaming and take to the nearby hills, pursued by the shooting Europeans. Some fall dead on the road, others run on wounded. The houses behind go up in flames. A few Chinamen who had lingered are seen running through smoke and fire toward the hills covering their heads with blankets and quilts held in their extended arms as a protection against bullets. The whites pursue. Few escape. If one appears, he is hunted down.

One hundred and fifty are killed.

At night the white workers return to the camp and burn all the fifty houses.

The law carries on its task slowly.

Six Chinese commissioners leave San Francisco under guard to investigate the crime.

The white miners go free and confer with the Union Pacific officers. They demand of the company a decision not to employ Chinese in the mines, a proposal the company does not accept.

The coal pits are deserted and the Knights of Labor announce that they will back with all their strength Union Pacific's white workers and will see to it that their demand be accepted. Either the Chinese are fired or the railroad will be minus coal.

THE INDUSTRIAL DEPRESSION

IN the United States this [labor] problem presents itself, as everything does here, suddenly and on a colossal scale. Here, when there is force, it is overpowering, when there is hunger, it is great . . . It is a well-known fact that this motley population is only American in its more recent stratum, the last generation, and in some places not even that.

Without the brakes of patriotism, therefore, which even among scoundrels has much strength, this medley of Irish, Scotch, Germans, Swedes — meat-eating, beer-drinking people, with shoulders and hands like Atlas' — rush quickly and unbridled, restrained only by fear or the instinct of self-preservation, to the conquest of what they consider theirs: their right to a larger part of the product of a wealth of which they consider themselves the main factor and of which they are not the main beneficiaries. This advancing mass might be held back, often justly held back. They might be made to understand that though they are an indispensable part in the production of wealth, on the other hand the accumulation of capital, against the hateful abuses of which they justly rebel, is just as important a part. They might be made to realize that it is not merely a question of maladjustment in the distribution of industrial products that often creates unemployment or underpayment of labor, but rather the enormous production due to the accelerated turn-out of machines, the excess of production over needs, the competition of foreign countries, which is fatal to countries which, like the United States, charge high customs duties on their imports, and the errors of industry itself — which feeds the laboring masses — who, fearing to have their own domestic market invaded by the products of free trade countries, advocate the con-

Part of an article dated New York, April 27, 1886, published in *La Nación* Buenos Aires, June 4, 1886.

tinuance of high import tariffs, thus making it impossible for industry to compete successfully in rival markets.

Now Uncle Sam is adjusting his suspenders, pulling at his beard, passing his top hat from hand to hand, wiping with his cotton handkerchief his sweaty brow, from which for the first time drops of blood begin to ooze, while he faces this formidable problem brought about by his having protected himself too much.

Uncle Sam provides himself with everything, he owns forests of factories of all kinds, but is himself obliged to buy all that he manufactures. But where will he put it all? What will he do with so much? Where will he get the money to go on feeding his factories? What will he do with his millions of workers, who do not stand by to look at the problem, but see that business is rich while they are poor, who want better wages, more security, more respect?

All this could be said to the laboring masses to hold them back or to postpone until a more propitious occasion their demands for industrial reorganization. But as they have already drawn up their bill of rights, well founded on reason; as they see that their ills spring partly from organized capital's insolence and disdain, from its illegal practices, from a system of unfair distribution of profits which keeps the working man a perpetual pauper; as they do not feel it is just that railroad workers should earn barely enough for a morsel of food and a blanket in order that the companies' bosses and henchmen may share in Gargantuan dividends; that for every thousand dollars of actual investment in the business twenty thousand dollars worth of shares is issued, so that, since profits are naturally proportionate to capital investment, there is never enough with the profit of a thousand to pay dividends on twenty thousand; furthermore, as the holy poison of human dignity has gotten into men's veins and is there to stay, swelling them, pushing them on, we have come to a state where, a justice done here, a violence there, workers are on their feet, having decided not to sit down except on a hand-in-hand basis with capital.

Then things get worse, unhappily. None feel the need of being masters more than slaves do, and as the working classes have had so much to suffer at the hands of the masters who employ them, they have developed a despotic inclination and are not content with becoming the equals of those who have made them suffer, but going beyond all reason would raise themselves above them, submit them to terms which would deprive their employers of the very dignity and human freedom which they claim for themselves.

There, in their own injustice, lies their weakness, and from this, at least this once, stems their defeat.

RELIGION

EVIDENTLY pompous institutions are not enough, nor are fine systems, impressive statistics, benevolent laws, vast schools, and external paraphernalia sufficient to counterbalance the impetus of a nation that disdainfully passes all this by, swept along with a complacent, selfish conception of life. It seems that this public defect, which in Mexico they are beginning to call *"dinerismo"* (money-mindedness), this unbounded craving for material wealth, this contempt for whoever lacks wealth, this unworthy adoration of anyone who has accumulated it, even if it has been at the expense of his honor or through criminal action, is brutalizing and corrupting nations. Doubtless those who practice or favor the cult of wealth should be deprived of social esteem and looked upon as disguised enemies of the commonwealth, as blotches, as Iagos. It is a glorious thing to accumulate wealth through honest, hard work, but to amass wealth by violent or sly means, which dishonor the one who employs them and corrupt the nation where they are practiced, is palpable proof of incapacity and shamelessness, a crime worthy of the severest penalty. Rich people, like thoroughbred horses, should display for everyone to see the pedigree of their fortune.

Now, all this becomes apparent here. But even as the study of nature, considered hostile to spirituality, foments a more vigorous and resplendent spirituality cleansed of superstition and strengthened with facts; even as great oppressions engender great rebellions; even as the lands most devoid of natural poetry breed, because of the very vehemence with which they crave it, the profoundest and most sensitive poets, thus do emerge here — due to the general lack of the finer conditions of

From two articles, one dated New York, April 8, 1888, published in *La Nación,* Buenos Aires, May 17, 1888, and the other dated New York, March 4, 1890, published in *El Partido Liberal,* Mexico City.

character — fervent propagandists, enthusiastic, ardent, mad saints, soap-box redeemers, sitting-room apostles, aggressive priestesses, all sorts of spiritual workers of the most eccentric and ludicrous varieties. It can be said, without fear of contradiction, that the official clergy, nowadays as competitive in serving the rich as they once were in the interpretation of the Scriptures, are the least helpful in this task of uplifting the fallen soul of the nation. It is an improvised clergy that provokes thinking, sees misfortune at closer range, and more eloquently preaches charity toward man and faith in God: a former medicine peddler, with eagle nose and eyes, clean-shaven upper lip and a long beard who now, in his riding boots and frock-coat down to his ankles, hits the town to "preach the Gospel"; a repentant ruffian who builds a church where once stood his own house of shame; a journeyman; an inspired boatman; a stevedore; a poor woman so familiar with misfortune that unhappy people end up by turning her house into a temple which they enter to have their hearts' sores healed with a soothing, charitable word.

Thus are religions founded here, new temples erected under Christian advocacy, the menaced and half putrescent moral character rekindled, religious educators chosen through a sort of non-written suffrage. What is imposed upon a community is always vain, what is free is vivifying.

An eighty-four-year-old town preacher . . . has condemned men's fear of telling the truth lest they offend those whom they count upon as friends in business and politics. "My horror of lying is such that next Sunday I shall preach in this my church my own funeral oration before the bier that will be mine." And he did. People came from all the neighboring towns.

The coffin was placed at the foot of the dais. On a bench, in deep mourning suitable to the occasion, sat his family. Funeral chants were entoned. Pastor Pridgeon scourged in his two-hour sermon his own "carnal scurrilities" and praised the "victories of his spirit." The congregation sometimes wept, sometimes laughed. He proclaimed: "No man should remain a bachelor for even a moment when there are so many deserving females anxious to find good husbands."

One preacher speaks about the influence of science on re-

ligion. . . . Another distributes flour from a barrel among the
neighborhood poor while he imparts during Lent picturesque lessons on the Bible to women and children in his ungrammatical
language and using examples from his own life. Children become
absorbed. A husband who on arriving home has found the table
unset furiously pulls his wife out of the class. The preacher sides
with the culprit and makes a joke, to which the irate husband
retorts with a curse while he pushes out that "rascally idler."
. . . In another temple, improvised in a brewery celler, even the
water cup is tied to a chain and on the mossy wall hangs a sign
that reads: "The Lord is our shepherd; He shall take care of
His sheep," next to another warning: "Please do not chew
tobacco in this hall." . . .

What is all this compared to the "conversions," the thousand
conversions the Methodist Harrison [1] has gotten in a week as
though he pulled souls out of hell with his own hands? Who
knows where this thirty-year-old preacher has come from? Since
he was eight he has been in the business of saving souls through
the fervor of his eloquence. . . . He starts converting in the
morning and it is past midnight when the police have to clear
the tabernacle by sheer force. . . .

The service, this extravagant, titanic service ends only to
begin again. "Let him come, let him come!" A breathless old
man approaches pushing his way through the crowd so that the
pastor may "lay his hands" upon him. "One more, one more
snatched from the Devil, one more star for heaven, one more
blue flame on the road to salvation!" "There were eight hundred," he says, "now we are eight hundred and one."

The preacher breaks out in tears. Women weep. Men stamp
their feet on the ground. People embrace each other, tell each
other aloud their sins. The service starts again. "Let us pray!"
and the screaming and sighing subside. . . . The prayer is short.
The hymns follow. . . . From the platform they cry out re-
quests to those in back to move closer. The preacher and his
lieutenant run up and down the platform clapping their hands,
yelling out coarse jokes, giving orders with their outstretched
arms. Then the hymn. What is going on? Harrison has stopped,
advanced his right leg, leaned his body forward, stooped to
listen as though he heard something from afar. Now he pulls

his hair, presses his palms against his temples so hard it seems he might squeeze his eyeballs out of their sockets.

Finally he steps forward with outstretched, trembling arms raised high over his head . . . The singing stops but not the weeping and sighing, the *hallelujahs* and *amens.* Reclining over the open Bible on the lectern, Harrison is about to deliver his sermon. . . . He starts in a low voice. . . . He goes on speaking as though to himself, one can scarcely make out what he says, when all of a sudden he leaps away from the lectern as though to bounce upon the crowds that press at his feet. "Didn't you hear what I said?" he yells. "God just told me! Didn't you hear what I said?" The public with bowed heads sob as would a dog beaten by his master. Then he breaks out with his peculiar eloquence, peculiar not because of what he says, which is the theological jargon, but because of his sudden changes of voice, the anecdotes he interpolates in the middle of a point on divinity, his seeming to draw tears from his eyes and scatter them like pearls over his convulsed followers, his mysterious insistance upon an insignificant phrase which by mere repetition seems to acquire a prophetic, frightful meaning. . . . Step by step he evokes the throne of light upon which the Eternal One sits, a description he begins almost prone upon the platform, as though he were gradually pulling it out of the ground, and on completing the picture on the tips of his toes and raising both arms toward heaven, suddenly he drops his arms, advancing toward the audience, stamps his foot hard and cries: "They tell me shopkeepers will give up cursing this very day."

The platform seems too small to hold him. He jumps off into the crowd. "All those who have been saved, stand up!" "All those who would be converted come to me!" A stream of tears flows from his eyes. His assistant whoops up the cries. He embraces everyone. He kneels next to them. They touch his garments, kiss his hand. One can actually see the man grow. And when he leaps back onto the platform with his harvest of converts, he tries to speak but cannot. He turns pale, he seems about to swoon. His assistant helps him to a chair where he leaves him holding his head in his hands, sobbing. He has been "smitten by the glory of God."

What is it that draws crowds to rich Trinity Church, while there
are cries in the Stock Exchange and brokers collide with each
other on the streets and bankers figure out quotations on
gold . . . ? The church fills like no theatre does. Tight-mouthed
clergymen, young bespectacled men, freshly-graduated lawyers,
harsh, frowning believers, famous preachers, bald-headed potentates in their fur coats, pale, bearded employees storm all doors
to gain entrance. They are attracted by faith, curiosity, emula-
tion. Ten old ones to each young one. The young ones, with
either mystic or inquisitive eyes, come to hear the preacher. The
old ones, in their tight-fitting greatcoats, whisper about famous
preachers: ah, Channing! [2] ah, Edwards! [3] ah Beecher's father! [4]
ah, Beecher! [5] The church is bursting with people. Reporters at
their tables facing the pulpit, sharpen their pencils. Daylight
filters like music through the stained-glass windows. Above the
main altar rises a window representing the twelve Apostles.
There is no more standing room even in the aisles. Those who
are seated read the papers, take notes, chat naturally but quietly . . . . A ray of light illumines a white dove that seems to
stand out against the pulpit's gray shell.

On Phillips Brooks' [6] entrance the congregation rises. There
are people even on the altar dais and outside the doors. He
winds his way with bowed head through the crowd, yet taller
than the rest. He holds a prayer book against his chest, his white
alb reaches to his feet, a black stole draped down both sides. He
steps quickly, silently. With a sigh he ascends the pulpit. He
holds his chin in his two hands, leans forth as though to speak
and calls for the hymn. His two strong, chubby hands firmly
hold a red hymnal. A spotlight reveals to us his features: close-
shaven; fiery eyes; straight, silver hair; toothless mouth. How
can that feline manner of walking and that Napoleonic head be
reconciled? The congregation standing sing the hymn and then
say the "Our Father": rich men, preachers, the merely curious,
office workers, young and old, clergymen, reporters, all join in
the "Our Father" with equal fervor, a childish fervor. What
are not men willing to give for one hour of purity, for that in-
stant in which once again they are as when they chased butterflies? The "Our Father" is childhood. The congregation sits.

Brooks is not one for formalities: without announcing his text, as customary, he reads it off fluently. But that is not his real text.

He knows that the whole city has been talking about him; that uptown potentates, in the lounges of their clubs, made blue with smoke, have interrupted their whist for a few minutes to discuss his sermons and that one of them even refused to play for once; that the papers have commented favorably on his rapid oratory, his farsighted Christianity, his sweeping, felicitous metaphors, his tremulous voice which pierces, like wounded birds, his listeners' hearts. The day before, a certain man has arrived late to hear him and only succeeded in doing so from where he could neither see the preacher nor grasp the meaning of his words, but back in his office he had dropped into his chair and wept: he knew that no one since Beecher has been able to shake souls as this man does, nor been less theatrical, nor availed himself less of worldly themes, nor spoken on religious matters with a greater semblance of freedom and reason.

For Christianity seems as though it were about to die on the threshold of a new church in which, under the sky's canopy, will sit the Catholic Christ and the Hindu Christ, flanked by Confucius on one side and Wotan on the other, where there will be no clergy other than the sense of duty, nor candelabra other than the sun's rays, nor incense burners other than the chalices of flowers. For in this agony of the Christian dogma, which persists in what it contains of morality and universality but, as creed, only survives in the wings of owls, some Christians would ransack the world calling the faithful to arise and brand with hell's iron those who disbelieve or merely question before believing, as in the times of Torquemada [7] or Calvin,[8] while others, like Brooks, hold that, if what is essential, i.e. religious authority, is to be saved, Christians should not be obliged to believe in what their reason condemns, but that Christianity should be presented so no one can deny it, as that sweet yet fearful sense of dependence which every creature feels toward the unknown Creator and that peace which surges from acting disinterestedly and lovingly as did Christ. "Let us picture," say the liberal Christians, "the religious sentiment which never dies in man and let us call it Christianity. By doing so, man will not deny us what is in him, and our churches will not be emptied, as they are now being emptied."

MOB VIOLENCE IN NEW ORLEANS

FROM this day on no person who has known pity will set foot in New Orleans without horror. Here and there groups of murderers still appear and disappear, their rifles on their shoulders. Another group made up of lawyers and tradesmen, broad-shouldered, blue-eyed, can be seen with guns at their hips and a leaf on their lapels — a leaf from the tree on which they have hanged a dead man, a dead Italian, one of the nineteen Italians that had been jailed under suspicion of having murdered Chief of Police Hennessy. An American jury had acquitted four of the nineteen, the trials of others had been interrupted because of errors, still others had not yet been indicted.

A few hours after the acquittal a committee of worthies appointed by the Mayor to assist in punishing the assassination, headed by the leader of one of the city's political factions, called a meeting of citizens by means of printed public convocations one day in advance. The meeting was held at the foot of Henry Clay's statue. They attack the parish jail, with scarcely a semblance of resistance on the part of the police, the militia, the mayor, or the governor. The mob tears down the yielding doors of the jail; screaming they pour into the corridors along which the hunted Italians flee, with their rifle butts they smash in the heads of the Italian political boss and of a banker who was Bolivian consul accused of complicity with a secret band of Mafia assassins, . . . others are murdered against the walls, in nooks, on the floor, at guns' end. The deed over, the citizens cheer their leader, the lawyer, and parade him on their shoulders.

Are these the streets of flowery homes with hypnaceae creeping up the white lattices, of mulatto women in turbans and aprons hanging out colored Indian baskets on trellissed balconies, of Creole belles on their way to the lake to lunch on pearly,

Dated New York, March 26, 1891, published in *La Nación*, Buenos Aires, May 20, 1891.

golden fish, a flowerlet pinned to their bodice and in their black tresses an orange blossom? Is this the city of oaks on which the Spanish moss grows like a silvery filigree, of honey-distilling date trees, of weeping willows mirrored in the river? Is this the New Orleans of Carnival mirth, all torch and castanets, which on Mardi gras parades Mexico's romance on a float festooned with lilies and carnations, on another the lovable heroes of Lalla Rookh in bejeweled costumes and on still another Prince Charming in orange satin waking a glittering-gowned Sleeping Beauty?

Can this be the Orleans of fishing canoes, of the charming suburbs, of the noisy, beaming market place, of dandies with felt hats down to their ears and grey goatees who gather at the Poetry café to chatter about duels and sweethearts? . . . Shots blast out; Bagnetto, the dead Italian, is hoisted to a limb; they riddle his face with bullets, a policeman tosses his hat into the air; some watch the scene with opera glasses from balconies and roof tops.

The governor "cannot be reached." The militia, "no one has called it out." A branch is sawed down, another is cut down with an ax; they shake off the leaves which fall upon the compact crowd gathered to take home as souvenirs a splinter of wood or a leaf still fresh at the foot of the oak tree from which an Italian covered with blood hangs swinging.

The city of New Orleans, for the pleasure of it or through cowardice, headed by its leading lawyers and businessmen, marched to the jail from which were to be released the recently acquitted prisoners. . . . The city led by lawyers, journalists, bankers, judges . . . struck down . . . the acquitted Italians: a New Orleaner of Italian descent; a rich man of the world who controlled the votes of the Italian colony; a father of six sons, wealthy partner of a well-known firm; a spirited Sicilian who a few months back had been fired at by an Irishman; a shoemaker who was influential in his neighborhood; a cobbler under suspicion of having killed a compatriot of his; several fruit vendors.

Italians are prone to fight among themselves, as are the feuding gangs in Kansas, where no governor has been able to bring peace in half a century, as are the Southern creoles, who inherit their family hatreds. Twenty years ago the father of this Hennessy had fallen by the hand of a certain Guerin for meddling into the affairs of the Italians or for wanting to deprive them, on the pretext of their quarrels, of the ascendency they had gained by their voting power. The killer of the elder Hennessy had been shot to death by a trader in votes who marched as one of the ringleaders in today's assault. The grey-eyed politicians hated the dark-eyed politicians. The Irish, who live mostly on politics, wanted to eliminate the Italians from politics.

They called them "Dagos," a nickname that makes a Sicilian's blood boil. If during these quarrels someone was killed they said he "had been sentenced by the *Maffia*." They spoke of the political executions by the *Maffia* when it conspired a century ago against the Bourbons as though they were sheer crimes committed now.

In spite of the fact that Hennessy had once had no better friend "to make the rounds of the gambling tables in the clubs or to partake of a good gumbo" than Macheca, the stylish, wealthy Italian — the one whose head now lies all battered in — our Hennessy then declared war without quarter on the Italians. There had been some killing in the Italian section. The police had followed up the investigation until they got a statement from one Italian, who next morning was found dead, telling them all they wanted to know about a society of assassins called the *Stiletto* and another called the *Stopaliagien*. Now, they announced, they held "complete evidence about the terrible *Maffia*, its death sentences, its thousands of members." One night, at the door of his house — a house with two rose bushes in the hallway — Hennessy fell brandishing his revolver against a band of assassins.

They found eleven bullets in his body. His death was declared "a *Maffia* vengeance." The most convincing proofs were promised. The Mayor himself appointed a committee of fifty citizens — politicians, lawyers, merchants, journalists — to assist the judiciary in its investigations. An impeccable jury was chosen from among the citizens with English family names. A few professional troublemakers among the Sicilians were jailed, along with two men who were the wealthiest and had the greatest control over the Italian voters.

The Italian population, from the Gulf to the Pacific, stood up for them: their press denied, as did their prominent men, that there was a *Maffia,* or a *Stiletto,* or a *Stopaliagien* society, or any possibility of proving such a thing, or any sense in holding for murder men of banker Macheca's or merchant Caruso's position. They insisted that the root of this vicious persecution was to be found in the political rivalries, in the determination to intimidate the Italians who would not submit to the will of their persecutors to get them out of New Orleans and out of the polls. They declared that a devilishly political conspiracy was being hatched.

The jury, after months of public trial, of reciprocal accusations, of witnesses going mad or committing perjury, talk of bribery, of scandal, acquitted the prisoners. Surely enough there were hostile bands among the New Orleans Sicilians. . . . Surely enough the streets were often strewn with Italian blood shed by Italians. But . . . it does not follow that all "Dagos" who live as their burning sun commands, loving and hating each other, giving their life for a kiss or taking a life for an insult "are an organized school of murderers."

New Orleans received the verdict with ire and threats. . . . But in Chicago the red shirts' neighborhood was aglow with lights; in the Providence suburbs they struck work to dance and make merry; the Bowery Italians in New York lined their fruit stands with fresh paper, stuck their flag in the burnished boots that hung to mark their bootblacks' chairs and women paraded their well-combed hair and their coral earrings — until the telegraph announced the awful news! That New Orleans was in mutiny, that the jail was surrounded, that Bagnetto had been hanged, Macheca killed! Women ran out of shanties and alleys screaming, or set down their babies and sat on the curbs to weep, or untied their tresses and pulled them, or waked their men, insulting them if they tarried, or ran about with their hands on their heads. In front of newspaper buildings the streets teemed with men and women. For the first time their journalists, as a rule disunited, gathered to harangue them; "Let us stand together, Italians, in this grief!" "Revenge, Italians, revenge!" And they read sighing the horrible telegrams. Women fell on their knees in the streets. Men brushed away a tear with their callused hands.

The ringleaders against the court were court people — judges,

district attorneys, defenders. The leaders at the killing were
delegates of the Mayor who abstained from sending his own
forces against the killers. Not a call for pity, not a woman's sup-
plication, not a clergyman's petition, not a protest from the
press: just "Kill the Dagos." "To arms, good citizens!" . . . At
one o'clock the streets leading to Clay's statue were crowded.
They say the militia was with them, that militiamen in plain
clothes were around, that there was a house full of picks and
axes, that a carload of beams to knock down doors was dumped
yesterday behind the jail, that the plan was all laid down yesterday by the committee of fifty, the leaders appointed, the arms
distributed. Some cheer Wyckliffe; all, Parkerson. . . . Parkerson, a man of law, a political leader, a young man, speaks: "To
arms, citizens! Crimes should be speedily punished, but where-
ever and whenever courts fail or juries break their oath or brib-
ing appears it behooves the people to do what courts and juries
have left undone!" "We're with you, Parkerson!" "What will
our resolution be? Action?" "Action! You lead! We're with
you!" "Ready?" "Ready!"

Then appears Denegre, a lawyer and proprietor. . . . Then
Wyckliffe speaks, a lawyer and newspaper owner . . .

The column marches at a rapid pace. Parkerson, the Democratic boss, leads. There's also Honston, another boss, the man
who twenty years ago killed the first Hennessy's killer. Wyckliffe, former district attorney, is second in command. There are
three wagons in the lead with ropes and ladders. From a post
on one hangs a noose.

Two hundred men shouldering rifles bring up the rear in war-
like formation. They are followed and surrounded by crowds,
some carrying shotguns, others revolvers. There is a stamping of
feet. "They smile, as on the way to a picnic." When they reach
the jail, a masonry building with balconies, each door is stormed
by a different picket, evidently following orders. Amidst yelling
and whistling the warden denies them the keys. They ram the
main door with the beams. Its panels begin to yield and then a
Negro hacks them down with an ax. Fifty enter; all would like
to. "Here's the key," cries the deputy warden . . .

The fifty hold council. From an open cell come some prisoners' trembling voices. A deathlike face can be seen through the

bars of another. "Those ain't the ones," says one of the custodians politely, "they're upstairs in the women's department," and hands them the appropriate key. "Easy, gentlemen, easy!" cries Parkerson. "Anybody knows them? Only the *Dagos*." They overrun the empty corridor; the scaly, whitish hand of an eighty-year-old negress points to a corner and a flight of narrow steps up which the quick stamping of feet is soon heard. "Hurrah, hurrah, hurrah!" cries one of the hunters; the rest, waving their hats, repeat the three hurrahs and follow him up. "Let 'em have it!" yells one. A volley is heard and the last of the fugitives reels in the air and falls with a bullet in his skull. The uproar outside drowns the noise of the shooting: "Hurrah for Parkerson!" "Hurray for Wyckliffe!" They haven't even time to beg for mercy. Guachi and Caruso fall riddled like sieves. Romero is on his knees, his head touching the ground when he is killed. His hat is like a mesh of ribbons, the back of his jacket is ripped to shreds.

Bullets fly everywhere. Macheca, corralled, falls under a blow on the head and is finished off amidst the feet of men — businessmen, lawyers — who crush him with the butts of their rifles. Angry shouts rang horribly from without: "Bring them outside! Kill them where we can see!" The square is full, the surrounding streets are full. There are women and children: "Bring them out to us! Bring them out!"

A squadron appears at one of the doors pushing before them Polozzi, the mad witness who reels as though he were drunk. They can scarcely hold him on his feet.

Two men insult and strike each other over which can handle the noose better. A cluster of men are strung on one rope. Those standing around empty their revolvers upon them. There are streams of blood on their chests. Bagnetto is carried out, his face covered with wounds. Around his neck, still warm in death, the new noose is placed. They leave him swinging from the branch of a tree. Later the adjoining branches will be pruned off and they will wear the leaves as emblems — women, on their hats; men, on their lapels. One pulls out his watch: "We've made good time: forty-five minutes." From roof tops and balconies people look on through their opera glasses.

ON THE INDIAN QUESTION

OF the reports submitted by the secretaries the best . . . was that of the Cabinet's "dreamer," "idealist," "vagabond," Secretary of the Interior Lamar,[1] accused of being a lover of romance, of letting his fancy fly at times, and on occasions of raising his eyes to heaven.

Indeed, there are more rats on earth than eagles . . . and Lamar is one of the eagles. His report is so cautious, so clear, so based on fact, so well adapted to the practical problems at hand, that for once we no longer hear it said that Lamar is unfit for his position because he reads poems or writes them, wears his hair long, is versed in antiquity and numismatics, and often sits glancing at the sparkling logs in his chimney place — pondering no doubt on ruffianly politicians!

About forty out of the report's ninety pages are devoted to the Indian problem. He feels it is high time the United States settle this now critical question. He does not even defend himself against being called a philanthropist: everybody is now giving preferential attention to the Indian question.

Though savages live in diverse degrees of civilization, they live like savages. They are not, as before, in far-off lands from which they can flee or from which they can be displaced. They are in the very lands the Government gave them in exchange for those it gradually took from them and of which they cannot be deprived without committing an infamy and breaking contracts. The Indian territories and reservations are by now completely surrounded by the white men's cultivated lands.

What is to be done, then?

Exterminate the savages? Corrupt them as a means to their extermination? Or compensate them, through civilized care, which they neither reject nor demand, for their wild freedom

---

From an article dated New York, January 16, 1886, published in *La Nación,* Buenos Aires, February 18, 1886.

among the native hills, the pleasures of hunting, their tribal life, the ancestral habitation where their mothers bore them in pain and where their ancestors knew lordship and happiness?

Since the lands are theirs, the Government must uphold them in their possession. If they are forced by agents to lease their lands to cattle ranchers for a low rental or for none at all, such fraudulent agreements should not be authorized under the law.

The fact that there are regions . . . like that of the Apaches,[2] where some hundred hardheaded, nomadic Indians resist being moved and living in subjection . . . is no reason to maltreat the five civilized tribes: the Cherokees,[3] the Choktaws,[4] the Chickasaws,[5] the Creeks,[6] and the brave Florida Seminoles.[7] The Apaches represent the excessive form of Indian vengeance. Where is the just idea that does not have its fanatics? What justice does not engender exaggerations? Why should it be surprising to find in men still close to nature sins which are inherent to human nature?

The Government may remove to the Pacific Islands the two hundred Apaches who are a constant source of trouble in the state of Arizona . . . but it is imperative to attract, once and for all, to a definitive civilized state the 200,000, the meagre 200,000 Indians, some already quite advanced, who live inserted among the white states, who are progressing under the present guardianship system, at a cost to the Government of some four to seven million dollars a year . . .

Secretary Lamar suggests that the Indians be educated by Indians; that, instead of sending them, against their parents' wishes, to far-off schools, they be sent to the Cheyennes'[8] excellent schools, where most of the teachers are Indian, which were founded and maintained by Indians and not by the Government, and where teaching, in the levels covered, as well as study methods, are as good as in the best New England schools — so says Secretary Lamar.

As to land, the Sioux[9] already possess theirs separately and are happy with the system. But Indians have been pushed about and their contracts with the Government often violated. Their natural fear that any new promise will be forgotten is great, and their loyalty to the racial traditions is alive and legitimate and all the more ardent the more menaced they are felt to be. Land tenure in common is one of their most inbred and cherished customs. Now, Secretary Lamar says land must be divided, for there is no better way to uplift a man than by making him his own creator and the owner of something, but that this must be done at first without too much violence to the racial customs and by taking care that, after the land is parcelled out to individuals, preying contractors or covetous white landholders do not snatch it from them.

Part of the lands now held under contract by each tribe is to be divided into personal farms; the rest will be bought by the Government from the Indians at a fair price and held in reserve for future improvement. For a period sufficient for the Indians to learn the value of their holdings they will not be allowed to sell or mortgage their land or lease it to anyone but an Indian of their own tribe.

For the Umatilla [10] tribe he proposes that they have a clergyman and recommends that they, who are ignorant of the advantages and satisfactions of individual property and never thought of it before except as a fearsome revolution in their customs induced by the deceitful white man, divide their land up in eighty-acre individual lots; that a group of ten or fifteen young Indians be selected and taught farm cultivation and management and be put to work as a team on the farms of each and all, under practical teachers, at a cost of $7,000 a year. At the end of this preparatory year each farm would be turned over to its proprietor, now trained to make it profitable, while another is being prepared for the following year, and so forth until the whole tribe is trained.

The Secretary does not favor fixed agents who apply an even system to tribes who have reached different degrees of civilization. He believes rather that each case should be handled according to its special requirements: that the Indian of the reservations, who has scarcely any meat to eat and little clothing to wear, is justified in not wanting to contribute to the public expenses of a civilization which benefits him not at all and whose laws are written in a language he does not understand. The Cheyennes, on the other hand, who have long been governing themselves with undeniable wisdom, will not only not be exempt from local taxes, but they have voluntarily and under no outside

pressure or suggestion, decided to contribute, out of the annuity
which the Government has agreed to pay them, $6,000 towards
the maintenance of the tribe's schools.

It so happens that in 1886 the same recommendations are
being made to solve the Indian problem — oh, human vanity! —
as were made in an ordinance of 1787 . . . , the same which
that brainy Southerner John Calhoun [11] suggested in a report of
1822: "a system of education which is the base for everything,
the reduction of their territories and the division of land property." Calhoun, also a Secretary, had already noted: "The tribes
not only do not resist, but request education for their children.
Teachers' reports are unanimously favorable. The progress made
by Indian children is entirely equal to that of white children of
the same age, and they seem equally capable of acquiring the
disposition to work." [12]

Lamar ends by recommending that they not be removed
from the places they now inhabit, because, fearful of being
ousted from the lands cultivated by them, they would not devote
themselves wholeheartedly to the task to which they were definitely assigned. No railroad company will be allowed to run its
lines over Indian land without full compensation. New individual farms will be recorded like any other property of a citizen
of the Republic and the proper title issued to each respective
Indian owner.

Thus, educated by teachers of his own race, attached lovingly
to his labor on land which is definitely his, helped rather than
bloodily mocked by his conquerors, assured of peace and the
benefits of property, reconciling the customs of his race with a
civilized life, uplifted by an instructed mind, the Indian will
endure — a useful, original, picturesque element among the people who interrupted the course of his civilization and wrenched
from him his land.

A GLANCE AT THE
NORTH AMERICAN'S SOUL TODAY

LAMAR'S [1] report goes on to make a suggestion which has been highly praised: a suggestion truly befitting in one given to romancing, addicted to poetry and ancient coins, who discovers things while he stares fixedly at the eloquent flames that rise from the sparkling logs in the hearth!

Washington, Madison, Jefferson, and Adams had all suggested what the new Secretary is now suggesting for reasons which he discretely refrains from mentioning. As he does, they all had recommended the creation of a national university.

It is evident, though he does not say so, that the general spiritual crudeness that afflicts to such large degree expansive, delicate minds, makes him suffer. It is each man for himself. Fortune, the only object of life. Woman, a luxury toy. A woman's love, a sort of caprice of fancy or a necessity for social adjustment. Man, a routine mechanism, very skillful in the occupation of his choice, but shutting out from himself all knowledge of commerce with and sympathy for things human. Such is the direct result of an elementary and exclusively practical education. In this gigantic nation there doesn't seem to be enough soul, that marvelous cohesive stuff without which everything in a nation comes crashing down catastrophically.

Men, despite all appearances, are tied together here only by interests, by the cordial hatred that exists between those who are bargaining for the same prize. It is imperative that they be united by something more lasting. A common atmosphere must be found for these souls in dispersion. It is urgent to feed the lamp of light and reduce the beast.

From an article dated New York, January 16, 1886, published in *La Nación,* Buenos Aires, February 18, 1886. From the same article as "The Indian Question."

It is strikingly evident that, apart from business and outside of a privileged circle, men here have nothing to say to each other, nor fine thoughts with which to regale and uplift each other, nor can they even, apart from instinct and habit, draw to themselves their women's flighty, imaginative souls.

Public schools do not go beyond reading, writing, and arithmetic. And from the public school they go on to their jobs, to the spectacle of luxury and the desire of possessing it, the vanity of exhibiting it, and to the cruel and ignoble anguish of competing with their neighbors.

It is imperative that these souls be rescued from such withering decay. In every man, no doubt, the role of merchant should be fostered, but his priestly side must be nurtured as well.

A man is not a figure sculpted on a hard dollar, with greedy eyes, smacking lips, and a diamond stud in his shirt front. Man is a living duty, a depository of forces which he must not allow to become stultified; man is like a wing.

The reading of things beautiful, the knowledge of the harmony of the universe, the mental contact with great ideas and noble deeds, the intimate acquaintance with the better things the human mind has been pouring out through the ages, stimulate and broaden the intelligence, place in man's hands the reins to control the simple, fugitive pleasures, to produce much deeper and more delicate satisfactions that the mere possession of fortune, to sweeten and ennoble the lives of those who are without fortune and create, by uniting equal men on a high level, the national soul.

The Secretary calls for a general higher education as an immediate national necessity. He believes that the dry, practically-oriented school is not enough. He wants a great national university organized on the basis of the various scientific corporations the Government now runs separately, but completing the picture of earthly forces caught and put to work, with the knowledge derived from man loving and aspiring upon this earth, man whose knowledge must not be only of that on which he stands, but of what he carries within.

A nation is not a complex of wheels, nor a wild horse race, but a stride upward concerted by real men.

NOTES

SELECTED BIBLIOGRAPHY

NOTES

WALT WHITMAN

1 Walt Whitman (1819–1892), born in West Hills, Long Island, N.Y.
2 William Ewart Gladstone (1809–1898), British statesman; Prime Minister (1868–74; 1880–85; 1886; 1892–94).
3 Walt Whitman, *Leaves of Grass* (New York: Pellegrini and Cudahy, 1948), I, 430. Poem "So Long!"
4. "So Long!" "Myriads of youths, beautiful, gigantic, sweet-blooded . . ." *Ibid.*, p. 430.
5 *Song of Myself,* Poem 6. *Ibid.*, p. 67.
6 Title of poem. *Ibid.*, p. 148.
7 A paraphrase. Whitman's text: "Knowing the perfect fitness and equanimity of things, while they discuss I am silent, and go bathe and admire myself." Poem 3, *Ibid.*, p. 64.
8 "I do not say these things for a dollar or to fill up the time while I wait for a boat." *Song of Myself,* Poem 47, *Ibid.*, p. 110.
9 "I am satisfied — I see, dance, laugh, sing." *Song of Myself,* Poem 3, *Ibid.*, p. 64.
10 *Song of Myself,* Poem 46, *Ibid.*, p. 108.
11 Victor Hugo (1802–1885), French romantic poet, novelist, dramatist.
12 Ralph Waldo Emerson (1803–1882), American essayist and poet. See article.
13 Alfred (Lord) Tennyson (1809–1892), English poet laureate.
14 Robert Williams Buchanan (1841–1901), English poet, novelist, and playwright.
15 "Crossing Brooklyn Ferry," Whitman, *op. cit.*, p. 169. Whitman's mentions of Manhattan are numerous.
16 "But I will sing you a song of what I behold, Libertad." *Ibid.*, p. 234. *Libertad* is Spanish for Freedom. Whitman makes much use of Spanish words.
17 Also a frequent expression of Whitman's. "My lovers, my dear friends" ("On the Terrible Doubt of Appearances"), *Ibid.*, p. 137; "his dear friends, his lovers," ("Recorders Ages Hence"), *Ibid.*, p. 138; "the undiminished faith — the groups of loving friends," "A Carol Closing Sixty-nine"), *Ibid.*, p. 433.

18 The expressions "young men" and "camerados" (apparently a corruption of the Spanish *camaradas*, equivalent to *comrades*) are obsessively repeated in Whitman's poems.
19 A series of fifty poems. Whitman, *op. cit.*, pp. 131–221. According to Webster's Dictionary, *calamus* is a very large and aromatic grass often called *sweet flag*, which grows in the northern and middle States.
20 Part of the poem *City of Orgies* (*Calamus*), *Ibid.*, p. 141.
21 *Songs of Parting, Ibid.*, p. 430.
22 *Song of Myself*, Poem 26, *Ibid.*, p. 85.
23 *Song of Myself*, Poem 8, *Ibid.*, p. 68.
24 *Song of Myself*, Poem 8, *Ibid.*, p. 69.
25 From poem entitled *When Lilacs last in the Dooryard Bloom'd* of the series *Memories of President Lincoln* in *Leaves of Grass. Ibid.*, p. 298.
26 *Song of Myself*, Poem 3, *Ibid.*, p. 72.
27 *Song of Myself*, Poem 48, *Ibid.*, p. 111.
28 *Song of Myself*, Poem 32, *Ibid.*, p. 89.
29 *Song of Myself*, Poem 21, *Ibid.*, p. 79.
30 *Song of Myself*, Poem 40, *Ibid.*, p. 101.
31 A paraphrase. Cf. *By the Roadside*, poem "Gods," *Ibid.*, p. 225.
32 Greek erotic woman poet, *circa* 600 B.C.
33 This quotation has not been found.
34 Virgil (70–19 B.C.), Roman poet.
35 Horace (65–8 B.C.), Roman poet.
36 A series of poems which are a part of *Leaves of Grass*. Whitman, *op. cit.*, pp. 114–31.
37 In Greek mythology, a race of women warriors with whom, according to legend, the Greeks had frequent encounters.
38 *Song of Myself*, Whitman, *op. cit.*, p. 102.
39 *Children of Adam*, Poem 1, *Ibid.*, p. 116.
40 *By the Roadside, Ibid.*, p. 259.
41 *By the Roadside, Ibid.*, p. 259.
42 *Song of Myself*, Poem 16. "My joints the limberest joints on earth and the sternest joints on earth." *Ibid.*, p. 76.
43 *Song of Myself*, Poem 22, *Ibid.*, p. 80.
44 Whitman's text: "Walt Whitman, a kosmos, of Manhattan the son, / Turbulent, fleshy, sensual, eating, drinking and breeding, / No sentimentalist, no stander above men and women or apart from them, . . ." *Song of Myself*, Poem 24, *Ibid.*, p. 82
45 "Oh, to die advancing on!" *Birds of Paradise*, poem "Pioneers! Oh,

Pioneers!" *Ibid.*, p. 225.
46 *Song of Myself*, Poem 14, *Ibid.*, p. 73.
47 *Song of Myself*, Poem 32, *Ibid.*, p. 89.
48 *Song of Myself*, Poem 23, *Ibid.*, p. 82.
49 *Song of the Broad-Axe*, Poem 6, *Ibid.*, p. 191.
50 "Birds of Paradise," *Song of the Universal, Ibid.*, p. 221.
51 *Song of Myself*, Poem 47, *Ibid.*, p. 109.
52 "The dirt receding before my prophetical screams." *Song of Myself*, Poem 25, *Ibid.*, p. 84.
53 "To conclude, I announce what comes after me." *Song of Parting*, poem "So Long!" *Ibid.*, p. 429.
54 *Song of Myself*, Poem 40, *Ibid.*, p. 100.
55 *Song of Myself*, Poem 52, *Ibid.*, p. 113.
56 *Songs of Parting*, poem "So Long!" *Ibid.*, p. 432.

PRESIDENT GARFIELD

1 James Abram Garfield (1831–1881). Twentieth President of the United States. Mortally wounded by a fanatic office seeker, Charles J. Guiteau, in Washington, on July 6, 1881. Died Sept. 19, 1881 at Elberton, N.J.
2 A report of this deathbed scene can be found in the *New York Times* for Sept. 20 and 21, 1881.
3 Peter Cooper. See article on Peter Cooper.
4 Josiah Gilbert Holland (1819–1881), *Kathrina, her Life and Mine*, a book of poetry published in 1867.
5 On Sept. 22, 1881 the *New York Times* reported thus on events of the previous day in Chicago: "Considerable excitement was caused in the vicinity of Canal and Sixteenth Streets this morning by an effigy of Guiteau, which was suspended from the viaduct. Hundreds of excited men and boys gathered about it cursing, shouting and throwing stones at the image of the assassin. The excitement was so great that the Police was compelled to disperse the mob."
6 Chester Alan Arthur (1830–1886), Twenty-first President of the United States.
7 James Gillespie Blaine (1830–1893), American congressman, senator, secretary of State and presidential candidate.
8 Job 14:1.
9 From prayer said by Rev. Ross N. Houghton. See *New York Times*, Sept. 27, 1881, p. 1, col. 2.
10 The Vocal Society of Cleveland.

11   The words of Mendelssohn's *Saint Paul* oratorio, sung on this occasion are slightly different: "In Thee I live, in Thee I die . . ."
12   This is a paraphrase of parts of the hymn "Oh, Reapers of Life's Harvest."
13   Spanish poet and historian (1503–1575).
14   Spanish poet (*circa* 1490–1542).

JESSE JAMES

1   Jesse Woodson James (1847–1882), born in Clay County, Mo.; a noted outlaw.
2   The reference is to Fernando Alvarez de Toledo, Duke of Alba (1507–1582) who, as brilliant military leader in Spain's days of glory under Charles V and Philip II, was noted for demanding of his troops strict discipline and boundless courage.
3   Francisco Pizarro (*circa* 1475–1541), Spanish conqueror of Peru
4   It is said Jesse James's family had suffered greatly at the hands of the Union forces and that, by way of retaliation, he had turned informer and later, when he was only fifteen years of age, had joined the guerrilla forces of W. C. Quantrill.
5   Governor Crittenden of Missouri offered a reward of $10,000 for the capture of Jesse James, dead or alive. Two members of his own band, Robert and Charles Ford, turned traitors and shot and instantly killed him in his home at St. Joseph, Mo., April 3, 1882.

LONGFELLOW

1   Henry Wadsworth Longfellow (1807–1882), American poet, born in Portland, Me.
2   "A Psalm of Life," in *Longfellow's Writings,* vol. 3 (Cambridge: The Riverside Press, 1886), p. 21.
3   Oliver Wendell Holmes (1809–1894), American physician, poet, and humorist, born in Cambridge, Mass.
4   The reference may be to George William Curtis (1824–1892), American author and editor.
5   William Dean Howells (1837–1920), American novelist and critic, born at Martin's Ferry, Ohio.
6   Louis Agassiz, son of Jean Louis Rodolphe Agassiz (1807–1873), Swiss-American naturalist, founder of Harvard's Agassiz Museum.
7   John Greenleaf Whittier (1807–1892), American poet and abolitionist.
8   See Martí's article on Emerson.

EMERSON

1 Ralph Waldo Emerson (1803–1882), American essayist, poet, and philosopher. Born in Boston, Mass. One of the leaders of Transcendentalism.

2 In Whitman's "By Emerson's Grave" in Louis Untermeyer, *The Poetry and Prose of Walt Whitman* (New York: Simon and Schuster, 1949), p. 800, we read: "How shall I henceforth dwell on the blessed hours when, not long since, I saw that benign face . . ."

3 Edmund Clarence Stedman (1833–1908), American author and critic. The exact phrase has not been found, but there are several instances in which this critic refers to Emerson's poetry as "light and air." See E. C. Stedman, *The Nature and Elements of Poetry* (Boston: Houghton, Mifflin and Co., 1892), p. 58, where he says: "Of Emerson I have said elsewhere that his prose was poetry, and his poetry light and air."

4 "Misfortune to have lived not knowing thee!" in a dedicatory poem. See H. Bronson Alcott, *Ralph Waldo Emerson, an estimate of his character and genious* (Boston: A. Williams and Co., 1882).

5 The reference is to Phryne, a wealthy courtesan of Athens in the fourth century B.C., who on occasions exposed her physical charms to the sight of the public and her judges.

6 *Nature*, Emerson's first book, was published in 1836.

7 Essay "The Over-soul," in *The Complete Writings of Ralph Waldo Emerson* (New York: William H. Wise and Co., 1929), I, 206.

8 *Ibid.*, p. 20.

9 "First innuendoes, then broad hints, then smart taps are given, suggesting that nothing stands still in nature but death; that creation is on wheels, in transit, always passing into something else, streaming into something higher . . ." *The Complete Writings of Ralph Waldo Emerson*, II, 727.

10 Published in 1853.

11 The *Essays* were published in two series, the first in 1841 and the second in 1844.

12 In his poem "Wealth" (*Nature,* in *op. cit.*, II, 915) Emerson writes: ". . . Which bind the strengths of Nature wild / To the conscience of a child."

13 John Tyndall (1820–1893), British physicist, best known for his researches on radiant heat, born in County Carlow, Ireland.

14 A paraphrase. Cf. *Nature* in *op. cit.*, I, 23: "The axis of vision is

not coincident with the axis of things, and so they appear not transparent but opaque."

15 The passage nearest to this quotation which has been found reads: (Every universal truth) ". . . is like a great circle, comprising all possible circles; which, however, may be drawn and comprise it in like manner." *Nature* in *op. cit.*, I, 14.
16 *Op. cit.*, I, 3.
17 *Op. cit.*, I, 15.
18 From essay "Montaigne; or the Skeptic," *op. cit.*, I, 377.
19 From essay "Self-reliance," *op. cit.*, I, 142.
20 "Leonidas and his three hundred martyrs consume one day in dying," *op. cit.*, I, 6.
21 *Op. cit.*, I, 8.
22 The exact sentence quoted has not been found, but the expression "the insanity of dialectics" used in the essay on "Race" (*op. cit.*, I, 434) seems to express the same idea.
23 The Spanish original reads: "Suyos son los únicos versos poémicos que consagran la lucha magna de esta tierra." The meaning is open to conjecture.

PETER COOPER

1 Peter Cooper (1791–1883), American manufacturer, inventor, and philanthropist. Founder of Cooper Union in New York City, the city of his birth.
2 Cooper Union, an educational institution at Cooper Square, New York City, founded by Peter Cooper in 1859. The Hewitt and Carnegie families and others later increased the Union's financial resources.
3 In about 1828 Peter Cooper built the Canton ironworks in Baltimore, Md., the foundation of his great fortune.
4 Peter Cooper designed and constructed in 1830 the first steam locomotive built in the U.S., "Tom Thumb," which was about the size of a modern handcar.
5 The reference is apparently to the War of 1812.
6 1854.
7 Cooper was president of the New York, Newfoundland, and London Telegraph company and the North American Telegraph company.

WENDELL PHILLIPS

1 Besides this article, Martí published an appreciation of Wendell Phillips in the March 1884 number of *La América*. In the following May number of the same publication a note by Martí appeared in which he says, among other things: "As criteria vary from race to race" (he means a Latin American's point of view may be different from that of an Anglo American) "and as *La América* is more inclined to be excessively benevolent rather than too critical, we had feared that our appreciation of Wendell Phillips might differ greatly from that of his own compatriots. But now we see with satisfaction there is a point-by-point coincidence, both in praise and in the finding of certain deficiencies, between *La América's* evaluation and that of George W. Curtis, who kindly writes us: 'I am happy to note that your appreciation of the great orator and mine do not differ in the least.'" In a previous paragraph he speaks in highly laudatory terms of Curtis and states that he was the man chosen to deliver the funeral oration in honor of Wendell Phillips. The following much quoted aphorisms of Martí also appear in said note: "An orator shines for what he speaks, but he endures for what he does. If his words are not upheld by his deeds, he will collapse even before he dies, for he has been standing on columes of smoke."

2 These references are to the public appearances of Jesse James' widow and of one of the Ford brothers, the famous outlaw's murderers. See Martí's article on Jesse James.

3 Wendell Phillips (1811–1884), noted orator and abolitionist, born in Boston, Mass.; educated at Harvard; president of the Anti-slavery Society (1865–1870); advocate of woman suffrage and of penal and labor reforms.

4 John Bright (1811–1889), English orator and statesman.

5 William E. Channing (1780–1842), American clergyman, writer, and philanthropist. One of the chief founders of Unitarianism in the U.S.

6 Elijah Lovejoy (1802–1837), American journalist, born in Albion, Me. He published *The Observer*, a religious paper, in St. Louis, Mo., but was forced to move his press across the river to Alton, Ill. where mobs destroyed it several times until he was killed in its defense, for which he has been called "the martyr abolitionist."

7 James T. Austin (1784–1870), Attorney-General—not governor—of the state of Massachusetts (1832–1843) at the time of the Faneuil Hall meeting, held December 8, 1837.

8 In Martí's metaphors one of the most frequently recurring images is that of the *wing,* as also are those conveyed by the words *mountain, eagle, sky,* etc. expressive of flight or loftiness.

9 John Lothrop Mottley (1814–1877), American diplomat and historian, was Wendell Phillips' close boyhood friend.

10 William Lloyd Garrison (1805–1879), antislavery leader born at Newburypoint, Mass. He drafted the declaration of principles of the American Antislavery Society and in 1835 was dragged through the streets of Boston by a mob.

11 John Caldwell Calhoun (1782–1850), American statesman and political philosopher, born in Abeville, S.C. Ardent advocate of states' rights.

12 Charles Sumner (1811–1874), American statesman. Was assaulted in the Senate by Preston Brooks for his abolitionist ideas.

13 This is not a literal quotation, but it summarizes Phillips' thought as expressed in many writings. Cf., for instance, his speech on "Progress" in *Wendell Phillips' Speeches, Lectures and Letters,* American Culture Series (Boston: Lee and Shepard, 1884), p. 417.

14 Phillips, in his speech "Surrender of Sims," relates that a certain Pelez Sprague, sixteen or seventeen years before, at Faneuil Hall had pointed to a portrait of Washington and called him "that slaveholder." *Ibid.,* p. 60.

15 Cf. W. Phillips' speech on "The Philosophy of the Abolition Movement," delivered before the Massachusetts Antislavery Society at Boston on Jan. 27, 1853 in *Ibid.,* p. 113.

16 A paraphrase. Phillips writes: "See to it, when Nature has provided you a monster like Webster, that you exhibit him—himself a whole menagerie—throughout the country." Cf. Phillips' review of Webster's speech on slavery in *Ibid.,* p. 48. Also his lecture on "Public Opinion," *Ibid.,* p. 49, where we read: "He bowed his vassal head to the temptations of the flesh and lucre. He gave himself up into the lap of the Delilah of slavery, for the mere promise of a nomination, . . ."

17 Pope Formosus (*circa* 816–896), Pontif from 891 to 896. Was disinterred by his successor Stephen VII and submitted to trial for alledged crimes, his election as pope being declared invalid.

18 "Poisoned with printer's ink, or choked with cotton dust, they stare at absolute right, as the dream of madmen." "The Lesson of the Hour," a lecture delivered by Wendell Phillips at Brooklyn, N.Y., Nov. 1, 1859 in James Redpath, *Echoes of Harper's Ferry* (Boston: Thayer and Eldridge, 1860), p. 45.

19 The exact equivalents of these quotations have not been found.

GROVER CLEVELAND

1 Stephen Grover Cleveland (1837–1908), born in Caldwell, N.J., Twenty-second and twenty-fourth President of the United States.

HENRY WARD BEECHER

1 Henry Ward Beecher (1813–1887), American clergyman and abolitionist, born in Litchfield, Conn.
2 Plymouth Congregational Church. His sermons there were published weekly, beginning in 1859, in a publication entitled *Plymouth Pulpit*. He also edited *The Independent* (1861–1863) to which he contributed for twenty years and *The Christian Union* (later *The Outlook*), between 1870 and 1881.
3 Suit was brought against H. W. Beecher by one Theodore Filton for alienation of his wife's affections.
4 Lyman Beecher (1775–1863), American clergyman, born in New Haven, Conn.
5 Thomas Paine (1737–1809), English-American author and humanitarian, born in Thetford, Norfolk, England.
6 Harriet Beecher Stowe (1811–1896), American writer and philanthropist, born in Litchfield, Conn., author of *Uncle Tom's Cabin*.
7 Beecher was pastor in Indianapolis from 1839 to 1847.
8 Preston Brooks. See note 12 to article on Wendell Phillips.
9 *Ibid.*
10 His speeches in England were published in London as *Speeches on the American Rebellion* (1864).
11 In Greek mythology, Zeus, to seduce Danaë, took the form of a shower of gold which descended upon her.

GENERAL SHERIDAN

1 Philip Henry Sheridan (1831–1888). Born in Albany, N.Y. Union officer during the American Civil War.
2 William Stark Rosecrans (1819–1898). Born in Kingston, Ohio. Union officer during the American Civil War.
3 Frank A. Burr and Richard J. Hinton, *The Life of Gen. Philip H. Sheridan: its Romance and Reality* (New York: Hurst and Co., 1890).
4 This is probably a free rendition of Gen. Sheridan's words. Joseph Hergesheimer in his *Sheridan* (Boston and New York: Houghton

Mifflin Co., 1931) says: "When, the winter of 1888, Gen. Sheridan visited Boston, he was repeatedly mentioned, among other possible Republican candidates, for the Presidency, although there is no existing proof that it was done with his consent. On February 19 of the same year, the Washington agent of the Associated Press interviewed the General about such a possibility, and he completely denied it."

5   Probably a free version of Sheridan's words: "We'll lick 'em out of their boots, boys!" Burr and Hinton, p. 431.

6   Joseph Hergesheimer, p. 250.

7   "Men, by God, we'll whip them yet! We'll sleep in our old camp tonight!" *Ibid.*, p. 254. Other historians have other versions of the same expression.

8   P. H. Sheridan, in his *Personal Memoirs*, I, 53, says: "It was at this period (Oct., 1855) that the Yaquima Indian war broke out . . . " On page 97 we read: "In the summer of 1856, and while I was still on duty there, the Coquille Indians on the Siletz, and down near the Yaquima Bay, became, on account of hunger and prospective starvation, very much excited . . ." The Coquille and Yakima (the accepted spelling of the term; see Encyclopaedia Britannica Atlas) occupy parts of Washington and Oregon.

9   Burr and Hinton, p. 92.

10   For a fuller account of this episode see Burr and Hinton, pp. 47, 146, 150.

11   This episode is described in Joseph Hergesheimer, pp. 212, 302, and in General Henry E. Davies, *General Sherman* (New York: D. Appleton and Co., 1898), p. 183.

12   "After this affair (battle of July 1st), which had important results, Generals Rosecrans, Sullivan, Granger, Elliott, and Asboth then united in a telegraphic dispatch to General Halleck urging Sheridan's promotion as brigadier, declaring that 'he is worth his weight in gold.' " Burr and Hinton, p. 66.

13   From a poem, *Sheridan's Ride*, Burr and Hinton, p. 236.

14   Sheridan said in a dispatch announcing this accomplishment that it was necessary to lay the valley so bare "that a crow flying over it must carry its rations." Burr and Hinton, p. 180.

15   Joseph Hergesheimer, p. 195.

16   The exact text has not been found, but there are many references in the various historians to his concern for the wounded, his troops in general, his horses. See, for instance, Burr and Hinton, p. 162.

THE CHARLESTON EARTHQUAKE

1 John Caldwell Calhoun (1782–1850). See note 11 to article on Wendell Phillips.

2 James Gadsden (1788–1858), American soldier, diplomat, and railroad president.

3 John Rutledge (1739–1800), American jurist and statesman, born and died in Charleston, S.C. Delegate to the Continental Congress (1772–1777).

4 The reference may be to any of the Pinckneys: Charles Cotesworth (1746–1825), Charles (1757–1823), Thomas (1750–1828), all born in Charleston, S.C., all soldiers in the War of Independence, diplomats, and statesmen; the first two, signatories of the Constitution.

5 A. G. McGarth, American district-attorney and collector in Charleston, S.C. See Samuel W. Crawford, *The History of the Fall of Fort Sumter* (New York: S. T. McLean and Co., 1898), pp. 14 *et seq.*

6 This and the following quotations are approximate versions of Negro spirituals most of which can be found in *Jubilee and Plantation Songs* (Boston: Oliver Ditson Company, 1887).

DEDICATION OF THE STATUE OF LIBERTY

1 Marquis de Lafayette (1757–1834), French statesman and soldier who fought for the independence of the United States.

2 See Brand Whitlock, *Lafayette* (New York: D. Appleton and Co., 1929), I, 67.

3 In a letter to the President of Congress Lafayette wrote: "After the sacrifices that I have made, I have the right to demand two favours; one is to serve at my own expense; the other to begin my service as a volunteer." Whitlock, p. 80.

4 Whitlock, p. 182.

5 "Old Maurepas (Jean Frédéric Maurepas, 1701–1781, French minister) complained that, to clothe the American army, the Marquis would gladly have stripped the palace at Versailles." Whitlock, p. 190.

6 Count de Rochambeau (1725–1807), French soldier, commander-in-chief of the troops that were sent to America. He participated in the actions that led to the Yorktown capitulation.

7 Count François Joseph Paul de Grasse (1722–1788), French naval

officer, in command of the French fleet during the War of Independence of the United States.

8   Charles Cornwallis (1734–1805), 2nd Earl and 1st Marquis Cornwallis, Commander-in-chief of the British forces during the War of Independence.

9   Frédéric Auguste Bartholdi (1834–1904), French sculptor whose most famous work is the statue of Liberty on Bedloe's Island in New York Harbor.

10 Edouard René Lefebvre de Laboulaye (1811–1883), French jurist, historian and politician.

11 Henri Martin (1810–1883), French historian.

12 Viscount Ferdinand Marie de Lesseps (1805–1894), French diplomat and financier who conceived and planned the Suez and Panama canals. He saw the former project completed, but not the latter, which was to be taken over by the United States.

13 The last part of this quotation does not coincide with Lesseps' words as recorded by the *New York Times*, Oct. 29, 1886, p. 2, col. 5, which were: "I hastened to come to avail myself of the gracious invitation which was given to me by the great American Republic. The idea of erecting the Statue of Liberty was a generous one. It does honor to those who conceived it, as it likewise does to those who executed it."

14 William Hepworth Dixon (1821–1879), English historian and traveler. His book *New America* was published in 1867.

15 The quotations in this paragraph were not all recorded by the *New York Times*.

16 Léon Michel Gambetta (1838–1882), French lawyer and statesman.

17 This bronze statue of the sun god, 105 ft. high, on the Island of Rhodes in the Aegean Sea, was the work of Chares, a pupil of Lysippus. It was demolished by an earthquake in 224 A.D. only 56 years after its completion. The notion that it stood astride the entrance to the harbor and that ships sailed under its legs is a mediaeval fiction.

18 Phidias' most celebrated work was the gold and ivory statue of Zeus at Olympia seven times life-size. Phidias, the most famous sculptor of ancient Greece, was born in Athens in 500 B.C., died 432 B.C.

19 Sumnat, also spelled Somnath. A colossal statue erected during the 11th or 12th century A.D. in the State of Gujerat, north of Bombay, India.

20 Martí may have had in mind the colossi of Memnon attached to the temple of Amenophis III which stood on the edge of the desert in western Thebes.

21 Ipsambul is another name for Abu Simbel, a group of temples of Ramses II (*circa* 1250 B.C.) on the west bank of the Nile in Aswan province, Egypt. The sitting colossi mentioned are carved in solid rock and measure 65 feet in height.

22 The colossal statue of Saint Charles Borromeo was erected in 1624 near his birth place Arona on the western shore of Lago Maggiore in northern Italy following the design of Giovanni Battista Crespi (c. 1576–1632), famous painter, architect, sculptor, called Il Cerano. The 77-foot bronze statue stands, including the pedestal, 112 feet high.

23 Characteristic of Le Puy in Haute-Loire, France, are two abrupt volcanic peaks that rise on the outskirts of the small town. On one a chapel has been erected, on the other, a statue of the Virgin Mary, known to the French as "Notre-Dame de France." The 50-foot high bronze statue is the work of Jean Marie Bonnassieux and was put up in 1860.

24 The Cheruscian Armenius in the Teutoborg Forest near Detmold, Germany took its author, Ernst von Bandel, forty years to erect. It commemorates the victory of Armenius over the Roman legions commanded by Varus.

25 The colossal national monument on the Niederwald near Rüdesheim, Germany, in commemoration of the War of 1870/71 was erected in 1883. The 33-foot bronze statue of Germania and its elaborate 82-foot high pedestal are the work of Johannes Schilling (1829–1910).

26 Ludwig von Schwanthaler (1802–1848), a neoclassic sculptor, was the author of the 60-foot statue of "Bavaria" near Munich, Germany.

27 Richard Salter Storrs (1821–1900), American Congregational minister.

28 William Maxwell Evarts (1818–1901), American statesman.

29 Chauncey Mitchell Depew (1834–1928), American lawyer, railway manager, orator; much admired as an after-dinner speaker. Martí, who mentions him many times, had little esteem for him.

30 The quotations from Depew's speech are not literal. See the *Chicago Tribune*, Oct. 29, 1886, p. 2, col. 3.

CENTENNIAL COMMEMORATION OF THE CONSTITUTION

1 An Italian word which means *mixture*, in this case *hodge-podge*.

2 Sir William Howe (1729–1814), Senior officer who led the British troops at Bunker Hill.

3 For the North. Probably an allusion to the Chilean José Victorino Lastarria's (1817–1888) characterization of the "Latin countries" as the "Dis-United States of America," in contrast to the United States of America.

4 Alexander Hamilton (1755–1804), delegate from New York to the Constitutional Convention of 1787. Political disputes with Aaron Burr led to a duel in which Hamilton was killed.

5 Plutarch (circa 46–120 A.D.), author of the Parallel Lives of the great men of antiquity.

6 James Madison (1751–1836), delegate from Virginia to the Constitutional Convention and fourth President of the United States.

7 Cleon (d. 422 B.C.), a Greek political leader who vigorously opposed Pericles.

8 Lycia, a federation of towns in Asia Minor noted in antiquity for its spirit of independence.

9 George Bancroft (1800–1891), author of the standard History of the United States.

10 Luther Martin (circa 1748–1826), American lawyer and dissenting member of the Constitutional Convention.

11 Gouverneur Morris (1752–1816), American statesman and diplomat, delegate from Pennsylvania to the Constitutional Convention.

12 William Paterson (1745–1806), delegate from New Jersey to the Constitutional Convention.

13 Edmund Randolph (1753–1813), delegate from Virginia to the Constitutional Convention, author of the "Virginia plan."

14 Nathaniel Gorham (1738–1796), merchant, public official, delegate from Massachusetts to the Constitutional Convention.

15 Rufus King (1755–1827), delegate from Massachusetts to the Constitutional Convention.

16 Oliver Ellsworth (1745–1807), delegate from Connecticut to the Constitutional Convention.

17 John Rutledge (1739–1800), delegate from South Carolina to the Constitutional Convention where he championed the cause of slavery.

18 James Wilson (1742–1798), Scottish-born lawyer, jurist, and politician who migrated to America in 1765. He became a member of Congress and was an active participant in the Constitutional Convention as delegate from Pennsylvania.

19 Roger Sherman (1721–1793), delegate from Massachusetts to the Constitutional Convention where he tried to mediate between the large states party and the small states party. Had served on the committee which drafted the Declaration of Independence and on that which drafted the Articles of Confederation.

20 William Samuel Johnson (1727–1819), jurist and educator, delegate from Connecticut to the Constitutional Convention.

21 Henri François d'Aguésseau (1668–1751), French jurist and statesman.

22 Charles Louis de Secondat Montesquieu (1689–1755), French political scientist, author of *De l'ésprit des lois* (*Spirit of the Laws*).

23 A paraphrase. Cf. Washington's letter to Dr. David Stewart of July 1, 1787, quoted in Joseph Dillaway Sawyer, *Washington* (New York: The Macmillan Co., 1927), II, 134 *et. seq.*

24 These are not literal quotations but reflect the conflicting positions of the large states and small states parties.

25 Probably not a literal quotation from any one speech by a delegate from a free state.

26 The foregoing quotations are probably not literal.

27 Not literal quotations.

28 William Ewart Gladstone (1809–1898), four times prime minister of Great Britain, called the "Grand Old Man of Liberalism."

29 William Jackson (1759–1828), known as "Major Jackson," a rank he won in the War of Independence, was nominated by Alexander Hamilton for secretary of the Constitutional Convention. At the close of its sessions the Convention ordered the records be burned, except the journal of the proceedings and the yea and nay votes, which are in Jackson's handwriting.

30 James Madison states (*Madison Papers,* p. 1624) that Dr. Franklin said to a group of friends, while the last members were signing: "I have often and often, in the course of the session, and in the vicissitudes of my hopes and fears as to its issues, looked at that (painted sun) behind the president, without being able to tell whether it was rising or setting; but now, at length, I have the happiness to know that it is a rising and not a setting sun."

31 Of the original states, the two last to ratify the Constitution were North Carolina (Nov. 21, 1789) and Rhode Island (May 29, 1790).

32 Samuel Freeman Miller (1816–1890), justice of the Supreme Court of the U.S., 1862–1890, born at Richmond, Ky.

33 James Gibbons (1834–1921), American Roman Catholic priest, born in Baltimore, Md. Made Cardinal in 1886 by Pope Leo XIII.

34 The Carlisle Indian School was established in southern Pennsylvania in 1879 by Captain R. H. Pratt; closed in 1918.

35 An Indian tribe of Nebraska.

CENTENNIAL OF WASHINGTON'S INAUGURATION: THE BALL

1 Eléonore François Elie Moustier (1751–1817), French diplomat and soldier. Appointed Ambassador to the United States in 1787.
2 Probably Bryan Fairfax (1737–1802), owner of a large estate in Virginia, who subsequently (1793) became the eighth Baron of Fairfax de Cameron.
3 John Jacob Astor (1763–1848), born in Heidelberg, Germany, founder of the Astor family, prominent in the United States and later in England also. He emmigrated to America in 1783 and amassed a great fortune in the fur-trapping business and exchanging furs for tea.
4 Cornelius Vanderbilt (1794–1877), born in Stapleton, N.Y., began his business career at the age of sixteen carrying produce and passengers in a sailboat between Staten Island and New York.
5 See article on Peter Cooper.
6 William Waldorf Astor (1848–1919).

THE GREAT "BUFFALO BILL"

1 William Frederic Cody (1846–1917), American scout, Indian fighter, and showman.

CONEY ISLAND

1 Aparejadas / van por las lomas / las cogujadas / y las palomas . . . Antonio García Gutiérrez (1812–1884), a Spanish romantic dramatist and lyric poet, was the author of *El trovador*, from which the libretto was taken for Verdi's opera *Il Trovatore*.
2 Pampas, vast prairies of South America.

THE THIRTEEN CLUB

1 William Darrah Kelly (1814–1890), Congressman from Pennsylvania, noted for his strong protectionist position.
2 The reference is to the recognition of the republican government in Brazil which followed the fall of Emperor Pedro II in November, 1889.
3 This may refer to some revelation regarding the campaign to secure Benjamin Harrison's nomination for the Presidency at the

Chicago Convention in 1888. He had been fourth on the first ballot and only nominated on the eighth, which led to speculation. Benjamin Harrison (1833–1901) had been senator from Indiana (1881–1887) and became the twenty-third President of the United States. Whatever irregularities might have occurred at the Convention, Harrison himself was considered free of all blame.

4 Roscoe Conkling (1829–1888), American lawyer and influential Republican member of Congress during the Reconstruction era. Resigned from the Senate in 1881 over a dispute with President Garfield. Martí wrote extensively on Roscoe Conkling.

5 Phineas Taylor Barnum (1810–1891), American circus proprietor, born in Bethel, Conn.

6 Robert Green Ingersoll (1833–1899), American orator, politician and lawyer, born in Dresden, N.Y.

7 *A Connecticut Yankee in King Arthur's Court* (1889).

ELECTIONEERING

1 William Waldorf Astor (1848–1919), American politician and diplomat, grandson of John Jacob Astor. W. W. Astor was born in New York, heir to the Astor millions, was appointed Minister to Italy in 1882. Became a British subject in 1899.

2 Roswell Pettibone Flower (1835–1899), born in Theresa, N.Y., was elected to Congress in 1881, 1888, and 1890, and served as governor of the State of New York from 1892 to 1895.

3 Seth Low (1850–1916), businessman, educator, political leader, born in Brooklyn, N.Y., was twice elected mayor of Brooklyn and, in 1901, mayor of greater New York. His name is associated with the growth of Columbia University of which he was president from 1890 to 1901.

4 Ulysses S. Grant (1822–1885), General-in-chief of the Union armies during the Civil War and ex-President of the United States, was at the time retired from public life and engaged in banking activities.

5 Roscoe Conkling. See note 4 to article on The Thirteen Club.

6 See article on Henry Ward Beecher.

ORIGIN OF THE REPUBLICAN PARTY

1 William Lloyd Garrison. See note 10 to article on Wendell Phillips.

2 William Cullen Bryant (1794–1878), American poet and journalist, born in Cummington, Mass.

3 *Uncle Tom's Cabin* by Harriet Beecher Stowe.

4   Horace Greeley (1811–1872), American newspaper editor and political leader, born near Amherst, N.H.
5   William E. Channing. See note 5 to article on Wendell Phillips.
6   Martí doubtless has in mind John Quincy Adams (1767–1848), born in Braintree, now Quincy, Mass., sixth President of the United States, statesman, diplomat, opposed to the expansion of slavery. He was twice elected to Congress.
7   Charles Sumner (1811–1874), American statesman, abolitionist, senator, born in Boston, Mass.
8   See article on Wendell Phillips.
9   The text nearest to these words that has been found is that in Wendell Phillips' speech on *Harper's Ferry* in Wendell Phillips, *Speeches, Lectures and Letters,* p. 282.
10 This quotation seems to be a synthesis of several of Whittier's verses. Cf. J. G. Whittier, *Anti-Slavery Poems: Songs of Labor and Reform,* III, 41. For instance: "Now, when our land to ruin's brink is verging, / In God's name, let us speak while there is time! / Now, when the padlocks for our lips are forging, / Silence is crime!" "From Wachuset, lone and bleak, / Unto Berkshire's tallest peak, / Let the flame-tongued heralds speak," p. 95.
11 Not a literal quotation. See the complete text of Webster's speech in *The Works of Daniel Webster* (Boston: Charles C. Little and James Brown, 1851), V, 325 *et seq.*
12 James Buchanan (1791–1868), fifteenth President of the United States (1856–1860), born near Mercersburg, Pa. He showed little courage in facing the slavery crisis.

HEATED CAMPAIGNING

1   Joseph Benson Foraker (1846–1917), American Senator, Governor of Ohio from 1885 to 1889.
2   Samuel Jones Tilden (1814–1886), American statesman, born at New Lebanon, N.Y. Democratic candidate to the presidency in the disputed election of 1876. He left a large fortune for the establishment and maintenance of a public library in New York City. This fund, combined with the Astor and Lenox libraries, formed the New York Public Library.
3   James Gillespie Blaine. See note 5 on Blaine and note 7 to article on President Garfield.
4   It has not been possible to check these versions of Foraker's speeches against the original texts.
5   James G. Blaine, on whom Martí wrote abundantly and critically.

6 Thomas Francis Bayard (1828–1898), American statesman, diplomat, and lawyer, born in Wilmington, Del. Was Secretary of State during Cleveland's first administration.

7 George Franklin Edmunds (1828–1919), born in Richmond, Vt., American senator from 1872 to 1891, except for one two year term. Was a candidate for the presidential nomination by the Republican party in 1880 and in 1884.

8 John Alexander Logan (1826–1886), American soldier and political leader, born in what is now Murphysboro, Ill. U.S. senator from 1871 to 1877 and from 1879 until his death. He ran for vice-president on the Republican ticket in 1884 with James G. Blaine.

9 John Sherman (1823–1900), American financier and statesman, born at Lancaster, Ohio. He was a brother of General W. T. Sherman. For various periods he was Republican member of the House and the Senate. Secretary of the Treasury in 1877.

10 Alfred Alexander (1848–1931) and Robert Love (1850–1912) Taylor, both born in Happy Valley, Tenn. "Bob" defeated "Al" in the election of 1886 for the governorship of Tennessee and served two terms (1887–1891); he already had served in Congress (1879–1881). Later, in 1901, "Al" was elected governor. Their picturesque campaign of 1886 was called "the War of the Roses." Both brothers drew large audiences on lecture tours which sometimes they made together.

11 Henry William Blair (1834–1920), born at Campton, N.H., introduced a bill in the Senate proposing a federal subsidy of $120,000,000 to be distributed to schools over a period of ten years for the erradication of illiteracy.

12 Henry George (1839–1897), American economist, born in Philadelphia, Pa., best known for his "single tax" theory. He barely lost to his Democratic opponent, Abram Hewitt, the election to the mayoralty of New York in 1886, but ran substantially ahead of the Republican candidate, Theodore Roosevelt.

RELIGION

1 The reference is to Thomas Harrison, mentioned by Bernard A. Weisberger in *They Gathered at the River* (Boston: Little, Brown and Co., 1958), as an innovator in the practice of revival at about the time Martí wrote. Harrison was born in Boston in 1854. He had devoted himself to evangelistic work since 1876, and was called "the boy preacher," because of his appearance rather than his age.

2 William Ellery Channing (1780–1842), American clergyman and author, born at Newport, R.I. He advocated Unitarianism.

3 Jonathan Edwards (1703–1758), American theologian, born at East Windsor, Conn.

4 Lyman Beecher. See note 4 to article on Henry Ward Beecher.

5 See article on Henry Ward Beecher.

6 Phillips Brooks (1835–1893), American Episcopal clergyman, born in Boston, Mass. He exercised his ministry mostly in his native city and in Philadelphia.

7 Tomás de Torquemada (1420–1498), Grand Inquisitor of Spain, noted for the ruthlessness with which he defended the Catholic Church against infidels.

8 John Calvin (1509–1564), Genevan theologian and religious reformer, often associated with religious intollerance, especially because of the burning at the stake of the Spaniard Miguel Servet (Michael Servetus), his dissentor in theological matters.

ON THE INDIAN QUESTION

1 Lucius Quintus Cincinnatus Lamar (1825–1893), American statesman, Supreme Court Justice and Secretary of the Interior (1885–1888), born in Putnam County, Ga. See article on The American Soul.

2 Apaches, the Athapaskan-speaking Indian tribes of southwestern North America.

3 Cherokees, Indians of Iroquoian lineage, originally located in eastern Tennessee and western North and South Carolina.

4 Choktaws, Indian tribe of Muskogee stock in southern Mississippi.

5 Chicasaws, Indian tribe of Muskogean linguistic stock residing originally in northern Mississippi and Alabama.

6 Creeks, Indian tribe originally living in Georgia and Alabama.

7 Seminoles, Indian tribe formed by splitting away from the Creeks. They occupy parts of Oklahoma and southern Florida.

8 Cheyennes, Algonkian-speaking Indian tribe living in the western Great Plains of the U.S.

9 Sioux, the largest tribe of the Siouan Indians which occupied various sections of what is now the United States. The Sioux are also called Dakota Indians.

10 Umatillas, Indian tribe of Oregon.

11 John C. Calhoun. See note 11 to article on Wendell Phillips.

12 These quotations are not literal. Calhoun's report of 1822 says, in part: "It may be affirmed, almost without qualification, that all

the tribes within our settlements and near our borders are even solicitous for the education of their children. . . . the reports of the teachers are almost uniformly favorable, both as to the capacity and docility of their youths. Their progress appears to be quite equal to that of white children of the same age, and they appear to be equally susceptible of acquiring habits of industry." See *The Works of John C. Calhoun,* ed. Richard K. Crallé (New York: D. Appleton and Co., 1888), V, 104–8.

A GLANCE AT THE NORTH AMERICAN'S SOUL TODAY

1   L. Q. C. Lamar. See note 1 to article on The Indian Question.

SELECTED BIBLIOGRAPHY

COLLECTED WORKS

There are numerous collections of Martí's works. The two most complete to date are:

Obras completas de Martí. 74 vols. Havana: Editorial Trópico, 1936–1953.

Martí, José, Obras completas. 2 vols. Havana: Editorial Lex, 1946.

SELECTIONS

Among the many selections from Martí's writings published in Spanish may be mentioned those edited by:

Argilagos, Rafael G. *Granos do oro.* Havana: Soc. Ed. Cuba Contemporánea, 1918.

González, Manuel Pedro and Ivan A. Schulman. *José Martí: esquema ideológico.* Mexico: Ed. Cultura, T. G., S. A., 1961.

Henríquez Ureña, Max. *Páginas escogidas.* Paris; Garnier, 1919.

Méndez, M. Isidro. *Ideario.* Havana: Colección de libros cubanos, 1930.

In other languages have appeared:

Tuya, Other Verses and Translations from José Martí. English trans. by Cecil Charles. New York: J. E. Richardson, 1898.

The America of José Martí. English trans. by Juan de Onís. New York: Noonday Press, 1954.

América. French trans. by Francis de Miomandre. Paris: Institut International de Coopération Intellectuelle, 1935.

Pages choisies. French trans. by Max Daireaux, José Carner, and Emilie Noulet. Paris: Editions Nagel, 1953.

Páginas escolhidas. Portuguese trans. by Silvio Júlio. Rio de Janeiro: Alba, 1956.

Selected works. Russian trans. by several authors. Moscow, 1956.

BIOGRAPHIES AND BOOKS OF GENERAL INTEREST

Baralt, Blanca Z. de. *El Martí que yo conocí.* Havana: Editorial Trópico, 1945.

González, Manuel Pedro. *José Martí, Epic Chronicler of the United States in the Eighties.* Chapel Hill: University of North Carolina Press, 1953.

Iduarte, Andrés. *Martí, escritor.* Havana: Dirección de Cultura, 1951.

Lizaso, Félix. *Martí, Martyr of Cuban Independence.* English trans. by E. E. Shuler. Albuquerque: University of New Mexico Press, 1953.

Mañach, Jorge. *Martí, Apostle of Freedom.* English trans. by C. Taylor. New York: Devin-Adair, 1960.

Vitier, Medardo. *Martí, estudio integral.* Havana: Com. Nac. del Centenario, 1954.

BIBLIOGRAPHIES

González, Manuel Pedro. *Fuentes para el estudio de José Martí; ensayo de bibliografía clasificada.* Havana: Dirección de Cultura, 1950.

Peraza, Fermín. *Bibliografía martiana, 1853–1953.* Havana: Com. Nac. del Centenario, 1954.